Management Accounting Best Practices

A Guide for the Professional Accountant

MANAGEMENT ACCOUNTING BEST PRACTICES

A Guide for the Professional Accountant

STEVEN M. BRAGG

BICENTENNIAL
1807
WILEY
2007
BICENTENNIAL

John Wiley & Sons, Inc.

Library of Congress Cataloging-in-Publication Data:

ISBN: 978–0471–74347–7

Printed in the United States of America
10   9   8   7   6   5   4   3   2   1

*To the crew at Wiley, with whom I have
worked since the previous century:
Sheck, John, Judy, Natasha,
Helen, and Brandon.*

Contents

Preface   xi

About the Author   xiii

Free Online Resources by Steve Bragg   xv

1 Budgeting Decisions   1

How Does the System of Interlocking Budgets Work?   1
What Does a Sample Budget Look Like?   10
How Does Flex Budgeting Work?   28
What Best Practices Can I Apply to the Budgeting Process?   29
How Can I Integrate the Budget into the Corporate Control System?   35
How Do Throughput Concepts Impact the Budget?   37

2 Capital Budgeting Decisions   44

How Does a Constrained Resource Impact Capital Budgeting Decisions?   44
What Is the True Cost of a Capacity Constraint?   45
How Do I Identify a Constrained Resource?   47
When Should I Invest in a Constrained Resource?   49
Should I Increase Sprint Capacity?   49
How Closely Should I Link Capital Expenditures to Strategy?   50
What Format Should I Use for a Capital Request Form?   51
Should I Judge Capital Proposals Based on Their
  Discounted Cash Flows?   51
How Do I Calculate the Cost of Capital?   54
When Should I Use the Incremental Cost of Capital?   58
How Do I Use Net Present Value in Capital Budgeting?   60
What Proposal Form Should I Require for a Cash Flow Analysis?   62
Should I Use the Payback Period in Capital Budgeting?   64
How Can a Post-Completion Analysis Help Me?   65
What Factors Should I Consider for a Site Selection?   67

3 Credit and Collection Decisions   69

How Do I Create and Maintain a Credit Policy?   70
When Should I Require a Credit Application?   72
How Do I Obtain Financial Information About Customers?   73
How Does a Credit Granting System Work?   74
What Payment Terms Should I Offer to Customers?   76

When Should I Review Customer Credit Levels?   77
How Can I Adjust the Invoice Content and
   Layout to Improve Collections?   78
How Can I Adjust Billing Delivery to Improve Collections?   80
How Do I Accelerate Cash Collections?   81
Should I Offer Early Payment Discounts?   82
How Do I Optimize Customer Contacts?   82
How Do I Manage Customer Contact Information?   83
How Do I Involve the Sales Staff in Collections?   85
How Do I Handle Payment Deductions?   86
How Do I Collect Overdue Payments?   88
When Should I Take Legal Action to Collect from a Customer?   90

4 **Control System Decisions   92**

Why Do I Need Controls?   92
How Do I Control Order Entry?   93
How Do I Control Credit Management?   94
How Do I Control Purchasing?   95
How Do I Control Procurement Cards?   96
How Do I Control Payables?   100
How Do I Control Inventory?   101
How Do I Control Billings?   102
How Do I Control Cash Receipts?   103
How Do I Control Payroll?   104
How Do I Control Fixed Assets?   106

5 **Financial Analysis Decisions   110**

How Do I Calculate the Breakeven Point?   110
What Is the Impact of Fixed Costs on the Breakeven Point?   112
What is the Impact of Variable Cost Changes on the Breakeven Point?   113
How Do Pricing Changes Alter the Breakeven Point?   114
How Can the Product Mix Alter Profitability?   115
How Do I Conduct a "What-If" Analysis with a Single Variable?   116
How Do I Conduct a "What-If" Analysis with Double Variables?   118
How Do I Calculate Cost Variances?   121
How Do I Conduct a Profitability Analysis for Services?   128
How Are Profits Affected by the Number of Days in a Month?   130
How Do I Decide Which Research and Development
   Projects to Fund?   131
How Do I Create a Throughput Analysis Model?   133
How Do I Determine whether More Volume at a Lower Price
   Creates More Profit?   135
Should I Outsource Production?   137

Should I Add Staff to the Bottleneck Operation? 137
Should I Produce a New Product? 139

6 Payroll Decisions 143

How Can I Automate Time Clock Data Collection? 144
How Do I Collect Time Information by Telephone? 145
How Can I Simplify Payroll Deductions? 146
How Do Employees Enter Their Own Payroll Changes? 147
How Do I Automate Payroll Form Distribution? 148
Should I Pay Employees via Direct Deposit? 149
How Do Paycards Compare with Payments by Direct Deposit? 150
What Issues Should I Consider When Setting Up a Paycard Program? 152
How Do I Make Electronic Child Support Payments? 152
How Do I Automate Payroll Remittances? 153
Should I Outsource Payroll? 153
Can I Outsource Employment Verifications? 155
Can I Outsource Benefits Administration? 156
How Many Payroll Cycles Should I Have? 157
How Can I Reduce the Number of Employee Payroll–Related Inquiries? 158

7 Inventory Decisions 160

How Do I Manage Inventory Accuracy? 160
How Do I Identify Obsolete Inventory? 165
How Do I Dispose of Obsolete Inventory? 167
How Do I Set Up a Lower of Cost or Market System? 169
Which Inventory Costing System Should I Use? 170
Which Inventory Controls Should I Install? 183
What Types of Performance Measurements Should I Use? 186
How Do I Maintain Service Levels with Low Inventory? 192
Should I Shift Inventory Ownership to Suppliers? 194
How Do I Avoid Price Protection Costs? 195

8 Cost Allocation Decisions 197

What Is the Basic Method for Calculating Overhead? 197
How Does Activity-Based Costing Work? 199
How Should I Use Activity-Based Costing? 206
Are There Any Problems with Activity-Based Costing? 207
How Do Just-in-Time Systems Impact Cost Allocation? 209
How Does Overhead Allocation Impact Automated Production
   Systems? 211
How Does Overhead Allocation Impact Low-Volume Products? 211
How Does Overhead Allocation Impact Low-Profit Products? 211
How Do I Allocate Joint and Byproduct Costs? 213

9 Performance Responsibility Accounting Decisions 217

What Is Responsibility Accounting? 217
What Are the Types of Responsibility Centers? 218
Should Allocated Costs Be Included in Responsibility Reports? 221
What Is Balanced Scorecard Reporting? 222
How Does Benchmarking Work? 224

10 Product Design Decisions 227

How Do I Make Funding Decisions for Research and
    Development Projects? 227
How Does Target Costing Work? 229
What Is Value Engineering? 230
How Does Target Costing Impact Profitability? 233
Are There Any Problems with Target Costing? 235
What Is the Accountant's Role in a Target Costing Environment? 236
What Data is Needed for a Target Costing Analysis? 237
How Do I Control the Target Costing Process? 239
Under What Scenarios Is Target Costing Useful? 240
How Can I Incorporate Target Costing into the Budget? 241
How Can I Measure the Success of a Target Costing Program? 241

11 Pricing Decisions 243

What Is the Lowest Price that I Should Accept? 243
How Do I Set Long-Range Prices? 245
How Should I Set Prices Over the Life of a Product? 247
How Do I Determine Cost-Plus Pricing? 249
How Should I Set Prices Against a Price Leader? 249
How Do I Handle a Price War? 250
How Do I Handle Predatory Pricing by a Competitor? 252
How Do I Handle Dumping by a Foreign Competitor? 253
When Is Transfer Pricing Important? 254
How Do Transfer Prices Alter Corporate Decision Making? 255
What Transfer Pricing Method Should I Use? 256

12 Quality Decisions 264

What Are the Various Types of Quality? 264
How Do I Create a Quality Reporting System? 269
What Is the Cost of Scrap? 277
How Should I Measure Post-Constraint Scrap? 279
Where Should I Place Quality Review Workstations? 280

Index 281

Preface

The typical accountant receives a thorough grounding in accounting standards in school, but then arrives on the job and asks—*What do I do now?* The unfortunate realization strikes that only a small proportion of the accounting job involves that painfully acquired knowledge of accounting standards. Instead, many other questions arise, with no obvious answers:

- How do I create a budget?
- What is a bottleneck asset, and should I invest in it?
- Should I approve a request for a capital expenditure?
- How do I grant credit to customers?
- How do I accelerate cash collections?
- Which controls should I set up?
- How do I conduct a throughput analysis?
- Should we outsource work?
- How do I collect payroll information?
- How do I achieve accurate inventory records?
- How do I allocate costs?
- What kinds of responsibility reports should I use?
- Should I set up a target costing system to assist the development of a new product?
- How do I set product prices?
- Where do I place quality review stations to improve profitability?

Management Accounting Best Practices provides the answers to all of these questions (and over 100 more) that show both the aspiring and seasoned accountant how to set up and manage an accounting department. Furthermore, when other members of the management team come calling with questions, the answers now lie on the accountant's bookshelf.

The information in this book is culled from eight of the author's best-selling books: *Accounting Control Best Practices, Billing and Collections Best Practices, Cost Accounting, Financial Analysis, Inventory Accounting, Payroll Best Practices, Throughput Accounting,* and the *Ultimate Accountants' Reference.* The new question-and-answer format in which this information is presented makes it easier to locate information on key accounting topics, and should make *Management Accounting Best Practices* a well-thumbed addition to any accountant's library.

STEVEN M. BRAGG
Centennial, Colorado
February 2007

About the Author

Steven Bragg, CPA, CMA, CIA, CPIM, has been the chief financial officer or controller of four companies, as well as a consulting manager at Ernst & Young and auditor at Deloitte & Touche. He received a Master's degree in Finance from Bentley College, an MBA from Babson College, and a Bachelor's degree in Economics from the University of Maine. He has been the two-time President of the Colorado Mountain Club, and is an avid alpine skier, mountain biker, and certified master diver. Mr. Bragg resides in Centennial, Colorado. He has written the following books through John Wiley & Sons:

Accounting and Finance for Your Small Business
Accounting Best Practices
Accounting Control Best Practices
Accounting Reference Desktop
Billing and Collections Best Practices
Business Ratios and Formulas
Controller's Guide to Costing
Controller's Guide to Planning and Controlling Operations
Controller's Guide: Roles and Responsibilities for the New Controller
Controllership
Cost Accounting
Design and Maintenance of Accounting Manuals
Essentials of Payroll
Fast Close
Financial Analysis
GAAP Guide
GAAP Implementation Guide
Inventory Accounting
Inventory Best Practices
Just-in-Time Accounting
Management Accounting Best Practices
Managing Explosive Corporate Growth
Outsourcing
Payroll Accounting
Payroll Best Practices
Revenue Recognition
Sales and Operations for Your Small Business
The Controller's Function

The New CFO Financial Leadership Manual

The Ultimate Accountants' Reference
Throughput Accounting

Also:

Advanced Accounting Systems (Institute of Internal Auditors)
Run the Rockies (CMC Press)

Free Online Resources
by Steve Bragg

Steve issues a free accounting best practices newsletter and an accounting best practices podcast. You can sign up for both at *www.stevebragg.com*, or access the podcast through iTunes.

Chapter 1

Budgeting Decisions

The most common method for creating a budget is to simply print out the financial statements, adjust historical expenses for inflationary increases, add some projected revenue adjustments, and *voila*—instant budget. Unfortunately, this rough method ignores a massive number of interlocking factors that would probably have resulted in a very different budget. Without a carefully compiled budget, there is a strong chance that a company will find itself acting on budget assumptions that are so incorrect that it may find itself in serious financial straits in short order.

To avoid these problems, the accountant must determine the proper format of a budget, find the best way to adjust it when revenue volumes change, ensure that the budgeting process is efficient, factor bottleneck operations into the budget, and use it to improve company control systems. This chapter provides answers to all of these key questions. The following table itemizes the section number in which the answers to each question can be found:

Section	Decision
1-1	How does the system of interlocking budgets work?
1-2	What does a sample budget look like?
1-3	How does flex budgeting work?
1-4	What best practices can I apply to the budgeting process?
1-5	How can I integrate the budget into the corporate control system?
1-6	How do throughput concepts impact the budget?

1-1 HOW DOES THE SYSTEM OF INTERLOCKING BUDGETS WORK?

A properly designed budget is a complex web of spreadsheets that account for the activities of virtually all areas within a company. As noted in Exhibit 1.1, the budget begins in two places, with both the revenue budget and research and development (R&D) budget. The revenue budget contains the revenue figures that the company believes it can achieve for each upcoming reporting period. These estimates come partially from the sales staff, which is responsible for estimates of sales levels for existing products within their current territories. Estimates for the sales of new products that have not yet been released, and for existing products in new markets, will come from a combination of the sales and marketing staffs, who will use their experience with related product sales to derive estimates. The greatest fallacy in any budget is to impose a revenue budget from the top management level without any input from the

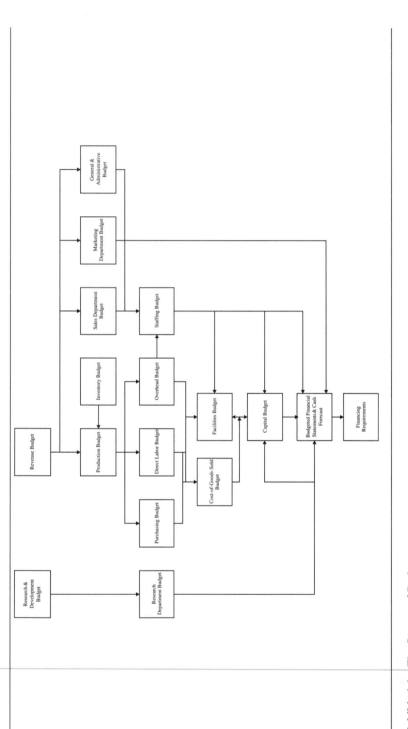

Exhibit 1.1 The System of Budgets

sales staff, since this can result in a companywide budget that is geared toward a sales level that is most unlikely to be reached.

A revenue budget requires prior consideration of a number of issues. For example, a general market share target will drive several other items within the budget, since greater market share may come at the cost of lower unit prices or higher credit costs. Another issue is the compensation strategy for the sales staff, since a shift to higher or lower commissions for specific products or regions will be a strong incentive for the sales staff to alter their selling behavior, resulting in some changes in estimated sales levels. Yet another consideration is which sales territories are to be entered during the budget period—those with high target populations may yield very high sales per hour of sales effort, while the reverse will be true if the remaining untapped regions have smaller target populations. It is also necessary to review the price points that will be offered during the budget period, especially in relation to the pricing strategies that are anticipated from competitors. If there is a strategy to increase market share as well as to raise unit prices, then the budget may fail due to conflicting activities. Another major factor is the terms of sale, which can be extended, along with easy credit, to attract more marginal customers; conversely, they can be retracted in order to reduce credit costs and focus company resources on a few key customers. A final point is that the budget should address any changes in the type of customer to whom sales will be made. If an entirely new type of customer will be added to the range of sales targets during the budget period, then the revenue budget should reflect a gradual ramp-up that will be required for the sales staff to work through the sales cycle of the new customers.

Once all of these factors have been ruminated upon and combined to create a preliminary budget, the sales staff should also compare the budgeted sales level per person to the actual sales level that has been experienced in the recent past to see if the company has the existing capability to make the budgeted sales. If not, the revenue budget should be ramped up to reflect the time it will take to hire and train additional sales staff. The same cross-check can be conducted for the amount of sales budgeted per customer, to see if historical experience validates the sales levels noted in the new budget.

Another budget that initiates other activities within the system of budgets is the research and development budget. This is not related to the sales level at all (as opposed to most other budgets), but instead is a discretionary budget that is based on the company's strategy to derive new or improved products. The decision to fund a certain amount of project-related activity in this area will drive a departmental staffing and capital budget that is, for the most part, completely unrelated to the activity conducted by the rest of the company. However, there can be a feedback loop between this budget and the cash budget, since financing limitations may require management to prune some projects from this area. If so, the management team must work with the R&D manager to determine the correct mix of projects with both short-range and long-range payoffs that will still be funded.

The production budget is largely driven by the sales estimates contained within the revenue budget. However, it is also driven by the inventory-level assumptions in the inventory budget. The inventory budget contains estimates by the materials management supervisor regarding the inventory levels that will be required for the upcoming budget period. For example, a new goal may be to reduce the level of finished goods inventory from 10 turns per year to 15. If so, some of the products required by the revenue budget can be bled off from the existing finished goods inventory stock, yielding smaller production requirements during the budget period. Alternatively, if there is a strong focus on improving the level of customer service, then it may be necessary to keep more finished goods in stock, which will require more production than is strictly called for by the revenue budget. This concept can also be extended to work-in-process (WIP) inventory, where the installation of advanced production planning systems, such as manufacturing resources planning or just-in-time, can be used to reduce the level of required inventory. Also, just-in-time purchasing techniques can be used to reduce the amount of raw materials inventory that is kept on hand. All of these assumptions should be clearly delineated in the inventory budget, so that the management team is clear about what systemic changes will be required in order to effect altered inventory turnover levels. Also, be aware that any advanced production planning system takes a considerable amount of time to install and tune, so it is best if the inventory budget contains a gradual ramp-up to different planned levels of inventory.

Given this input from the inventory budget, the production budget is used to derive the unit quantity of required products that must be manufactured in order to meet revenue targets for each budget period. This involves a number of interrelated factors, such as the availability of sufficient capacity for production needs. Of particular concern should be the amount of capacity at the bottleneck operation. Since this tends to be the most expensive capital item, it is important to budget a sufficient quantity of funding to ensure that this operation includes enough equipment to meet the targeted production goals. If the bottleneck operation involves skilled labor, rather than equipment, then the human resources staff should be consulted regarding its ability to bring in the necessary personnel in time to improve the bottleneck capacity in a timely manner.

Another factor that drives the budgeted costs contained within the production budget is the anticipated size of production batches. If the batch size is expected to decrease, then more overhead costs should be budgeted in the production scheduling, materials handling, and machine setup staffing areas. If longer batch sizes are planned then there may be a possibility of proportionally reducing overhead costs in these areas. This is a key consideration that is frequently overlooked, but which can have an outsized impact on overhead costs. If management attempts to contain overhead costs in this area while still using smaller batch sizes, then it will likely run into larger scrap quantities and quality issues that are caused by rushed batch setups and the allocation of incorrect materials to production jobs.

Step costing is also an important consideration when creating the production budget. Costs will increase in large increments when certain capacity levels are reached. The management team should be fully aware of when these capacity levels will be reached, so that it can plan appropriately for the incurrence of added costs. For example, the addition of a second shift to the production area will call for added costs in the areas of supervisory staff, an increased pay rate, and higher maintenance costs. The inverse of this condition can also occur, where step costs can decline suddenly if capacity levels fall below a specific point.

Production levels may also be impacted by any lengthy tooling setups or change-overs to replacement equipment. These changes may halt all production for extended periods, and so must be carefully planned for. This is the responsibility of the industrial engineering staff. The accountant would do well to review the company's past history of actual equipment setup times to see whether the current engineering estimates are sufficiently lengthy.

The expense items included in the production budget should be driven by a set of subsidiary budgets, which are the purchasing, direct labor, and overhead budgets. These budgets can be simply included in the production budget, but they typically involve such a large proportion of company costs that it is best to lay them out separately in greater detail in separate budgets. Comments on these budgets are as follows:

- *Purchasing budget.* The purchasing budget is driven by several factors, first of which is the bill of materials that comprises the products that are planned for production during the budget period. These bills must be accurate, or else the purchasing budget can include seriously incorrect information. In addition, there should be a plan for controlling material costs, perhaps through the use of concentrated buying through few suppliers, or perhaps through the use of long-term contracts. If materials are highly subject to market pressures, comprise a large proportion of total product costs, and have a history of sharp price swings, then best-case and worst-case costing scenarios should be added to the budget so that managers can review the impact of costing issues in this area. If a just-in-time delivery system from suppliers is contemplated, then the purchasing budget should reflect a possible increase in material costs caused by the increased number of deliveries from suppliers. It is also worthwhile to budget for a raw material scrap and obsolescence expense; there should be a history of costs in these areas that can be extrapolated based on projected purchasing volumes.

- *Direct labor budget.* Do not make the mistake of budgeting for direct labor as a fully variable cost. The production volume from day to day tends to be relatively fixed, and requires a set number of direct labor personnel on a continuing basis to operate production equipment and manually assemble products. Further, the production manager will realize much greater production efficiencies by holding onto an experienced production staff, rather than by letting them go as soon as production volumes make small incremental drops. Accordingly, it is better to budget based on reality, which is that direct labor personnel are usually retained, even if there are ongoing fluctuations in the level of production. Thus, direct labor should be shown in the budget as a fixed cost of production, within certain production volume parameters.

  Also, this budget should describe staffing levels by type of direct labor position; this is driven by labor routings, which are documents that describe the exact type and quantity of staffing needed to produce a product. When multiplied by the unit volumes located in the production budget, this results in an expected level of staffing by direct labor position. This information is most useful for the human resources staff, which is responsible for staffing the positions.

The direct labor budget should also account for any contractually mandated changes in hourly rates, which may be itemized in a union agreement. Such an agreement may also have restrictions on layoffs, which should be accounted for in the budget if this will keep labor levels from dropping in proportion with budgeted reductions in production levels. Such an agreement may also require that layoffs be conducted in order of seniority, which may force higher-paid employees into positions that would normally be budgeted for less expensive laborers. Thus, the presence of a union contract can result in a much more complex direct labor budget than would normally be the case.

The direct labor budget may also contain features related to changes in the efficiency of employees, and any resulting changes in pay. For example, one possible pay arrangement is to pay employees based on a piece rate, which directly ties their performance to the level of production achieved. If so, this will probably apply only to portions of the workforce, so the direct labor budget may involve pay rates based on both piece rates and hourly pay. Another issue is that any drastic increases in the budgeted level of direct labor personnel will likely result in some initial declines in labor efficiency, since it takes time for new employees to learn their tasks. If this is the case, the budget should reflect a low level of initial efficiency, with a ramp-up over time to higher levels that will result in greater initial direct labor costs. Finally, efficiency improvements may be rewarded with staff bonuses from time to time; if so, these bonuses should be included in the budget.

- *Overhead budget.* The overhead budget can be a simple one to create if there are no significant changes in production volume from the preceding year, because this involves a large quantity of static costs that will not vary much over time. Included in this category are machine maintenance, utilities, supervisory salaries, wages for the materials management, production scheduling, quality assurance personnel, facilities maintenance, and depreciation expenses. Under the no-change scenario, the most likely budgetary alterations will be to machinery or facilities maintenance, which are dependent on the condition and level of usage of company property.

  If there is a significant change in the expected level of production volume, or if new production lines are to be added, then one should examine this budget in great detail, for the underlying production volumes may cause a ripple effect that results in wholesale changes to many areas of the overhead budget. Of particular concern is the number of overhead-related personnel who must be either laid off or added when capacity levels reach certain critical points, such as the addition or subtraction of extra work shifts. Costs also tend to rise substantially when a facility is operating at very close to 100 percent capacity, since this tends to call for an inordinate amount of effort to maintain on an ongoing basis.

The purchasing, direct labor, and overhead budgets can then be summarized into a cost-of-goods-sold budget. This budget should incorporate, as a single line item, the total amount of revenue, so that all manufacturing costs can be deducted from it to yield a gross profit margin on the same document. This budget is referred to constantly during the budget creation process, since it tells management whether its budgeting assumptions are yielding an acceptable gross margin result. Since it is a summary-level budget for the production side of the budgeting process, this is also a good place to itemize any production-related statistics, such as the average hourly cost of direct labor, inventory turnover rates, and the amount of revenue dollars per production person.

Thus far, we have reviewed the series of budgets that descend in turn from the revenue budget and then through the production budget. However, there are other expenses that are unrelated to production. These are categories in a separate set of budgets. The first is the sales department budget. This includes the expenses that the sales staff must incur in order to achieve the revenue budget, such as travel and entertainment, as well as sales training. Of particular concern in this budget is the amount of budgeted headcount that is required to meet the sales target. It is essential that the actual sales per salesperson from the most recent completed year of operations be compared with the same calculation in the budget to ensure that there is a sufficiently large budget available for an adequate number of sales personnel. This is a common problem, for companies will make the false assumption that the existing sales staff can make heroic efforts to wildly exceed its previous-year sales efforts. Furthermore, the budget must account for a sufficient time period in which new sales personnel can be trained and form an adequate base of customer contacts to create a meaningful stream of revenue for the company. In some industries, this learning curve may be only a few days, but it can be the better part of a year if considerable technical knowledge is required to make a sale. If the latter situation is the case, it is likely that the procurement and retention of qualified sales staff is the key element of success for a company, which makes the sales department budget one of the most important elements of the entire budget.

The marketing budget is also closely tied to the revenue budget, for it contains all of the funding required to roll out new products, merchandise them properly, advertise for them, test new products, and so on. A key issue here is to ensure that the marketing budget is fully funded to support any increases in sales noted in the revenue budget. It may be necessary to increase this budget by a disproportionate amount if one is trying to create a new brand, issue a new product, or distribute an existing product in a new market. These costs can easily exceed any associated revenues for some time. A common budgeting problem is not to provide sufficient funding in these instances, leading to a significant drop in expected revenues.

Another nonproduction budget that is integral to the success of the corporation is the general and administrative budget. This contains the cost of the corporate management staff, plus all accounting, finance, and human resources personnel. Since this is a cost center, the general inclination is to reduce these costs to the bare minimum. However, in order to do so, there must be a significant investment in technology in order to achieve reductions in the manual labor usually required to process transactions; thus, there must be some provision in the capital budget for this area.

There is a feedback loop between the staffing and direct labor budgets and the general and administrative budget, because the human resources department must staff itself based on the amount of hiring or layoffs that are anticipated elsewhere in the company. Similarly, a major change in the revenue volume will alter the budget for the accounting department, since many of the activities in this area are driven by the volume of sales transactions. Thus, the general and administrative budget generally requires a number of iterations in response to changes in many other parts of the budget.

Though salaries and wages should be listed in each of the departmental budgets, it is useful to list the total headcount for each position through all budget periods in a separate staffing budget. By doing so, the human resources staff can tell when specific positions must be filled, so that they can time their recruiting efforts most appropriately. This budget also provides good information for the person responsible for the facilities budget, since he or she can use it to determine the timing and amount of square footage requirements for office space. Rather than being a standalone budget, the staffing budget tends to be one whose formulas are closely intertwined with those of all other departmental budgets, so that a change in headcount information on this budget will automatically translate into a change in the salaries expense on other budgets. It is also a good place to store the average pay rates, overtime percentages, and average benefit costs for all positions. By centralizing this cost information, the human resources staff can more easily update budget information. Since salary-related costs tend to comprise the highest proportion of costs in a company (excluding materials costs), this tends to be a heavily used budget.

The facilities budget is based on the level of activity that is estimated in many of the budgets just described. For this reason, it is one of the last budgets to be completed. This budget is closely linked to the capital budget, since expenditures for additional facilities will require more maintenance expenses in the facilities budget. This budget typically contains expense line items for building insurance, maintenance, repairs, janitorial services, utilities, and the salaries of the maintenance personnel employed in this function. It is crucial to estimate the need for any upcoming major repairs to facilities when constructing this budget, since these can greatly amplify the total budgeted expense.

Another budget that includes input from virtually all areas of a company is the capital budget. This should comprise either a summary listing of all main fixed asset categories for which purchases are anticipated, or else a detailed listing of the same information; the latter case is recommended only if there are comparatively few items to be purchased. The capital budget is of great importance to the calculation of corporate financing requirements, since it can involve the expenditure of sums far beyond those that are normally encountered through daily cash flows. This topic is addressed in greater detail in Chapter 2, Capital Budgeting Decisions.

The end result of all the budgets just described is a set of financial statements that reflect the impact on the company of the upcoming budget. At a minimum, these statements should include the income statement and cash flow statement, since these are the best evidence of fiscal health during the budget period. The balance sheet is less necessary, since the key factors upon which it reports are related to cash, and that information is already contained within the cash flow statement. These reports should be directly linked to all the other budgets, so that any changes to the budgets will immediately appear in the financial statements. The management team will closely examine these statements and make numerous adjustments to the budgets in order to arrive at a satisfactory financial result.

The budget-linked financial statements are also a good place to store related operational and financial ratios, so that the management team can review this information and revise the budgets in order to alter the ratios to match benchmarking or industry standards that may have been set as goals. Typical measurements in this area can include revenue and income per person, inventory turnover ratios, and gross margin percentages. This type of information is also useful for lenders, who may have required minimum financial performance results as part of loan agreements, such as a minimum current ratio or debt-to-equity ratio.

The cash forecast is of exceptional importance, for it tells company managers whether the proposed budget model will be feasible. If cash projects result in major cash needs that cannot be met by any possible financing, then the model must be changed. The assumptions that go into the cash forecast should be based on strict historical fact, rather than the wishes of managers. This stricture is particularly important in the case of cash receipts from accounts receivable. If the assumptions are changed in the model to reflect an advanced rate of cash receipts that exceeds anything that the company has heretofore experienced, then it is very unlikely that it will be achieved during the budget period. Instead, it is better to use proven collection periods as assumptions and alter other parts of the budget to ensure that cash flows remain positive.

The cash forecast is a particularly good area in which to spot the impact of changes in credit policy. For example, if a company wishes to expand its share of the market by allowing easy credit to marginal customers, then it should lengthen the assumed collection period in the cash forecast to see if there is a significant downgrading of the resulting cash flows.

The other key factor in the cash forecast is the use of delays in budgeted accounts payable payments. It is common for managers to budget for extended payment terms in order to fund other cash flow needs, but there are several problems that can result from this policy. One is the possible loss of key suppliers who will not tolerate late payments. Another is the risk of being charged interest on late payments to suppliers. A third problem is that suppliers may relegate a company to a lower level on their lists of shipment priorities, since they are being paid late. Finally, suppliers may simply raise their prices in order to absorb the cost of the late payments. Consequently, the late payment strategy must be followed with great care, using it only on those suppliers who do not appear to notice, and otherwise doing it only after prior negotiation with targeted suppliers to make the changed terms part of the standard buying agreement.

The last document in the system of budgets is the discussion of financing alternatives. This is not strictly a budget, though it will contain a single line item, derived from the cash forecast, which itemizes funding needs during each period itemized in the budget. In all other respects, it is simply a discussion of financing alternatives, which can be quite varied. This may involve a mix of debt, supplier financing, preferred stock, common stock, or some other, more innovative approach. The document should contain a discussion of the cost of each form of financing, the ability of the company to obtain it, and when it can be obtained. Managers may find that there are so few financing alternatives available, or that the cost of financing is so high, that the entire budget must be restructured in order to avoid the negative cash flow that calls for the financing. There may also be a need for feedback from this document back into the budgeted financial statements in order to account for the cost of obtaining the funding, as well as any related interest costs.

1-2 WHAT DOES A SAMPLE BUDGET LOOK LIKE?

In response this question, we will review several variations on how a budget can be constructed, using a number of examples. The first budget covered is the revenue budget, which is shown in Exhibit 1.2. The exhibit uses quarterly revenue figures for a budget year rather than monthly, in order to conserve space. It contains revenue estimates for three different product lines that are designated as Alpha, Beta, and Charlie.

The Alpha product line uses a budgeting format that identifies the specific quantities that are expected to be sold in each quarter, as well as the average price per unit sold. This format is most useful when there are not so many products that such a detailed delineation would create an excessively lengthy budget. It is a very useful format, for the sales staff can go into the budget model and alter unit volumes and prices quite easily. An alternative format is to reveal this level of detail for only the most important products, and to lump the revenue from other products into a single line item, as is the case for the Beta product line.

The most common budgeting format is used for the Beta product line, where we avoid the use of detailed unit volumes and prices in favor of a single lump-sum revenue total for each reporting period. This format is used when there are multiple products within each product line, making it cumbersome to create a detailed list of individual products. However, this format is the least informative and gives no easy way to update the supporting information.

Yet another budgeting format is shown for the Charlie product line, where projected sales are grouped by region. This format is most useful when there are many sales personnel, each of whom has been assigned a specific territory in which to operate. This budget can then be used to judge the ongoing performance of each salesperson.

Exhibit 1.2 Revenue Budget for the Fiscal Year Ended xx/xx/07

	Quarter 1	Quarter 2	Quarter 3	Quarter 4	Totals
Product Line Alpha:					
Unit Price	$15.00	$14.85	$14.80	$14.75	—
Unit Volume	14,000	21,000	25,000	31,000	91,000
Revenue Subtotal	$210,000	$311,850	$370,000	$457,250	$1,349,100
Product Line Beta:					
Revenue Subtotal	$1,048,000	$1,057,000	$1,061,000	$1,053,000	$4,219,000
Product Line Charlie:					
Region 1	$123,000	$95,000	$82,000	$70,000	$370,000
Region 2	$80,000	$89,000	$95,000	$101,000	$365,000
Region 3	$95,000	$95,000	$65,000	$16,000	$271,000
Region 4	$265,000	$265,000	$320,000	$375,000	$1,225,000
Revenue Subtotal	$563,000	$544,000	$562,000	$562,000	$2,231,000
Revenue Grand Total	$1,821,000	$1,912,850	$1,993,000	$2,072,250	$7,799,100
Quarterly Revenue Proportion	23.3%	24.5%	25.6%	26.6%	100.0%
Statistics:					
Product Line Proportion:					
Alpha	11.5%	16.3%	18.6%	22.1%	17.3%
Beta	57.6%	55.3%	53.2%	50.8%	54.1%
Charlie	30.9%	28.4%	28.2%	27.1%	28.6%
Product Line Total	100.0%	100.0%	100.0%	100.0%	100.0%

Exhibit 1.3   Production & Inventory Budget for the Fiscal Year Ended xx/xx/07

	Quarter 1	Quarter 2	Quarter 3	Quarter 4	Totals
Inventory Turnover Goals:					
Raw Materials Turnover	4.0	4.5	5.0	5.5	4.8
W-I-P Turnover	12.0	15.0	18.0	21.0	16.5
Finished Goods Turnover	6.0	6.0	9.0	9.0	7.5
Product Line Alpha Production:					
Beginning Inventory Units	15,000	21,000	20,000	15,000	—
Unit Sales Budget	14,000	21,000	25,000	31,000	91,000
Planned Production	20,000	20,000	20,000	27,375	87,375
Ending Inventory Units	21,000	20,000	15,000	11,375	
Bottleneck Unit Capacity	20,000	20,000	20,000	40,000	
Bottleneck Utilization	100%	100%	100%	68%	
Planned Finished Goods Turnover	15,167	15,167	11,375	11,375	

These revenue reporting formats can also be combined, so that the product line detail for the Alpha product can be used as underlying detail for the sales regions used for the Charlie product line—though this will result in a very lengthy budget document.

There is also a statistics section at the bottom of the revenue budget that itemizes the proportion of total sales that occurs in each quarter, plus the proportion of product line sales within each quarter. Though it is not necessary to use these exact measurements, it is useful to include some type of measure that informs the reader of any variations in sales from period to period.

Both the production and inventory budgets are shown in Exhibit 1.3. The inventory budget is itemized at the top of the exhibit, where we itemize the amount of planned inventory turnover in all three inventory categories. There is a considerable ramp-up in work-in-process inventory turnover, indicating the planned installation of a manufacturing planning system of some kind that will control the flow of materials through the facility.

The production budget for just the Alpha product line is shown directly below the inventory goals. This budget is not concerned with the cost of production, but rather with the number of units that will be produced. In this instance, we begin with an on-hand inventory of 15,000 units, and try to keep enough units on hand through the remainder of the budget year to meet both the finished goods inventory goal at the top of the exhibit and the number of required units to be sold, which is referenced from the revenue budget. The main problem is that the maximum capacity of the bottleneck operation is 20,000 units per quarter. In order to meet the revenue target, we must run that operation at full bore through the first three quarters, irrespective of the inventory turnover target. This is especially important because the budget indicates a jump in bottleneck capacity in the fourth quarter from 20,000 to 40,000 units—this will occur when the bottleneck operation is stopped for a short time while additional equipment is added to it. During this stoppage, there must be enough excess inventory on hand to cover any sales that will arise. Consequently, production is planned for 20,000 units per quarter for the first three quarters, followed by a more precisely derived figure in the fourth quarter that will result in inventory turns of 9.0 at the end of the year, exactly as planned.

The production budget can be enhanced with the incorporation of planned machine downtime for maintenance, as well as for the planned loss of production units to scrap. It is also useful to plan for the capacity needs of nonbottleneck work centers, since these areas will require varying levels of staffing, depending on the number of production shifts needed.

The purchasing budget is shown in Exhibit 1.4. This contains several different formats for planning budgeted purchases for the Alpha product line. The first option summarizes the planned production for each quarter; this information is brought forward from the production budget. We then multiply this by the standard unit cost of materials to arrive at the total amount of purchases that must be made in order to adequately support sales. The second option identifies the specific cost of each component of the product, so that management can see where cost increases are expected to occur. Though this version provides more information, it occupies a great deal of space on the budget if there are many components in each product, or many products. A third option is shown at the bottom of the exhibit that summarizes all purchases by commodity type. This format is most useful for the company's buyers, who usually specialize in certain commodity types.

The purchasing budget can be enhanced by adding a scrap factor for budgeted production, which will result in slightly higher quantities to buy, thereby leaving less chance of running out of raw materials. Another upgrade to the exhibit would be to schedule purchases for planned production some time in advance of the actual manufacturing date, so that the purchasing staff will be assured of having the parts on hand when manufacturing begins. A third enhancement is to round off the purchasing volumes for each item into the actual buying volumes that can be obtained on the open market. For example, it may be possible to buy the required labels only in volumes of 100,000 at a time, which would result in a planned purchase at the beginning of the year that would be large enough to cover all production needs through the end of the year.

The direct labor budget is shown in Exhibit 1.5. This budget assumes that only one labor category will vary directly with revenue volume; that category is the final assembly department, where a percentage in the far right column indicates that the cost in this area will be budgeted at a fixed 3.5 percent of total revenues. In all other cases, there are assumptions for a fixed number of personnel in each position within each production department. All of the wage figures for each department (except for final assembly) are derived from the planned hourly rates and headcount figures noted

Exhibit 1.4 Purchasing Budget for the Fiscal Year Ended xx/xx/07

	Quarter 1	Quarter 2	Quarter 3	Quarter 4	Totals
Inventory Turnover Goals:					
Raw Materials Turnover	4.0	4.5	5.0	5.5	4.8
Product Line Alpha Purchasing (Option 1):					
Planned Production	20,000	20,000	20,000	27,375	
Standard Materials Cost/Unit	$5.42	$5.42	$5.67	$5.67	
Total Material Cost	$108,400	$108,400	$113,400	$155,216	$485,416
Product Line Alpha Purchasing (Option 2):					
Planned Production	20,000	20,000	20,000	27,375	
Molded Part	$4.62	$4.62	$4.85	$4.85	
Labels	$0.42	$0.42	$0.42	$0.42	
Fittings & Fasteners	$0.38	$0.38	$0.40	$0.40	
Total Cost of Components	$5.42	$5.42	$5.67	$5.67	
Product Line Alpha Purchasing (Option 2):					
Plastic Commodities					
Molded Parts Units	20,000	20,000	20,000	27,375	
Molded Parts Cost	$4.62	$4.62	$4.85	$4.85	
Adhesives Commodity					
Labels Units	20,000	20,000	20,000	27,375	
Labels Cost	$0.42	$0.42	$0.42	$0.42	
Fasteners Commodity					
Fasteners Units	20,000	20,000	20,000	27,375	
Fasteners Cost	$0.38	$0.38	$0.40	$0.40	
Statistics:					
Materials as Percent of Revenue	36%	36%	38%	38%	

at the bottom of the page. This budget can be enhanced with the addition of separate line items for payroll tax percentages, benefits, shift differential payments, and overtime expenses. The cost of the final assembly department can also be adjusted to account for worker efficiency, which will be lower during production ramp-up periods when new, untrained employees are added to the workforce.

A sample of the overhead budget is shown in Exhibit 1.6. In this exhibit, we see that the overhead budget is really made up of a number of subsidiary departments, such as maintenance, materials management, and quality assurance. If the budgets of any of these departments are large enough, it makes a great deal of sense to split them off into a separate budget, so that the managers of those departments can see their budgeted expectations more clearly. Of particular interest in this exhibit is the valid

Exhibit 1.5   Direct Labor Budget for the Fiscal Year Ended xx/xx/07

	Quarter 1	Quarter 2	Quarter 3	Quarter 4	Totals	Notes
Machining Department:						
Sr. Machine Operator	$15,120	$15,372	$23,058	$23,058	$76,608	
Machining Apprentice	$4,914	$4,964	$9,929	$9,929	$29,736	
Expense Subtotal	$20,034	$20,336	$32,987	$32,987	$106,344	
Paint Department:						
Sr. Paint Shop Staff	$15,876	$16,128	$16,128	$16,128	$64,260	
Painter Apprentice	$5,065	$5,216	$5,216	$5,216	$20,714	
Expense Subtotal	$20,941	$21,344	$21,344	$21,344	$84,974	
Polishing Department:						
Sr. Polishing Staff	$16,632	$11,844	$11,844	$11,844	$52,164	
Polishing Apprentice	$4,360	$4,511	$4,511	$4,511	$17,892	
Expense Subtotal	$20,992	$16,355	$16,355	$16,355	$70,056	
Final Assembly Department:						
General Laborer	$63,735	$66,950	$69,755	$72,529	$272,969	3.5%
Expense Subtotal	$63,735	$66,950	$69,755	$72,529	$272,969	
Expense Grand Total	$125,702	$124,985	$140,441	$143,215	$534,343	
Statistics:						
Union Hourly Rates:						
Sr. Machine Operator	$15.00	$15.25	$15.25	$15.25		
Machining Apprentice	$9.75	$9.85	$9.85	$9.85		
Sr. Paint Shop Staff	$15.75	$16.00	$16.00	$16.00		
Painter Apprentice	$10.05	$10.35	$10.35	$10.35		
Sr. Polishing Staff	$11.00	$11.75	$11.75	$11.75		
Polishing Apprentice	$8.65	$8.95	$8.95	$8.95		
Headcount by Position:						
Sr. Machine Operator	2	2	3	3		
Machining Apprentice	1	1	2	2		
Sr. Paint Shop Staff	2	2	2	2		
Painter Apprentice	1	1	1	1		
Sr. Polishing Staff	3	2	2	2		
Polishing Apprentice	1	1	1	1		

Exhibit 1.6   Overhead Budget for the Fiscal Year Ended xx/xx/07

	Quarter 1	Quarter 2	Quarter 3	Quarter 4	Totals	Valid Capacity Range
Supervision:						
Production Manager Salary	$16,250	$16,250	$16,250	$16,250	$65,000	—
Shift Manager Salaries	$22,000	$22,000	$23,500	$23,500	$91,000	40%–70%
Expense Subtotal	$38,250	$38,250	$39,750	$39,750	$156,000	
Maintenance Department:						
Equipment Maint. Staff	$54,000	$56,500	$58,000	$60,250	$228,750	40%–70%
Facilities Maint. Staff	$8,250	$8,250	$8,500	$8,500	$33,500	40%–70%
Equipment Repairs	$225,000	$225,000	$275,000	$225,000	$950,000	40%–70%
Facility Repairs	$78,000	$29,000	$12,000	$54,000	$173,000	40%–70%
Expense Subtotal	$365,250	$318,750	$353,500	$347,750	$1,385,250	
Materials Management Department:						
Manager Salary	$18,750	$18,750	$18,750	$18,750	$75,000	—
Purchasing Staff	$28,125	$18,750	$18,750	$18,750	$84,375	40%–70%
Materials Mgmt. Staff	$28,000	$35,000	$35,000	$35,000	$133,000	40%–70%
Production Control Staff	$11,250	$11,250	$11,250	$11,250	$45,000	40%–70%
Expense Subtotal	$86,125	$83,750	$83,750	$83,750	$337,375	
Quality Department:						
Manager Salary	$13,750	$13,750	$13,750	$13,750	$55,000	—
Quality Staff	$16,250	$16,250	$16,250	$24,375	$73,125	40%–70%
Lab Testing Supplies	$5,000	$4,500	$4,500	$4,500	$18,500	40%–70%
Expense Subtotal	$35,000	$34,500	$34,500	$42,625	$146,625	
Other Expenses:						
Depreciation	$14,000	$15,750	$15,750	$15,750	$61,250	—
Utilities	$60,000	$55,000	$55,000	$60,000	$230,000	40%–70%
Boiler Insurance	$3,200	$3,200	$3,200	$3,200	$12,800	—
Expense Subtotal	$77,200	$73,950	$73,950	$78,950	$304,050	
Expense Grand Total	$601,825	$549,200	$585,450	$592,825	$2,329,300	

capacity range noted on the far-right side of the exhibit. This signifies the production activity level within which the budgeted overhead costs are accurate. If the actual capacity utilization were to fall outside of this range, either high or low, a separate overhead budget should be constructed with costs that are expected to be incurred within those ranges.

A sample cost-of-goods-sold budget is shown in Exhibit 1.7. This format splits out each of the product lines noted in the revenue budget for reporting purposes, and subtracts from each one the materials costs that are noted in the purchases budget. This results in a contribution margin for each product line that is the clearest representation of the impact of direct costs (usually direct material costs) on each one. We then summarize these individual contribution margins into a summary-level contribution margin, and then subtract the total direct labor and overhead costs (as referenced from the direct labor and overhead budgets) to arrive at a total gross margin. The statistics section also notes the number of production personnel budgeted for each quarterly reporting period, plus the average annual revenue per production employee—these statistics can be replaced with any operational information that management wants to see at a summary level for the production function, such as efficiency levels, capacity utilization, or inventory turnover.

The sales department budget is shown in Exhibit 1.8. This budget shows several different ways in which to organize the budget information. At the top of the budget is a block of line items that lists the expenses for those overhead costs within the department that cannot be specifically linked to a salesperson or region. In cases where the number of sales staff is quite small, *all* of the department's costs may be listed in this area.

Another alternative is shown in the second block of expense line items in the middle of the sales department budget, where all of the sales costs for an entire product line are lumped together into a single line item. If each person on the sales staff is exclusively assigned to a single product line, then it may make sense to break down the budget into separate budget pages for each product line, and list all of the expenses associated with each product line on a separate page.

A third alternative is shown next in the exhibit, where we list a summary of expenses for each sales person. This format works well when combined with the departmental overhead expenses at the top of the budget, since this accounts for all of the departmental costs. However, this format brings up a confidentiality issue, since the compensation of each sales person can be inferred from the report. Also, this format would include the commission expense paid to each sales person; since commissions are a variable cost that is directly associated with each incremental dollar of sales, they should be itemized as a separate line item within the cost of goods sold.

A final option listed at the bottom of the example is to itemize expenses by sales region. This format works best when there are a number of sales personnel within the department who are clustered into a number of clearly identifiable regions. If there were no obvious regions or if there were only one salesperson per region, then the better format would be to list expenses by salesperson.

Exhibit 1.7   Cost-of-Goods-Sold Budget for the Fiscal Year Ended xx/xx/07

	Quarter 1	Quarter 2	Quarter 3	Quarter 4	Totals
Product Line Alpha:					
Revenue	$210,000	$311,850	$370,000	$457,250	$1,349,100
Materials Expense	$108,400	$108,400	$113,400	$155,216	$485,416
Contribution Margin $$	$101,600	$203,450	$256,600	$302,034	$863,684
Contribution Margin %	48%	65%	69%	66%	64%
Product Line Beta:					
Revenue	$1,048,000	$1,057,000	$1,061,000	$1,053,000	$4,219,000
Materials Expense	$12,000	$14,000	$15,000	$13,250	$54,250
Contribution Margin $$	$1,036,000	$1,043,000	$1,046,000	$1,039,750	$4,164,750
Contribution Margin %	99%	99%	99%	99%	99%
Revenue—Product Line Charlie:					
Revenue	$563,000	$544,000	$562,000	$562,000	$2,231,000
Materials Expense	$268,000	$200,000	$220,000	$230,000	$918,000
Contribution Margin $$	$295,000	$344,000	$342,000	$332,000	$1,313,000
Contribution Margin %	52%	63%	61%	59%	59%
Total Contribution Margin $$	$1,432,600	$1,590,450	$1,644,600	$1,673,784	$6,341,434
Total Contribution Margin %	79%	83%	83%	81%	81%
Direct Labor Expense:	$125,702	$124,985	$140,441	$143,215	$534,343
Overhead Expense:	$601,825	$549,200	$585,450	$592,825	$2,329,300
Total Gross Margin $$	$705,073	$916,265	$918,709	$937,744	$3,477,791
Total Gross Margin %	39%	48%	46%	45%	44%
Statistics:					
No. of Production Staff*	23	22	22	23	
Ave. Annual Revenue per Production Employee	$316,696	$347,791	$362,364	$360,391	

*Not including general assembly staff.

At the bottom of the budget is the usual statistics section. The sales department budget is concerned only with making sales, so it should be no surprise that revenue per salesperson is the first item listed. Also, since the primary sales cost associated with this department is usually travel costs, the other statistical item is the travel and entertainment cost per person.

Exhibit 1.8   Sales Department Budget for the Fiscal Year Ended xx/xx/07

	Quarter 1	Quarter 2	Quarter 3	Quarter 4	Totals
Departmental Overhead:					
Depreciation	$500	$500	$500	$500	$2,000
Office Supplies	$750	$600	$650	$600	$2,600
Payroll Taxes	$2,945	$5,240	$5,240	$8,186	$21,611
Salaries	$38,500	$68,500	$68,500	$107,000	$282,500
Travel & Entertainment	$1,500	$1,500	$1,500	$2,000	$6,500
Expense Subtotal	$44,195	$76,340	$76,390	$118,286	$315,211
Product Line Alpha:	$32,000	$18,000	$0	$21,000	$71,000
Expenses by Salesperson:					
Jones, Milbert	$14,000	$16,500	$17,000	$12,000	$59,500
Smidley, Jefferson	$1,000	$9,000	$8,000	$12,000	$30,000
Verity, Jonas	$7,000	$9,000	$14,000	$12,000	$42,000
Expense Subtotal	$22,000	$34,500	$39,000	$36,000	$131,500
Expenses by Region:					
East Coast	$52,000	$71,000	$15,000	$0	$138,000
Midwest Coast	$8,000	$14,000	$6,000	$12,000	$40,000
West Coast	$11,000	$10,000	$12,000	$24,000	$57,000
Expense Subtotal	$71,000	$95,000	$33,000	$36,000	$235,000
Expense Grand Total	$137,195	$205,840	$148,390	$190,286	$681,711
Statistics:					
Revenue per Salesperson	$607,000	$637,617	$664,333	$690,750	$2,599,700
T&E per Salesperson	$500	$500	$500	$667	$2,167

Exhibit 1.9 shows a sample marketing budget. As was the case for the sales department, this one also itemizes departmental overhead costs at the top, which leaves space in the middle for the itemization of campaign-specific costs in the middle. The campaign-specific costs can be lumped together for individual product lines, as is the case for product lines Alpha and Beta in the exhibit, or with subsidiary line items, as is shown for product line Charlie. A third possible format, which is to itemize marketing costs by marketing tool (e.g., advertising, promotional tour, coupon redemption, etc.) is generally not recommended if there is more than one product line, since there is no way for an analyst to determine the impact of individual marketing costs on specific product lines. The statistics at the bottom of the page attempt to compare marketing costs to sales; however, this should be treated as only an

Exhibit 1.9   Marketing Budget for the Fiscal Year Ended xx/xx/07

	Quarter 1	Quarter 2	Quarter 3	Quarter 4	Totals
Departmental Overhead:					
Depreciation	650	750	850	1,000	3,250
Office Supplies	200	200	200	200	800
Payroll Taxes	4,265	4,265	4,265	4,265	17,060
Salaries	$55,750	$55,750	$55,750	$55,750	223,000
Travel & Entertainment	5,000	6,500	7,250	7,250	26,000
Expense Subtotal	65,865	67,465	68,315	68,465	270,110
Campaign-Specific Expenses:					
Product Line Alpha	14,000	26,000	30,000	0	70,000
Product Line Beta	18,000	0	0	24,000	42,000
Product Line Charlie					0
Advertising	10,000	0	20,000	0	30,000
Promotional Tour	5,000	25,000	2,000	0	32,000
Coupon Redemption	2,000	4,000	4,500	1,200	11,700
Product Samples	2,750	5,250	1,250	0	9,250
Expense Subtotal	51,750	60,250	57,750	25,200	194,950
Expense Grand Total	117,615	127,715	126,065	93,665	465,060
Statistics:					
Expense as Percent of Total Sales	6.5%	6.7%	6.3%	4.5%	6.0%
Expense Proportion by Quarter	25.3%	27.5%	27.1%	20.1%	100.0%

approximation, since marketing efforts will usually not result in immediate sales, but rather will result in sales that build over time. Thus, there is a time lag after incurring a marketing cost that makes it difficult to determine the efficacy of marketing activities.

A sample general and administrative budget is shown in Exhibit 1.10. This budget can be quite lengthy, including such additional line items as postage, copier leases, and office repair. Many of these extra expenses have been pruned from the exhibit in order to provide a compressed view of the general format to be used. The exhibit does not lump together the costs of the various departments that are typically included in this budget, but rather identifies each one in separate blocks; this format is most useful when there are separate managers for the accounting and human resources functions, so that they will have a better understanding of their budgets. The statistics section at the bottom of the page itemizes a benchmark target of the total general and administrative cost as a proportion of revenue. This is a particularly useful statistic

Exhibit 1.10   General & Administrative Budget for the Fiscal Year Ended xx/xx/07

	Quarter 1	Quarter 2	Quarter 3	Quarter 4	Totals	Notes
Accounting Department:						
Depreciation	4,000	4,000	4,250	4,250	16,500	
Office Supplies	650	650	750	750	2,800	
Payroll Taxes	4,973	4,973	4,973	4,973	19,890	
Salaries	$65,000	$65,000	$65,000	$65,000	260,000	
Training	500	2,500	7,500	0	10,500	
Travel & Entertainment	0	750	4,500	500	5,750	
Expense Subtotal	75,123	77,873	86,973	75,473	315,440	
Corporate Expenses:						
Depreciation	450	500	550	600	2,100	
Office Supplies	1,000	850	750	1,250	3,850	
Payroll Taxes	6,598	6,598	6,598	6,598	26,393	
Salaries	$86,250	$86,250	$86,250	$86,250	345,000	
Insurance, Business	4,500	4,500	4,500	4,500	18,000	
Training	5,000	0	0	0	5,000	
Travel & Entertainment	2,000	500	500	0	3,000	
Expense Subtotal	105,798	99,198	99,148	99,198	403,343	
Human Resources Department:						
Benefits programs	7,284	7,651	7,972	8,289	31,196	**0.4%**
Depreciation	500	500	500	500	2,000	
Office Supplies	450	8,000	450	450	9,350	
Payroll Taxes	2,869	2,869	2,869	2,869	11,475	
Salaries	$37,500	$37,500	$37,500	$37,500	150,000	
Training	5,000	0	7,500	0	12,500	
Travel & Entertainment	2,000	1,000	3,500	1,000	7,500	
Expense Subtotal	55,603	57,520	60,291	50,608	224,021	
Expense Grand Total	236,523	234,591	246,411	225,278	942,804	
Statistics:						
Expense as Proportion of Revenue	13.0%	12.3%	12.4%	10.9%	12.1%	
Benchmark Comparison	11.5%	11.5%	11.5%	11.5%	11.5%	

to track, since the general and administrative function is a cost center, and requires such a comparison in order to inform management that these costs are being held in check.

A staffing budget is shown in Exhibit 1.11. This itemizes the expected headcount in every department by major job category. It does not attempt to identify individual

Exhibit 1.11   Staffing Budget for the Fiscal Year Ended xx/xx/07

	Quarter 1	Quarter 2	Quarter 3	Quarter 4	Average Salary	Overtime Percent
Sales Department:						
Regional Sales Manager	1	2	2	3	$120,000	0%
Salesperson	2	4	4	6	$65,000	0%
Sales Support Staff	1	1	1	2	$34,000	6%
Marketing Department:						
Marketing Manager	1	1	1	1	$85,000	0%
Marketing Researcher	2	2	2	2	$52,000	0%
Secretary	1	1	1	1	$34,000	6%
General & Administrative:						
President	1	1	1	1	$175,000	0%
Chief Operating Officer	1	1	1	1	$125,000	0%
Chief Financial Officer	1	1	1	1	$100,000	0%
Human Resources Mgr.	1	1	1	1	$80,000	0%
Accounting Staff	4	4	4	4	$40,000	10%
Human Resources Staff	2	2	2	2	$35,000	8%
Executive Secretary	1	1	1	1	$45,000	6%
Research Department:						
Chief Scientist	1	1	1	1	$100,000	0%
Senior Engineer Staff	3	3	3	4	$80,000	0%
Junior Engineer Staff	3	3	3	3	$60,000	0%
Overhead Budget:						
Production Manager	1	1	1	1	$65,000	0%
Quality Manager	1	1	1	1	$55,000	0%
Materials Manager	1	1	1	1	$75,000	0%
Production Scheduler	1	1	1	1	$45,000	0%
Quality Assurance Staff	2	2	2	3	$32,500	8%
Purchasing Staff	3	2	2	2	$37,500	8%
Materials Mgmt Staff	4	5	5	5	$28,000	8%
Total Headcount	39	42	42	48		

positions, since that can lead to an excessively lengthy list. Also, because there may be multiple positions identified within each job category, the *average* salary for each cluster of jobs is identified. If a position is subject to overtime pay, its expected overtime percentage is identified on the right side of the budget. Many sections of the budget should have linkages to this page, so that any changes in headcount here will be automatically reflected in the other sections. This budget may have to be restricted from general access, since it contains salary information that may be considered confidential information.

Exhibit 1.12   Facilities Budget for the Fiscal Year Ended xx/xx/07

	Quarter 1	Quarter 2	Quarter 3	Quarter 4	Totals
Facilty Expenses:					
Contracted Services	$5,500	$5,400	$5,000	$4,500	$20,400
Depreciation	$29,000	$29,000	$28,000	$28,000	$114,000
Electricity Charges	$4,500	$3,500	$3,500	$4,500	$16,000
Inspection Fees	$500	$0	$0	$500	$1,000
Insurance	$8,000	$0	$0	$0	$8,000
Maintenance Supplies	$3,000	$3,000	$3,000	$3,000	$12,000
Payroll Taxes	$1,148	$1,148	$1,148	$1,186	$4,628
Property Taxes	$0	$5,000	$0	$0	$5,000
Repairs	$15,000	$0	$29,000	$0	$44,000
Sewage Charges	$250	$250	$250	$250	$1,000
Trash Disposal	$3,000	$3,000	$3,000	$3,000	$12,000
Wages—Janitorial	$5,000	$5,000	$5,000	$5,500	$20,500
Wages—Maintenance	$10,000	$10,000	$10,000	$10,000	$40,000
Water Charges	$1,000	$1,000	$1,000	$1,000	$4,000
Expense Grand Total	$85,898	$66,298	$88,898	$61,436	$302,528
Statistics:					
Total Square Feet	52,000	52,000	78,000	78,000	
Square Feet/Employee	839	813	1,219	1,099	
Unused Square Footage	1,200	1,200	12,500	12,500	

The facilities budget tends to have the largest number of expense line items. A sample of this format is shown in Exhibit 1.12. These expenses may be offset by some rental or sub-lease revenues if a portion of the company facilities is rented out to other organizations. However, this revenue is shown in this budget only if the revenue amount is small; otherwise, it is more commonly found as an "other revenue" line item on the revenue budget. A statistics section is found at the bottom of this budget that refers to the total amount of square feet occupied by the facility. A very effective statistic is the amount of unused square footage, which can be used to conduct an ongoing program of selling off, renting, or consolidating company facilities.

The research department's budget is shown in Exhibit 1.13. It is most common to segregate the department-specific overhead that cannot be attributed to a specific project at the top of the budget, and then cluster costs by project below that. By doing so, the management team can see precisely how much money is being allocated to each project. This may be of use in determining which projects must be canceled or delayed as part of the budget review process. The statistics section at the bottom of the budget notes the proportion of planned expenses among the categories of overhead, research, and development. These proportions can be examined to see whether the company is allocating funds to the right balance of projects that most effectively meets it product development goals.

Exhibit 1.13　Research Department for the Fiscal Year Ended xx/xx/07

	Quarter 1	Quarter 2	Quarter 3	Quarter 4	Totals
Departmental Overhead:					
Depreciation	500	500	400	400	1,800
Office supplies	750	2,000	1,500	1,250	5,500
Payroll Taxes	9,945	9,945	9,945	11,475	41,310
Salaries	$130,000	$130,000	$130,000	$150,000	540,000
Travel & Entertainment	0	0	0	0	0
Expense Subtotal	141,195	142,445	141,845	163,125	588,610
Research-Specific Expenses:					
Gamma Project	20,000	43,500	35,000	12,500	111,000
Omega Project	5,000	6,000	7,500	9,000	27,500
Pi Project	14,000	7,000	7,500	4,500	33,000
Upsilon Project	500	2,500	5,000	0	8,000
Expense Subtotal	39,500	59,000	55,000	26,000	179,500
Development-Specific Expenses:					
Latin Project	28,000	29,000	30,000	15,000	102,000
Greek Project	14,000	14,500	15,000	7,500	51,000
Mabinogian Project	20,000	25,000	15,000	10,000	70,000
Old English Project	6,250	12,500	25,000	50,000	93,750
Expense Subtotal	68,250	81,000	85,000	82,500	316,750
Expense Grand Total	248,945	282,445	281,845	271,625	1,084,860
Statistics:					
Budgeted Number of Patent Applications Filed	2	0	1	1	4
Proportion of Expenses:					
Overhead	56.7%	50.4%	50.3%	60.1%	217.5%
Research	15.9%	20.9%	19.5%	9.6%	65.8%
Development	27.4%	28.7%	30.2%	30.4%	116.6%
Total Expenses	100.0%	100.0%	100.0%	100.0%	400.0%

The capital budget is shown in Exhibit 1.14. This format clusters capital expenditures by a number of categories. For example, the first category, entitled "bottleneck-related expenditures," clearly focuses attention on those outgoing payments that will increase the company's key productive capacity. The payments in the third quarter under this heading are directly related to the increase in bottleneck capacity that was shown the production budget for the fourth quarter. The budget also contains an automatic assumption of $7,000 in capital expenditures for any net

Exhibit 1.14   Capital Budget for the Fiscal Year Ended xx/xx/07

	Quarter 1	Quarter 2	Quarter 3	Quarter 4	Totals
Bottleneck-Related Expeditures:					
Stamping Machine			$150,000		$150,000
Facility for Machine			$72,000		$72,000
Headcount-Related Expenditures:					
Headcount Change x					
$7,000 Added Staff	$0	$21,000	$0	$42,000	$63,000
Profit-Related Expenditures:					
Blending Machine		$50,000			$50,000
Polishing Machine		$27,000			$27,000
Safety-Related Expenditures:					
Machine Shielding		$3,000	$3,000		$6,000
Handicapped Walkways	$8,000	$5,000			$13,000
Required Expenditures:					
Clean Air Scrubber			$42,000		$42,000
Other Expenditures:					
Tool Crib Expansion				$18,500	$18,500
Total Expenditures	$8,000	$106,000	$267,000	$60,500	$441,500

increase in non–direct labor headcount, which encompasses the cost of computer equipment and office furniture for each person. If the company's capitalization limit is set too high to list these expenditures on the capital budget, then a similar line item should be inserted into the general and administrative budget, so that the expense can be recognized under the office supplies or some similar account.

The capital budget also includes a category for profit-related expenditures. Any projects listed in this category should be subject to an intensive expenditure review to ensure that they return a sufficient cash flow to make their acquisition profitable to the company. Other categories in the budget cover expenditures for safety or required items, which tend to be purchased with no cash flow discounting review. An alternative to this grouping system is to list only the sum total of all capital expenditures in each category, which is most frequently done when there are far too many separate purchases to list on the budget. Another variation is to list only the largest expenditures on separate budget lines, and cluster together all smaller ones. The level of capital purchasing activity will determine the type of format used.

All of the preceding budgets roll up into the budgeted income and cash flow statement, which is noted in Exhibit 1.15. This format lists the grand totals from all preceding pages of the budget in order to arrive at a profit or loss for each budget quarter. In the example, we see that a large initial loss in the first quarter is gradually

Exhibit 1.15   Income and Cash Flow Statement for the Fiscal Year Ended xx/xx/07

	Quarter 1	Quarter 2	Quarter 3	Quarter 4	Totals
	$1,821,000	$1,912,850	$1,993,000	$2,072,250	$7,799,100
Revenue:					
Cost of Goods Sold:					
Materials	$388,400	$322,400	$348,400	$398,466	$1,457,666
Direct Labor	$125,702	$124,985	$140,441	$143,215	$534,343
Overhead					
Supervision	$38,250	$38,250	$39,750	$39,750	$156,000
Maintenance Department	$365,250	$318,750	$353,500	$347,750	$1,385,250
Materials Management	$86,125	$83,750	$83,750	$83,750	$337,375
Quality Department	$35,000	$34,500	$34,500	$42,625	$146,625
Other Expenses	$77,200	$73,950	$73,950	$78,950	$304,050
Total Cost of Goods Sold	$1,115,927	$996,585	$1,074,291	$1,134,506	$4,321,309
Gross Margin	$705,073	$916,265	$918,709	$937,744	$3,477,791
Operating Expenses:					
Sales Department	$137,195	$205,840	$148,390	$190,286	$681,711
General & Admin. Dept.					
Accounting	$75,123	$77,873	$86,973	$75,473	$315,440
Corporate	$105,798	$99,198	$99,148	$99,198	$403,343
Human Resources	$55,603	$57,520	$60,291	$50,608	$224,021
Marketing Department	$117,615	$127,715	$126,065	$93,665	$465,060
Facilities Department	$85,898	$66,298	$88,898	$61,436	$302,528
Research Department	$248,945	$282,445	$281,845	$271,625	$1,084,860
Total Operating Expenses	$826,176	$916,888	$891,609	$842,290	$3,476,963
Net Profit (Loss)	−$121,103	−$624	$27,100	$95,455	$828

	Quarter 1	Quarter 2	Quarter 3	Quarter 4	Totals
Cash Flow:					
Beginning Cash	$100,000	$20,497	−$34,627	−$223,727	
Net Profit (Loss)	−$121,103	−$624	$27,100	$95,455	$828
Add Depreciation	$49,600	$51,500	$50,800	$51,000	$202,900
Minus Capital Purchases	−$8,000	−$106,000	−$267,000	−$60,500	−$441,500
Ending Cash	$20,497	−$34,627	−$223,727	−$137,772	

offset by smaller gains in later quarters to arrive at a small profit for the year. However, the presentation continues with a cash flow statement that has less positive results. It begins with the net profit figure for each quarter, adds back the depreciation expense for all departments, and subtracts out all planned capital expenditures from the capital budget to arrive at cash flow needs for the year. This tells us that the company will

Exhibit 1.16   Financing Budget for the Fiscal Year Ended xx/xx/07

	Quarter 1	Quarter 2	Quarter 3	Quarter 4	Financing Cost
Cash Position:	$20,497	−$34,627	−$223,727	−$137,772	
Financing Option One:					
Additional Debt		$225,000			9.5%
Financing Option Two:					
Additional Preferred Stock	$225,000				8.0%
Financing Option Three:					
Additional Common Stock	$225,000				18.0%
Existing Capital Structure:					
Debt	400,000				9.0%
Preferred Stock	$150,000				7.5%
Common Stock	$500,000				18.0%
Existing Cost of Capital	11.8%				
Revised Cost of Capital:					
Financing Option One	10.7%				
Financing Option Two	11.2%				
Financing Option Three	12.9%				

Note: Tax rate equals 38%.

experience a maximum cash shortfall in the third quarter. This format can be made more precise by adding in time lag factors for the payment of accounts payable and the collection of accounts receivable.

The final document in the budget is an itemization of the finances needed to ensure that the rest of the budget can be achieved. An example is shown in Exhibit 1.16, which carries forward the final cash position at the end of each quarter that was the product of the preceding cash flow statement. This line shows that there will be a maximum shortfall of $223,727 by the end of the third quarter. The next section of the budget outlines several possible options for obtaining the required funds (which are rounded up to $225,000)—debt, preferred stock, or common stock. The financing cost of each one is noted in the far-right column, where we see that the interest cost on debt is 9.5 percent, the dividend on preferred stock is 8 percent, and the expected return by common stockholders is 18 percent.

The third section on the page lists the existing capital structure, its cost, and the net cost of capital. This is quite important, for anyone reviewing this document can see what impact the financing options will have on the capital structure if any of them are selected. For example, the management team may prefer the low cost of debt, but can also use the existing capital structure presentation to see that this will result in a very high proportion of debt to equity, which increases the risk that the company cannot afford to repay the debt to the lender.

The fourth and final part of the budget calculates any changes in the cost of capital that will arise if any of the three financing options are selected. A footnote points out the incremental corporate tax rate; this is of importance to the calculation of the cost of capital, because the interest cost of debt can be deducted as an expense, thereby reducing its net cost. In the exhibit, selecting additional debt as the preferred form of financing will result in a reduction in the cost of capital to 10.7 percent, whereas a selection of high-cost common stock will result in an increase in the cost of capital to 12.9 percent. These changes can have an impact on what types of capital projects are accepted in the future, for the cash flows associated with them must be discounted by the cost of capital in order to see if they result in positive cash flows. Accordingly, a reduction in the cost of capital will mean that projects with marginal cash flows will become more acceptable, while the reverse will be true for a higher cost of capital.

The budgeting examples shown here can be used as the format for a real-life corporate budget. However, it must be adjusted to include a company's chart of accounts and departmental structure, so that it more accurately reflects actual operations. Also, it should include a detailed benefits and payroll tax calculation page, which will itemize the cost of Social Security taxes, Medicare, unemployment insurance, worker's compensation insurance, medical insurance, and so on. These costs are a substantial part of a company's budget, and yet are commonly lumped together into a simplistic budget model that does not accurately reflect their true cost.

Though the budget model presented here may seem excessively large, it is necessary to provide detailed coverage of all aspects of the corporation, so that prospective changes to it can be accurately modeled through the budget. Thus, a detailed format is strongly recommended over a simple, summarized model.

1-3 HOW DOES FLEX BUDGETING WORK?

One problem with the traditional budget model is that many of the expenses listed in it are directly tied to the revenue level. If the actual revenue incurred is significantly different from the budgeted figure, then so many expenses will also shift in association with the revenue that the comparison of budgeted to actual expenses will not be valid. For example, if budgeted revenues are $1 million and budgeted material costs are $450,000, one would expect a corresponding drop in the actual cost of materials incurred if actual revenues drop to $800,000. A budget-to-actual comparison would then show a significant difference in the cost of materials, which would in turn cause a difference in the gross margin and net profit. This issue also arises for a number of other variable or semivariable expenses, such as salesperson commissions, production supplies, and maintenance costs. Also, if there are really large differences between actual and budgeted revenue levels, other costs that are more fixed in nature will also change, such as the salaries, office supplies, and even facilities maintenance (since facilities may be sold off or added to, depending on which direction actual revenues have gone). These represent large step cost changes that will skew actual expenses so far away from the budget that it is difficult to conduct any meaningful comparison between the two.

A good way to resolve this problem is to create a flexible budget, or "flex" budget that itemizes different expense levels depending upon changes in the amount of actual revenue. In its simplest form, the flex budget will use percentages of revenue for certain expenses, rather than the usual fixed numbers. This allows for an infinite series of changes in budgeted expenses that are directly tied to revenue volume. However, this approach ignores changes to other costs that do not change in accordance with small revenue variations. Consequently, a more sophisticated format will also incorporate changes to many additional expenses when certain larger revenue changes occur, thereby accounting for step costs. By making these changes to the budget, a company will have a tool for comparing actual with budgeted performance at many levels of activity.

Though the flex budget is a good tool, it can be difficult to formulate and administer. One problem with its formulation is that many costs are not fully variable, instead having a fixed cost component that must be included in the flex budget formula. Another issue is that a great deal of time can be spent developing step costs, which is more time than the typical accounting staff has available, especially when in the midst of creating the standard budget. Consequently, the flex budget tends to include only a small number of step costs, as well as variable costs whose fixed cost components are not fully recognized.

Implementation of the flex budget is also a problem, for very few accounting software packages incorporate any features that allow one to load in multiple versions of a budget that can be used at different revenue levels. Instead, some include the option to store a few additional budgets, which the user can then incorporate into the standard budget-to-actual comparison reports. This option does not yield the full benefits of a flex budget, since it allows for only a few changes in expenses based on a small number of revenue changes, rather than a set of expenses that will automatically change in proportion to actual revenue levels incurred. Furthermore, the option to enter several different budgets means that someone must enter this additional information into the accounting software, which can be a considerable chore if the number of budget line items is large. For these reasons, it is more common to see a flex budget incorporated into an electronic spreadsheet, with actual results being manually posted to it from other accounting reports.

1-4 WHAT BEST PRACTICES CAN I APPLY TO THE BUDGETING PROCESS?

The budgeting process is usually rife with delays, which are caused by several factors. One is that information must be input to the budget model from all parts of the company—some of which may not put a high priority on the submission of budgeting information. Another reason is that the budgeting process is highly iterative, sometimes requiring dozens of budget recalculations and changes in assumptions before the desired results are achieved. The typical budgeting process is represented in Exhibit 1.17, where we see that there is a sequential process that requires the completion of the revenue plan before the production plan can be completed, which in turn must be finished before the departmental expense budgets can be finished, which then yields a financing plan. If the results do not meet expectations, then the process starts over again at the top of the exhibit. This process is so time-consuming that the budget may not be completed before the budget period has already begun.

There are a number of best practices that can be used to create a more streamlined budgeting process, which are as follows:

- *Reduce the number of accounts.* The number of accounts included in the budget should be reduced, thereby greatly reducing the amount of time needed to enter and update data in the budget model.

- *Reduce the number of reporting periods.* Consolidate the 12 months shown in the typical budget into quarterly information, thereby eliminating two-thirds of the information in the budget. If the budget must later be reentered into the accounting system in order to provide budget-to-actual comparisons, then a simple formula can be used to divide the quarterly budget back into its monthly components—which is still much less work than maintaining 12 full months of budget information.

- *Use percentages for variable cost updates.* When key activities, such as revenues, are changed in the budget model, one must peruse the entire budget in order to determine what related expenses must change in concert with the key activities. A much easier approach is to use percentage-based calculations for variable costs in the budget model, so that these expenses will be updated automatically. They should also be color-coded in the budget model, so that they will not be mistaken for items that are manually changed.

- *Report on variables in one place.* A number of key variables will impact the typical budget model, such as the assumed rate of inflation in wages or purchased parts, tax rates for income, payroll, and worker's compensation, medical insurance rates, and so on. These variables are much easier to find if they are set up in a cluster within the budget, so that one can easily reference and alter them. Under this arrangement, it is also useful to show key results (such as net profits) on the same page with the variables, in order to make alterations to the variables and immediately see their impact without having to search through the budget model to find the information.

- *Use a budget procedure and timetable.* The budget process is plagued by many iterations, since the first results will nearly always yield profits or losses that do not meet a company's expectations. Furthermore, it requires input from all parts of a company, some of which may lag in sending in information in a timely manner. Accordingly, it is best to construct a budgeting procedure that specifically identifies

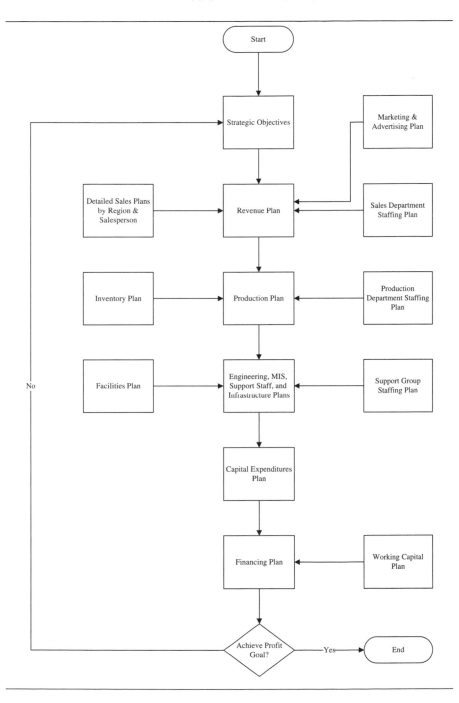

Exhibit 1.17 Traditional Budgeting Process

what job positions must send budgeting information to the budget coordinator, what information is required of each person, and when that information is due. Furthermore, there should be a clear timetable of events that is carefully adhered to, so that plenty of time is left at the end of the budgeting process for the calculation of multiple iterations of the budget.

In addition to these efficiency-improvement issues, there are other ways to modify the budgeting process so that it can be completed much more quickly. The following changes should be considered:

- *Preload budget line items.* Rather than requiring department managers to fill out a blank budget form for the upcoming budget year, have the accounting staff preload many of the budget line items with information from the current year. Most expenses are relatively fixed from year to year, or are easily linked to key drivers, such as headcount. Consequently, the accounting staff can probably arrive at more accurate budget numbers than a department manager for most line items. This approach leaves only a few of the larger and more variable accounts for managers to enter in the budget form. In some cases where a department is anticipating no major changes for the next budget year, it may even be possible for the accounting staff to create the entire department budget, so the department manager has only to make revisions to it.

- *Itemize the corporate strategy.* The strategy and related tactical goals that the company is trying to achieve should be listed at the beginning of the budget model. All too frequently, management loses sight of its predetermined strategy when going through the many iterations that are needed to develop a realistic budget. By itemizing the corporate strategy in the budget document, it is much less likely that the final budget model will deviate significantly from the company's strategic direction.

- *Identify step-costing change points.* The budget model should have notations incorporated into it that specify the capacity levels at which expenses are valid. For example, if the production level for product A exceeds 100,000 per year, then a warning flag should be generated by the budget model that informs the budget manager of the need to add an extra shift to accommodate the increased production requirements. Another example is to have the model generate a warning flag when the average revenue per salesperson exceeds $1,000,000, since this may be the maximum expectation for sales productivity, and will require the addition of more sales personnel to the budget. These flags can be clustered at the front of the budget model, so that problems will be readily apparent to the reader.

- *Specify maximum amounts of available funding.* One of the warning flags just noted should include the maximum level of funding that the company can obtain. If an iteration of the budget model results in excessively high cash requirements, then the flag will immediately point out the problem. It may be useful to note next to the warning flag the amount by which the maximum funding has been exceeded, so that this information is readily available for the next budget iteration.

- *Base expense changes on cost drivers.* Many expenses in the budget will vary in accordance with changes in various activities within the firm. As noted earlier in this section, expenses can be listed in the budget model as formulas, so that they vary in direct proportion to changes in budgeted revenue. This same concept can be taken a step further by listing other types of activities that drive cost behavior, and linking still other expenses to them with formulas. For example, the amount of telephone expense is directly related to the number of employees, so it can be linked to the total number of employees on the staffing budget. Another example is the number of machine setup personnel, which will change based on the planned number of production batches to be run during the year. This level of automation requires a significant degree of knowledge of how selected expenses interact with various activities within the company.

- *Budget by groups of staff positions.* A budget can rapidly become unwieldy if every position in the company is individually identified—especially if the names of all employees are listed. This format requires constant updating as the budget progresses through multiple iterations. A better approach is to itemize by job title, which allows one to vastly reduce the number of job positions listed in the budget.

- *Rank projects.* A more complex budget model can incorporate a ranking of all capital projects, so that any projects with a low ranking will be automatically eliminated by the model if the available amount of cash drops below the point where they could be funded. However, this variation requires that great attention be paid to the ranking of projects, since there may be some interrelationship between projects—if one is dropped but others are retained, then the ones retained may not be functional without the missing project.

- *Issue a summary-level model for use by senior management.* The senior management team is primarily concerned with the summary results of each department, product line, or operating division, and does not have time to wade through the details of individual revenue and expense accounts. Further, they may require an increased level of explanation from the budgeting staff if they *do* choose to examine these details. Accordingly, the speed of the iteration process can be enhanced by producing a summary-level budget that is directly linked to the main budget, so that all fields in it are updated automatically. The senior management team can more easily review this document, yielding faster updates to the model.

- *Link budget results to an employee goal and reward system.* The budgeting process does not end with the final approval of the budget model. Instead, it then passes to the human resources department, which uses it as the foundation for an employee goal and reward system. The trouble is that if budget approval is delayed, the human resources department will have very little time in which to create its goal and reward system. Accordingly, this add-on project should be incorporated directly into the budget model, so that it is approved alongside the rest of the budget. For example, a goals and rewards statement added to the budget can specify a bonus payment to the manager of the production department if he or she can create the number of units of product specified in the production budget. Similarly, the

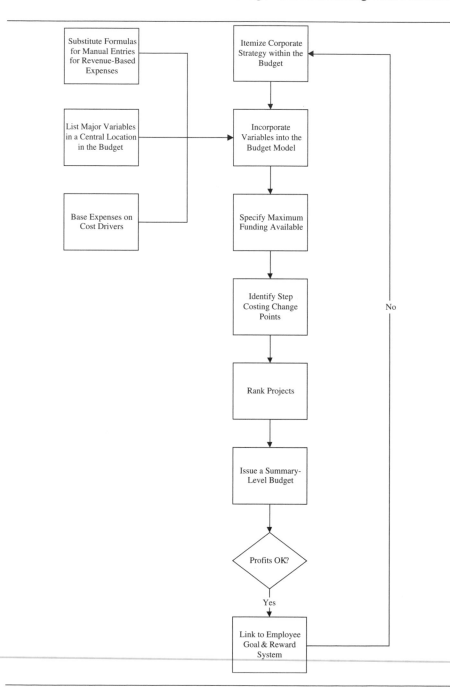

Exhibit 1.18   Streamlined Budgeting Process

sales manager can receive a bonus based on reaching the sales goals noted in the revenue budget. By inserting the bonus amounts in this page of the budget, the model can automatically link them to the final targets itemized in the plan, requiring minimal further adjustments by the human resources staff.

As a result of these improvements, the budgeting process will change to the format shown in Exhibit 1.18, where the emphasis moves away from many modeling iterations toward the incorporation of a considerable level of automation and streamlining into the structure of the budget model. By following this approach, the budget will require much less manual updating; this will allow it to sail through the smaller number of required iterations with much greater speed.

1-5 HOW CAN I INTEGRATE THE BUDGET INTO THE CORPORATE CONTROL SYSTEM?

There are several ways in which a budget can be used to enhance a company's control systems so that objectives are more easily met and it is more difficult for costs to stray from approved levels.

One of the best methods for controlling costs is to link the budget for each expense within each department to the purchasing system. By doing so, the computer system will automatically accumulate the total amount of purchase orders that have been issued thus far against a specific account, and will refuse any further purchase orders when the budgeted expense total has been reached. This approach can involve the comparison of the monthly budget to monthly costs, or compare costs with annual budgeted totals. The latter approach can cause difficulty for the inattentive manager, since actual expenses may be running well ahead of the budget for most of the year, but the system will not automatically flag the problem until the entire year's budget has been depleted. Alternatively, a comparison to monthly budgeted figures may result in so many warning flags on so many accounts that the purchasing staff is unable to purchase many items. One workaround for this problem is to use a fixed overage percentage by which purchases are allowed to exceed the budget; another possibility is to compare cumulative expenses only with quarterly budget totals, which reduces the total number of system warning flags.

Another budgetary control system is to compare actual with budgeted results for the specific purpose of evaluating the performance of employees. For example, the warehouse manager may be judged based on actual inventory turnover of $12\times$, which compares unfavorably to a budgeted turnover rate of $15\times$. Similarly, the manager of a cost center may receive a favorable review if the total monthly cost of her cost center averages no more than \$152,000. This also works for the sales staff, who can be assigned sales quotas that match the budgeted sales levels for their sales territories. In this manner, a large number of employees can have their compensation levels directly tied to the achievement of budgeted goals. This is a highly effective way to ensure that the budget becomes a fixture in the lives of employees.

However, there is also a problem with linking employee pay to performance levels as outlined in the budget. If employees realize that they will fall short of their bonus targets, they will be more likely to hoard their resources or possible sales for the next period, when they will have a better opportunity to achieve better performance and be paid a bonus. The result is wild swings in corporate performance from period to period as employees cycle through the hoard-to-splurge circuit. Employees may also stretch or break the accounting rules in a variety of ways to achieve the target. The solution is to link the budget to a sliding performance scale that contains no "hard" performance goals. The best example of the sliding bonus scale is what it is *not*—there are no specific goals at which the bonus target suddenly increases in size. Instead, the bonus is a constant percentage of the goal, such as 1 percent of sales or 5 percent of net after-tax profits. Also, there should be no upper boundary to the sliding scale, which would present employees with the disincentive to stop performing once they have reached a maximum bonus level. Similarly, there should theoretically be no lower limit to the bonus either, though it is more common to see a baseline level that is derived from the corporate breakeven point, on the grounds that employees must at least ensure that the company does not lose money. The sliding scale approach also makes it much easier to budget for the bonus expense at various activity levels, rather than trying to budget for the more common all-or-nothing bonus payment.

Yet another budgetary control system is to use it as a feedback loop to employees. This can be done by issuing a series of reports at the end of each reporting period that are specifically designed to match the responsibilities of each employee. For example, Exhibit 1.19 shows a single revenue line item that is reported to a salesperson for a single territory. The salesperson does not need to see any other detailed comparison with the budget, because he is not responsible for anything besides the specific line item that is reported to him. This reporting approach focuses the attention of many employees on just those segments of the budget over which they have control. Though this approach can result in the creation of dozens or even hundreds of reports by the accounting department, they can be automated on most packaged accounting software systems, so that only the initial report creation will take up much accounting time.

An additional control use for the budget is to detect fraud. The budget is usually based on several years of actual operating results, so unless there are major changes in activity levels, actual expense results should be fairly close to budgeted expectations. If not, variance analysis is frequently used to find out what happened. This process is an excellent means for discovering fraud, since this activity will usually result in a sudden surge in expense levels, which the resulting variance analysis will detect. The two instances in which this control will not work is when the fraud has been in existence for a long time (and so is incorporated into the budgeted expense numbers

Exhibit 1.19   Line Item Budget Reporting for Specific Employees

Account No.	Description	Actual Results	Budgeted Results	Variance
4500-010	Arizona Revenue	$43,529	$51,000	−$7,471

already) or the amount of fraud is so low that it will not create a variance large enough to warrant investigation.

1-6 HOW DO THROUGHPUT CONCEPTS IMPACT THE BUDGET?

In a traditional budget, the entire budget model is driven by the revenue forecast, since this information is needed to derive materials purchases, inventory and staffing levels, and operating expenses. The revenue forecast is usually summarized in one of two ways: either by total revenue dollars for each product, or by total revenue dollars by customer (which is more common when dealing with labor hour billings).

Though a valid way to obtain top-line revenue projections, this information lacks any clear linkage to directly variable costs, so managers cannot tell from the revenue budget alone how revenue projections will impact profitability. In addition, it does not show the impact of sales projections on the company's capacity constraint. A better approach is to develop a throughput forecast, either by product or customer, that clearly shows the impact on both profits and the capacity constraint.

Exhibit 1.20 shows a traditional revenue forecast for several products, followed by a revised forecast that reveals the individual and cumulative throughput levels for the same products and product quantities shown in the original forecast.

The traditional product revenue budget shown at the top of Exhibit 1.20 presents the usual itemization of estimated product sales that many of us are accustomed to seeing. However, this view has serious shortcomings when compared with the much richer set of information listed in the bottom half of the exhibit for throughput-based information. The latter portion of the exhibit reveals that the company is incapable of meeting its revenue budget, because there is not a sufficient amount of capacity available (based on 260 working days, at three shifts, assuming 80% efficiency) to meet its sales goals. A traditional budget would not have flagged this constraint problem anywhere, so the company would have constructed a fundamentally unsound budget and proceeded to implement it, with an essentially guaranteed revenue shortfall being the only possible outcome.

In addition, the enhanced budget shows that the company earns the least throughput per minute on its top-of-the-line carbon and titanium bikes; depending on the marketing effect of this decision, management could elect to drop production of both bikes, thereby bringing remaining estimated bike sales within range of the constraint limitation, while minimizing the resulting negative impact on throughput. Thus, the throughput approach to the revenue budget not only reveals problems with the initial forecast, but also presents a possible solution regarding how the sales mix might be modified.

A further note on the use of the throughput-based product revenue budget is to list the same product multiple times if it is forecasted to be sold to different customers at different prices (in which case it is useful to identify the customers in the budget for each line item). This makes it easier to see the throughput per unit at each price point.

Exhibit 1.20 Traditional Product Revenue Budget

Product Name	Unit Sales	Price/ Each	Extended Revenue	Variable Cost/Unit	Throughput per Unit	Total Throughput	Constraint Time/Unit	Total Time on Constraint	Throughput per Minute
1-speed road bike	2,850	$250	$712,500						
3-speed road bike	5,100	$400	$2,040,000						
24-speed road bike	4,800	$800	$3,840,000						
24-speed carbon road bike	450	$4,000	$1,800,000						
3-speed dual-shock mountain bike	8,750	$1,000	$8,750,000						
24-speed titanium mountain bike	650	$2,500	$1,625,000						
Totals	22,600		$18,767,500						

Throughput-Based Product Revenue Budget:

Product Name	Unit Sales	Price/ Each	Extended Revenue	Variable Cost/Unit	Throughput per Unit	Total Throughput	Constraint Time/Unit	Total Time on Constraint	Throughput per Minute
1-speed road bike	2,850	$250	$712,500	$70	$180	$513,000	5	14,250	$36.00
3-speed road bike	5,100	$400	$2,040,000	$125	$275	$1,402,500	11	56,100	$25.00
24-speed road bike	4,800	$800	$3,840,000	$225	$575	$2,760,000	13	62,400	$44.23
24-speed carbon road bike	450	$4,000	$1,800,000	$1,750	$2,250	$1,012,500	80	36,000	$28.13
3-speed dual-shock mountain bike	8,750	$1,000	$8,750,000	$350	$650	$5,687,500	22	192,500	$29.55
24-speed titanium mountain bike	650	$2,500	$1,625,000	$1,150	$1,350	$877,500	65	42,250	$20.77
Totals	22,600		$18,767,500			$12,253,000		403,500	

Maximum available constraint time (minutes)   299,520

The same approach can be taken with a revenue budget that is based on sales by customer. The example shown in Exhibit 1.21 assumes that sales are based on billable hours to customers.

The traditional revenue budgeting model shown in Exhibit 1.21 shows an estimate of revenues by customer, with no additional interpretive information. However, the throughput-based version at the bottom of the exhibit reveals a great deal more information. When variable costs (in this case, labor) are subtracted from the budgeted revenue to arrive at throughput, we find that there is a loss on the work being done for the Mining Safety Engineers customer, which may prompt a discussion of repricing this work or of dropping the customer. In addition, the model then summarizes the labor used in the various customer projects by labor category and calculates the amount of staffing required, based on the estimate of billable hours and an 80 percent billable percentage for each employee. This information tells management that it must hire additional staff in several labor categories in order to have sufficient staff to meet its revenue budget.

The main reason for a budget is to give management a model of how the company should operate during the budget period, based on the impact of operational and financial changes that management wants to implement during the budget period. However, the traditional budget model is designed to show results based on the local optimization of resources, rather than systemwide resources, which usually results in counterproductive budgeting decisions. For example, if expenses are projected to be too high, management may mandate an across-the-board 10 percent budget cut for all departments, which will likely both reduce the capacity of the constrained resource and shrink operating expenses to such an extent that the ability of the entire system to support the current level of throughput has now been reduced.

Unfortunately, it is very difficult to create a quantitative format for how a change in operating expenses will impact total system throughput, since in many cases there does not appear to be a direct or even an indirect link between some costs and the generation of throughput. Consequently, the creation of a budget where expenses support throughput generation requires an extremely detailed knowledge of how the entire system works together to create throughput.

In many cases where no link between an expense and throughput can be found, management is still able to wield a sharp budgeting axe in cutting expenses. Thus, there are considerable differences in how various budget line items should be treated, based on their impact on throughput. Any expense supporting throughput should be cut only after detailed review by a process analyst, while other expenses can be cut with much less review. This interpretation of the budget model results in a change in the budgeting format, which is shown in Exhibit 1.22. The exhibit shows a before-and-after department budget where the first version ignores the impact of throughput, while the second version splits operating expenses into those impacting throughput and those that do not. The expenses in the second version can be shifted between the two categories based on whether they affect the company's throughput capacity.

However, the exhibit clearly shows that *most* expenses will be attributable in some manner to throughput capacity, since most corporate expenses involve departments

Exhibit 1.21 Traditional Customer Revenue Budget:

Customer Name	Billable Hours	Price/Hour	Extended Revenue	Variable Cost/Hour	Throughput per Hour	Total Throughput	Staff Required*	Staff Available
Amber Distribution Corporation	2,000	$125	$250,000					
Bi-Way Valve Specialties	8,000	$85	$680,000					
Breaker Breaker Radio Design	2,700	$125	$337,500					
Hippo Weight Loss Clinics	4,100	$85	$348,500					
Mining Safety Engineers	10,500	$65	$682,500					
Vessel Insurance Brokers	500	$125	$62,500					
Totals	27,800		$2,361,000					

Throughput-Based Customer Revenue Budget:

Customer Name	Billable Hours	Price/Hour	Extended Revenue	Variable Cost/Hour	Throughput per Hour	Total Throughput	Staff Required*	Staff Available
Amber Distribution Corporation	2,000	$125	$250,000	$81.75	$43.25	$86,500		
Bi-Way Valve Specialties	8,000	$85	$680,000	$72.35	$12.65	$101,200		
Breaker Breaker Radio Design	2,700	$125	$337,500	$81.75	$43.25	$116,775		
Hippo Weight Loss Clinics	4,100	$85	$348,500	$72.35	$12.65	$51,865		
Mining Safety Engineers	10,500	$65	$682,500	$66.50	–$1.50	–$15,750		
Vessel Insurance Brokers	500	$125	$62,500	$81.75	$43.25	$21,625		
Totals	27,800		$2,361,000			$362,215		

Labor Category Aggregation	Billable Hours	Price/Hour	Extended Revenue	Variable Cost/Hour	Throughput per Hour	Total Throughput	Staff Required*	Staff Available
Expert Consultant	5,200	125	$650,000	$ 81.75	$43.25	$224,900	3.1	2
Senior Consultant	12,100	85	$1,028,500	$ 72.35	$12.65	$153,065	7.3	7
Junior Consultant	10,500	65	$682,500	$ 66.50	–$1.50	–$15,750	6.3	4
	27,800		$2,361,000			$362,215		

* Assumes 80% billable hours.

Exhibit 1.22   Before-and-After Throughput Expense Budget

	1st Quarter	2nd Quarter	3rd Quarter	4th Quarter	Total
Version 1:					
Bank fees	3,000	4,500	2,500	4,000	14,000
Legal fees	15,000	18,500	32,000	19,000	84,500
Promotional materials	82,000	0	48,000	28,500	158,500
Salaries, accounting	85,000	87,000	87,000	91,000	350,000
Salaries, corporate	105,000	110,000	143,000	141,000	499,000
Salaries, engineering	190,000	200,000	203,000	205,000	798,000
Salaries, marketing	20,000	21,000	21,000	22,000	84,000
Salaries, production	280,000	275,000	285,000	290,000	1,130,000
Salaries, sales	150,000	175,000	180,000	195,000	700,000
Supplies	17,500	16,000	13,500	19,000	66,000
Taxes, payroll	65,155	68,138	72,142	74,104	279,539
Trade shows	0	100,000	0	0	100,000
Travel & entertainment	10,500	14,500	17,000	12,000	54,000
Total	1,023,155	1,089,638	1,104,142	1,100,604	4,317,539
Version 2:					
Throughput-related:					
Promotional materials	82,000	0	48,000	28,500	158,500
Salaries, engineering	190,000	200,000	203,000	205,000	798,000
Salaries, marketing	20,000	21,000	21,000	22,000	84,000
Salaries, production	280,000	275,000	285,000	290,000	1,130,000
Salaries, sales	150,000	175,000	180,000	195,000	700,000
Trade shows	0	100,000	0	0	100,000
Travel & entertainment	8,000	10,000	16,000	6,000	40,000
Subtotal	730,000	781,000	753,000	746,500	3,010,500
Not throughput-supportive:					
Bank fees	3,000	4,500	2,500	4,000	14,000
Legal fees	15,000	18,500	32,000	19,000	84,500
Salaries, accounting	85,000	87,000	87,000	91,000	350,000
Salaries, corporate	105,000	110,000	143,000	141,000	499,000
Supplies	17,500	16,000	13,500	19,000	66,000
Taxes, payroll	65,155	68,138	72,142	74,104	279,539
Travel & entertainment	2,500	4,500	1,000	6,000	14,000
Subtotal	293,155	308,638	351,142	354,104	1,307,039
Grand total	1,023,155	1,089,638	1,104,142	1,100,604	4,317,539

that are directly related to the production of revenue, such as engineering, production, marketing, and sales. Only such classic overhead expenses as accounting, general corporate costs, and legal expenses can be reduced with some assurance that the reductions will not impact throughput.

Thus far, the discussion of operating expenses has primarily focused on a company's ability to cut expenses. However, how should the budgeting process handle requests for *increased* operating expenses? The primary guideline should be that the existing level of operating expenses is sufficient to handle not only existing but also any projected increases in throughput. If not, then some elements of operating expenses become the constraint, at which point increases in those expenses should be included in the budget.

The standard ways to budget for production staffing levels are to (1) incrementally adjust existing staffing levels based on forecasted revenue changes or (2) extrapolate labor requirements derived by multiplying the forecasted revenue for the budget period by the labor routings for each product listed in the forecast. Many companies start with the latter method and compare it with the results obtained from the first approach, and then adopt a hybrid solution. These techniques will yield reasonably accurate staffing levels for a company attempting to create locally optimized manufacturing operations. However, they will likely result in inadequate staffing levels when capacity constraints are taken into account.

When throughput is taken into account, it is necessary to hire additional employees when either of the following two circumstances arise:

1. When the sprint capacity of key workstations positioned upstream from the constrained resource is insufficient to recover from system downtime to such an extent that buffers are repeatedly penetrated
2. When the constrained resource could generate more throughput with the addition of more staff

It is entirely possible that the constrained resource is not in the production area or the marketplace at all (the two most common areas), but rather in the sales department. This problem is most evident when the company's sales funnel begins with a large number of prospective sales, but narrows down to a small number of completed sales due to a bottleneck somewhere in the sales conversion process. The identification of the constrained resource within the sales funnel can be determined as part of the budgeting process, usually with an analysis similar to the one shown in Exhibit 1.23.

Exhibit 1.23   Sales Funnel Bottleneck Identification

Steps in Sales Funnel	Actual Time Used (hours)	Theoretical Capacity (hours)
Initial identification	450	700
Customer qualification	120	240
Needs assessment	300	300
Letter of understanding	50	80
Product demonstration	620	800
Solution proposal	2,400	3,100
Negotiation	280	400
Closing	100	200

The exhibit shows the basic steps needed to advance through the sales funnel, from initial identification of the customer through closing the deal. For each step, the table shows the actual time used on various steps in the process, as compared with the theoretical amount of staff capacity available for each step. The table reveals that the constrained resource is the needs assessment, for which the actual time used has matched the theoretical maximum available. Thus, for budgeting purposes, management should bolster the ranks of the sales engineers who are responsible for creating needs assessments.

If a company does not perform this analysis, then it may budget for increases in the wrong types of sales positions, which will yield no new sales if the additions do not address the constraint.

Chapter 2

Capital Budgeting Decisions

The accountant is usually trained in the use of discounted cash flows to analyze funding requests for capital projects. A newer approach is constraint management, which instead focuses attention on allocating funding to bottleneck (constrained) operations. Both capital budgeting methodologies are presented in this chapter.

If the accountant were to use constraint-based capital budgeting, some key questions would involve how to determine the cost of a bottleneck operation, how to locate that operation, whether investments should be made in the operation, and when investments should be made outside of the bottleneck operation.

If the accountant were to instead use the traditional discounted cash flow method, some key questions would involve how to calculate and use the cost of capital, how to derive a project's net present value, and when to use payback periods and post-completion project analyses.

This chapter provides answers to all of these key questions. The following table itemizes the section number in which the answers to each question can be found:

Section	Decision
2-1	How does a constrained resource impact capital budgeting decisions?
2-2	What is the true cost of a capacity constraint?
2-3	How do I identify a constrained resource?
2-4	When should I invest in a constrained resource?
2-5	Should I increase sprint capacity?
2-6	How closely should I link capital expenditures to strategy?
2-7	What format should I use for a capital request form?
2-8	Should I judge capital proposals based on their discounted cash flows?
2-9	How do I calculate the cost of capital?
2-10	When should I use the incremental cost of capital?
2-11	How do I use net present value in capital budgeting?
2-12	What proposal form should I require for a cash flow analysis?
2-13	Should I use the payback period in capital budgeting?
2-14	How can a post-completion analysis help me?
2-15	What factors should I consider for a site selection?

2-1 HOW DOES A CONSTRAINED RESOURCE IMPACT CAPITAL BUDGETING DECISIONS?

Pareto analysis holds that 20 percent of events cause 80 percent of the results. For example, 20 percent of customers generate 80 percent of all profits, or 20 percent of all production issues cause 80 percent of the scrap. The theory of constraints, when reduced down to one guiding concept, states that 1 percent of all events cause 99 percent of the results. This conclusion is reached by viewing a company as one giant system designed to produce profits, with one constrained resource controlling the amount of those profits.

Under the theory of constraints, all management activities are centered on management of the bottleneck operation, or constrained resource. By focusing on making this resource more efficient and ensuring that all other company resources are oriented toward supporting it, a company will maximize its profits. The concept is shown in Exhibit 2.1, where the total production capacity of four work centers is shown, both before and after a series of efficiency improvements are made. Of the four work centers, the capacity of center C is the lowest, at 80 units per hour. Despite subsequent efficiency improvements to work centers A and B, the total output of the system remains at 80 units per hour, because of the restriction imposed by work center C.

This approach is substantially different from the traditional management technique of local optimization, where *all* company operations are to be made as efficient as possible, with machines and employees maximizing their work efforts at all times. The key difference between the two methodologies is the view of efficiency: Should it be maximized everywhere, or just at the constrained resource? The constraints-based approach holds that any local optimization of a nonconstraint resource will simply allow it to produce more than the constrained operation can handle, which results in excess inventory. For example, a furniture company discovers that its drum operation is its paint shop. The company cannot produce more than 300 tables per day, because that maximizes the capacity of the paint shop. If the company adds a lathe to produce more table legs, this will only result in the accumulation of an excessive quantity of table legs, rather than the production of a larger number of painted tables. Thus, the investment in efficiencies elsewhere than the constrained operation will only increase costs without improving sales or profits.

The preceding example shows that not only should efficiency improvements *not* be made in areas other than the constrained operation, but it is quite acceptable to not even be efficient in these other areas. It is better to stop work in a nonconstraint operation and idle its staff than to have it churn out more inventory than can be used by the constrained operation.

2-2 WHAT IS THE TRUE COST OF A CAPACITY CONSTRAINT?

If the use of the capacity constraint is not maximized, what is the opportunity cost to the company? In a traditional cost accounting system, the cost would be the forgone gross margin on any products that could not be produced by the operation. For example, a work center experiences downtime of one hour, because the machine operator is on a

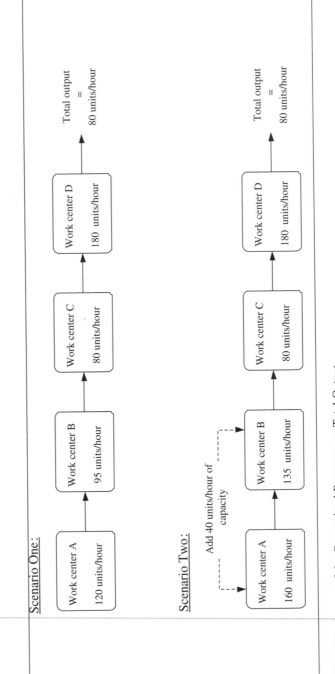

Exhibit 2.1 Impact of the Constrained Resource on Total Output

scheduled break. During that one hour, the work center could have created 20 products having a gross margin of $4.00 each. Traditional cost accounting tells us that this represents a loss of $80. Given this information, a manager might very well not backfill the machine operator, and allow the machine to stay idle for the one-hour break period.

However, throughput accounting uses a different calculation of the cost of the capacity constraint. Since the performance of the constraint drives the total throughput of the entire system, the opportunity cost of not running that operation is actually the total operating expense of running the entire facility, divided by the number of hours during which the capacity constraint is being operated. This is because it is not possible to speed up the constrained operation, resulting in the permanent loss of any units that are not produced. For example, if the monthly operating expenses of a facility are $1.2 million and the constrained resource is run for every hour of that month, or 720 hours (30 days × 24 hours/day), then the cost per hour of the operation is $1,667 ($1,200,000 divided by 720 hours). Given this much higher cost of not running the operation, a manager will be much more likely to find a replacement operator for break periods.

Thus, knowing the substantial cost of not running a constrained resource is extremely important when determining how much capital funding should be allocated to that resource.

2-3 HOW DO I IDENTIFY A CONSTRAINED RESOURCE?

The constrained resource may not be immediately apparent, especially in a large production environment with many products, routings, and work centers. It is this "noise in the system" that prevents us from easily identifying constraints. Here are some questions to ask that will help locate it:

- *Where is there a work backlog?* If there is an area where work virtually never catches up with demand, where expeditors are constantly hovering, and where there are large quantities of inventory piled up, this is a likely constraint area.

- *Where do most problems originate?* Management usually finds itself hovering around only a small number of work centers whose problems never seem to go away. Continuing problems are common at constrained resources, because they are so heavily utilized that there is never enough time to perform a sufficient level of maintenance, resulting in recurring breakdowns. In addition, there tends to be a fight over work priorities when there is not sufficient capacity, which also means that managers will be regularly called upon to determine these priorities among competing orders.

- *Where are the expediters?* An expediter physically steers a high-priority job through the production process. Because they frequently wait while their assigned jobs are being processed, their presence (especially several of them together) is a good indicator of a bottleneck where they must wait for available production time.

- *Which work centers have high utilization?* Many companies measure the utilization level of their work centers. If so, review the list to determine which ones have a continually high level of utilization over multiple months. If a work center only briefly attains high utilization, it could still be the constraint if the reason for the lower utilization is ongoing maintenance problems or employee absenteeism.

- *What happens to total throughput when the constraint capacity changes?* If we add to the capacity of the suspected constraint, is there a noticeable increase in throughput? Conversely, if we deliberately reduce the capacity of the targeted work center (not recommended as a testing technique!), does overall throughput decline? If throughput does alter as a result of these changes, then we have probably located the constrained resource.

If, after this analysis, a company picks the wrong operation as its constrained resource, the real constraint will soon appear because of changes in the inventory buffers in front of the real and fake constraints. If the real constraint is upstream from the fake constraint, then the inventory buffer in front of the fake constraint will disappear. This happens because management will focus its attention on improving the efficiency of the fake resource, thereby wiping out its backlog of work. The real constraint will be readily apparent, because it still has an inventory backlog. Conversely, if the real constraint is downstream from the fake constraint, then a larger inventory backlog will build in front of it. This happens because the same improvement in efficiency at the fake resource will result in a flood of additional inventory heading downstream, where it will dam up at the real constraint.

If products are engineered to order, then consider the engineering department to be part of the production process. This is important from the perspective of locating the constraint, because the constraint may not be in the traditional production area at all, but rather in the engineering department. Similarly, and for all types of product sales, the constraint may also reside in the sales department, where there may not be enough staff available to convert a large proportion of sales prospects into orders. This constraint is most evident when there are clearly many sales prospects at the top of the sales funnel, but there is a choke point somewhere in the sales conversion process, below which few orders are received. If this is the case, the solution is to enhance staffing for the sales positions specifically needed to improve handling of sales prospects at the choke point in the sales funnel.

Another constraint can also be raw materials. This problem arises during periods of excessive industry demand, resulting in materials allocations from suppliers. The location of this constraint will be immediately apparent to the materials management staff, which will have to reschedule production based on the shortage. However, this problem tends to be a short-term one, after which the constraint shifts back from the supplier and into the company.

It is also possible to *designate* a work center as the constrained resource. Taking this proactive approach is most useful when a work center requires a great deal of additional investment or highly skilled staffing to increase its capacity. By requiring that the constraint be focused on this area, management can profitably spend its time ensuring that the work center is fully utilized. It is also useful to avoid positioning the constraint on a resource that requires considerable management to operate properly, such as one where employee training or turnover levels are extremely high. Thus, positioning the constrained resource can be a management decision, rather than an incidental occurrence.

2-4 WHEN SHOULD I INVEST IN A CONSTRAINED RESOURCE?

At what point should a company invest in more of the constrained resource? In many cases, the company has specifically designated a resource to be its constraint, because it is so expensive to add more capacity, so this decision is not to be taken lightly. The decision process is to review the impact on the incremental change in throughput caused by the added investment, less any changes in operating expenses. Because this type of investment represents a considerable step cost (where costs and/or the investment will jump considerably as a result of the decision), management must usually make its decision based on the perceived level of long-term throughput changes, rather than smaller expected short-term throughput increases.

2-5 SHOULD I INCREASE SPRINT CAPACITY?

Sprint capacity is excess capacity built into a production operation that allows the facility to create excess inventory in the short term, usually to make up for sudden shortfalls in inventory levels. Sprint capacity is extremely useful for maintaining a sufficient flow of inventory into the constrained resource, since the system can quickly recover from a production shortfall. If there is a great deal of sprint capacity in a production system, then there is less need for an inventory buffer in front of the constrained resource, since new inventory stocks can be generated quickly.

It is not only useful, but necessary to have excess capacity levels available in a system. This controverts the traditional management approach of eliminating excess capacity in order to reduce the costs associated with maintaining that capacity. Instead, management should invest in nonconstraint resources when those resources have so little excess capacity that they have difficulty recovering from downtime. This can be a major problem if the lack of capacity constantly places the constrained resource in danger of running out of work. In this case, a good investment alternative is to invest in a sufficient amount of additional sprint capacity to ensure that the system can rapidly recover from a reasonable level of downtime. If a manager is applying for a capital investment based on this reasoning, he should attach to the proposal a chart showing the capacity level at which the targeted resource has been operating over the past few months, as well as the amount of downtime this has caused at the constrained resource.

Most companies do not experience a sudden increase in product sales; rather, they are subject to a slow, steady increase in demand that gradually fills the available amount of capacity throughout the production area. When this happens, management attention is rightly focused on maintaining a high level of throughput at the constrained resource. However, the increased demand also tends to gradually absorb excess capacity levels elsewhere in the plant. If this phenomenon continues for some time, management may be blindsided by what appears to be a sudden decrease in sprint capacity.

If sprint capacity declines to an excessive extent, it is likely that occasional upstream production problems will eventually result in shortages at the constraint and a reduction of throughput. To guard against the onset of this creeping reduction in capacity, the accountant should monitor nonconstraint usage levels, and warn management when there is a long-term reduction of sprint capacity that is not abating. This may very well call for additional capital investments in order to maintain a sufficient level of sprint capacity.

2-6 HOW CLOSELY SHOULD I LINK CAPITAL EXPENDITURES TO STRATEGY?

Companies tend not to spend money where their strategies indicate they should spend it. Instead, they tend to support their existing infrastructures with continuing investments in those areas. This tendency is largely due to the way in which the capital budgeting approval process is structured, whereby the managers in charge of this infrastructure are responsible not only for submitting capital requests, but also for approving them. The inevitable result is that the managers of new business units that are more closely tied to the company's long-term strategy will find themselves crowded out in the competition to obtain a limited amount of corporate funding. Another form of evidence of this tendency is when a company continually increases its asset base in an existing business in order to increase its efficiency levels, while competition forces its prices downward. The result is an inferior or negative return on investment.

A greatly preferable alternative is to have the senior management team that is responsible for setting strategy also be solely responsible for allocating funding to the various capital requests. By doing so, a company can more readily focus its capital funding on those potentially large markets with good growth rates, and in which the company stands the best chance of competing. From a purely financial perspective, this means that the company will be investing where its return on investments exceeds its cost of capital by the greatest amount, and eliminating assets where the return is negative.

2-7 WHAT FORMAT SHOULD I USE FOR A CAPITAL REQUEST FORM?

The summary-level capital budgeting form shown in Exhibit 2.2 splits capital budgeting requests into three categories: (1) constraint-related, (2) risk-related, and (3) non-constraint-related. The risk-related category covers all capital purchases for which the company must meet a legal requirement, or for which there is a perception that the company is subject to an undue amount of risk if it does *not* invest in an asset. All remaining requests that do not clearly fall into the constraint-related or risk-related categories drop into a catchall category at the bottom of the form. The intent of this format is to clearly differentiate among various types of approval requests, with each one requiring different types of analysis and management approval.

The approval levels vary significantly in the throughput-based capital request form. Approvals for constraint-related investments include a process analyst (who verifies that the request will actually impact the constraint), as well as generally higher-dollar approval levels for lower-level managers—the intent is to make it easier to approve capital requests that will improve the constrained resource. Approvals for risk-related projects first require the joint approval of the corporate attorney and chief risk officer, with added approvals for large expenditures. Finally, the approvals for non-constraint-related purchases involve lower-dollar approval levels, so the approval process is intentionally made more difficult.

Once approved as part of the budgeting process, capital requests can be segregated in the budget into the three categories just noted. The basic format of this portion of the budget is shown in Exhibit 2.3.

The capital budget example shows more expenditures for risk-related projects, but in most cases the bulk of funding should be focused squarely on constraint-related projects, with only minimal funding reserved for non-constraint-related projects. Also, the example contains an additional section at the bottom, in which is listed the incremental additional capacity of the constrained resource resulting from the new investments. In this section, the new capacity is listed with a time delay, so that a capital expenditure is fully installed before the resulting capacity is assumed to be available. Though most of the budget contains nothing but financial information, this operational information may have an impact on the company's ability to increase its sales later in the budget period, and so is extremely useful reference information.

2-8 SHOULD I JUDGE CAPITAL PROPOSALS BASED ON THEIR DISCOUNTED CASH FLOWS?

The traditional capital budgeting approach involves having the management team review a series of unrelated requests from throughout the company, each one asking for funding for various projects. Management decides whether to fund each request based on the discounted cash flows projected for each one. If there are not sufficient funds available for all requests having positive discounted cash flows, then those with

Project name: _____

Name of project sponsor: _____

Submission date: _____   Project number: _____

☐ **Constraint-Related Project**   <u>Approvals</u>

Initial expenditure: $ _____   All

                                                          _____
Additional annual expenditure: $ _____   Process Analyst

                                              $100,000   _____
Impact on throughput: $ _____   Supervisor

Impact on operating expenses: $ _____ $100,001–   _____
                                              $1,000,000   President
Impact on ROI: $ _____

                                              $1,000,000+ _____
(Attach calculations)   Board of Directors

☐ **Risk-Related Project**   <u>Approvals</u>

Initial expenditure: $ _____   _____
                                              < $50,000   Corporate Attorney
Additional annual expenditure: $ _____
                                                           _____
Description of legal requirement fulfilled or   Chief Risk Officer
risk issue mitigated (attach description as needed):

                                              $50,001+   _____
_____   President

_____ $1,000,000+ _____
                                                           Board of Directors

---

☐ **Non-Constraint-Related Project**   <u>Approvals</u>

Initial expenditure: $ _____   All
                                                           _____
Additional annual expenditure: $ _____   Process Analyst

☐ Improves sprint capacity?   <$10,000   _____
  Attach justification of sprint capacity increase   Supervisor

                                              $10,001–   _____
☐ Other request $100,000   President
  Attach justification for other request type
                                              $100,000+   _____
                                                           Board of Directors

---

Exhibit 2.2   Capital Request Form

Exhibit 2.3   Capital Budget

	1st Quarter	2nd Quarter	3rd Quarter	4th Quarter	Total
Constraint-related projects:					
Additional metal press	$500,000				$500,000
Refurbish old metal press			75,000		75,000
Conveyors into metal press		180,000			180,000
Subtotal	$500,000	$180,000	$75,000	$0	$755,000
Risk-related projects:					
Smokestack scrubber		850,000			850,000
Water filtration			175,000		175,000
Asbestos abatement				250,000	250,000
Subtotal	$0	$850,000	$175,000	$250,000	$1,275,000
Non-constraint-related projects:					
Automated stock carver			147,000		147,000
Paint booth replacement		263,000			263,000
Lamination department conveyors				82,000	82,000
Subtotal	$0	$263,000	$147,000	$82,000	$492,000
Grand Total	$500,000	$1,293,000	$397,000	$332,000	$2,522,000

	Incremental Improvement in Constraint Minutes			
	1st Quarter	2nd Quarter	3rd Quarter	4th Quarter
Operational impacts:				
Additional metal press		299,520	299,520	299,520
Refurbish old metal press				42,500
Conveyors into metal press			2,860	2,860
Total	0	299,520	302,380	344,880

the largest cash flows or highest percentage returns are usually accepted first, until the funds run out.

There are several problems with this type of capital budgeting. First and most important, there is no consideration of how each requested project fits into the entire system of production—instead, most requests involve the local optimization of specific work centers that may not contribute to the total throughput of the company. Second, there is no consideration of the constrained resource, so managers cannot tell which funding requests will result in an improvement to the efficiency of that operation. Third, managers tend to engage in a great deal of speculation regarding the budgeted cash flows resulting from their requests, resulting in inaccurate discounted cash flow projections. Since many requests involve unverifiable cash flow estimates, it is impossible to discern which projects are better than others.

A greater reliance on throughput accounting concepts eliminates most of these problems. In particular, the priority for funding should be placed squarely on any projects that can improve the capacity of the constrained resource, based on a comparison of the incremental additional throughput created with the incremental operating expenses and investment incurred.

Nonetheless, many companies have a long tradition of using discounted cash flows to determine which capital requests are to be accepted. If so, then at least include constraint analysis in the overall approval process, which may skew some funding allocations in favor of bottleneck operations that require additional capacity.

2-9 HOW DO I CALCULATE THE COST OF CAPITAL?

A company's cost of capital is used to discount the net present value of cash flows projected for prospective projects, and so is a key part of the capital budgeting process. The cost of capital is comprised of three elements, which are the costs of debt, preferred stock, and common stock.

When calculating the cost of debt, it is important to remember that the interest expense is tax deductible. This means that the tax paid by the company is reduced by the tax rate multiplied by the interest expense. An example is shown in Exhibit 2.4, where we assume that $1,000,000 of debt has a basic interest rate of 9.5 percent, and the corporate tax rate is 35 percent.

If a company is not currently turning a profit, and therefore not in a position to pay taxes, one may question whether the company should factor the impact of taxes into the interest calculation. The answer is still yes, because any net loss will carry forward to the next reporting period, when the company can offset future earnings against the accumulated loss to avoid paying taxes at that time. Thus, the reduction in interest costs caused by the tax deductibility of interest is still applicable even if a company is not currently in a position to pay income taxes.

Exhibit 2.4   Calculating the Interest Cost of Debt, Net of Taxes

$$\frac{(\text{Interest expense}) \times (1 - \text{Tax rate})}{\text{Amount of debt}} = \text{Net after-tax interest expense}$$

Or,

$$\frac{\$95,000 \times (1 - 0.35)}{\$1,000,000} = \text{Net after-tax interest expense}$$

$$\frac{\$61,750}{\$1,000,000} = 6.175\%$$

Exhibit 2.5 Calculating the Interest Cost of Debt, Net of Taxes, Fees, and Discounts

$$\frac{(\text{Interest expense}) \times (1 - \text{Tax rate})}{(\text{Amount of debt}) - (\text{Fees}) - (\text{Discount on sale of debt})} = \text{Net after-tax interest expense}$$

Or,

$$\frac{(95{,}000 \times (1 - 0.35)}{\$1{,}000{,}000 - \$25{,}000 - \$20{,}000} = \text{Net after-tax interest expense}$$

$$\frac{\$61{,}750}{\$955{,}000} = 6.466\%$$

Another issue is the cost of acquiring debt, and how this cost should be factored into the overall cost of debt calculation. When obtaining debt, there are usually extra fees involved, which may include placement or brokerage fees, documentation fees, or the price of a bank audit. In the case of a private placement, the company may set a fixed percentage interest payment on the debt, but find that prospective borrowers will not purchase the debt instruments unless they can do so at a discount, thereby effectively increasing the interest rate they will earn on the debt. In both cases, the company is receiving less cash than initially expected, but must still pay out the same amount of interest expense. In effect, this raises the cost of the debt. To carry forward the example in Exhibit 2.4 to Exhibit 2.5, we assume that the interest payments are the same, but that brokerage fees were $25,000 and that the debt was sold at a 2 percent discount. The result is an increase in the actual interest rate.

The cost of preferred stock is treated differently from debt, because under the tax laws, interest payments are treated as dividends instead of interest expense, which means that these payments are not tax deductible. This is a key issue, for it greatly increases the cost of funds for any company using preferred stock as a funding source. By way of comparison, if a company has a choice between issuing debt or preferred stock at the same rate, the difference in cost will be the tax savings on the debt. In the following example, a company issues $1,000,000 of debt and $1,000,000 of preferred stock, both at 9 percent interest rate, with an assumed 35 percent tax rate.

$$\text{Debt cost} = \text{Principal} \times (\text{Interest rate} \times (1 - \text{tax rate}))$$
$$\text{Debt cost} = \$1{,}000{,}000 \times (9\% \times (1 - .35))$$
$$\underline{\$58{,}500} = \$1{,}000{,}000 \times (9\% \times .65)$$

If the same information is used to calculate the cost of payments using preferred stock, we have the following result:

$$\text{Preferred stock interest cost} = \text{Principal} \times \text{Interest rate}$$
$$\text{Preferred stock interest cost} = \$1{,}000{,}000 \times 9\%$$
$$\underline{\$90{,}000} = \$1{,}000{,}000 \times 9\%$$

The final component of the cost of capital is common stock. The usual method for developing its cost is the capital asset pricing model (CAPM). The CAPM essentially derives the cost of capital by determining the relative risk of holding the stock of a specific company as compared with a mix of all stocks in the market. This risk is composed of three elements:

1. *The return that any investor can expect from a risk-free investment.* This is usually defined as the return on a U.S. government security.
2. *The return from a set of securities considered to have an average level of risk.* This can be the average return on a large *market basket* of stocks, such as the Standard & Poor's 500, the Dow Jones Industrials, or some other large cluster of stocks.
3. *The company's beta, which defines the amount by which a specific stock's returns vary from the returns of stocks with an average risk level.* This information is provided by several of the major investment services, such as Value Line. A beta of 1.0 means that a specific stock is exactly as risky as the average stock, while a beta of 0.8 would represent a lower level of risk and a beta of 1.4 would be higher.

When combined, this information yields the baseline return to be expected on any investment (the risk-free return), plus an added return that is based on the level of risk that an investor is assuming by purchasing a specific stock.

The calculation of the equity cost of capital using the CAPM methodology is relatively simple, once one has accumulated all the components of the equation. For example, if the risk-free cost of capital is 5 percent, the return on the Dow Jones Industrials is 12 percent, and ABC Company's beta is 1.5, the cost of equity for ABC Company would be:

$$\text{Cost of equity capital} = \text{Risk-free return} + \text{Beta (Average stock}$$
$$\text{return} - \text{risk-free return)}$$
$$\text{Cost of equity capital} = 5\% + 1.5(12\% - 5\%)$$
$$\text{Cost of equity capital} = 5\% + 1.5 \times 7\%$$
$$\text{Cost of equity capital} = 5\% + 10.5\%$$
$$\text{Cost of equity capital} = \underline{15.5\%}$$

Now that we have derived the costs of debt, preferred stock, and common stock, we can assemble all three costs into a weighted cost of capital. The following example shows the method by which the weighted cost of capital of the Canary Corporation is calculated.

The chief financial officer of the Canary Corporation, Mr. Birdsong, is interested in determining the company's weighted cost of capital. There are two debt offerings on the books. The first is $1,000,000 that was sold below par value, which garnered $980,000 in cash proceeds. The company must pay interest of 8.5 percent on this debt. The second is for $3,000,000 and was sold at par, but included legal fees of $25,000.

The interest rate on this debt is 10 percent. There is also $2,500,000 of preferred stock on the books, which requires annual interest (or dividend) payments amounting to 9 percent of the amount contributed to the company by investors. Finally, there is $4,000,000 of common stock on the books. The risk-free rate of interest, as defined by the return on current U.S. government securities, is 6 percent, while the return expected from a typical market basket of related stocks is 12 percent. The company's beta is 1.2, and it currently pays income taxes at a marginal rate of 35 percent. What is the Canary Company's weighted cost of capital?

The method we will use is to separately compile the percentage cost of each form of funding, and then calculate the weighted cost of capital, based on the amount of funding and percentage cost of each of the above forms of funding. We begin with the first debt item, which was $1,000,000 of debt that was sold for $20,000 less than par value, at 8.5 percent debt. The marginal income tax rate is 35 percent. The calculation is as follows.

$$\text{Net after-tax interest percent} = \frac{((\text{Interest expense}) \times (1 - \text{tax rate})) \times \text{Amount of debt}}{(\text{Amount of debt}) - (\text{Discount on sale of debt})}$$

$$\text{Net after-tax interest percent} = \frac{((8.5\%) \times (1 - .35)) \times \$1,000,000}{\$1,000,000 - \$20,000}$$

$$\text{Net after-tax interest percent} = \underline{5.638\%}$$

We employ the same method for the second debt instrument, for which there is $3,000,000 of debt that was sold at par: $25,000 in legal fees were incurred to place the debt, which pays 10 percent interest. The marginal income tax rate remains at 35 percent. The calculation is as follows:

$$\text{Net after-tax interest percent} = \frac{((\text{Interest expense}) \times (1 - \text{tax rate})) \times \text{Amount of debt}}{(\text{Amount of debt}) - (\text{Discount on sale of debt})}$$

$$\text{Net after-tax interest percent} = \frac{((10\%) \times (1 - .35)) \times \$3,000,000}{\$3,000,000 - \$25,000}$$

$$\text{Net after-tax interest percent} = \underline{7.091\%}$$

We now calculate the cost of the preferred stock. As noted above, there is $2,500,000 of preferred stock on the books, with an interest rate of 9 percent. The marginal corporate income tax does not apply, since the interest payments are treated like dividends, and are not deductible. The calculation is the simplest of all, for the answer is 9 percent, since there is no income tax to confuse the issue.

Exhibit 2.6　The Weighted Cost of Capital Calculation

Type of Funding	Amount of Funding	Percentage Cost	Dollar Cost
Debt number 1	$980,000	5.638%	$55,252
Debt number 2	2,975,000	7.091%	210,957
Preferred stock	2,500,000	9.000%	225,000
Common stock	4,000,000	13.200%	528,000
Totals	$10,455,000	**9.75%**	$1,019,209

To arrive at the cost of equity capital, we take from the example a return on risk-free securities of 6 percent, a return of 12 percent that is expected from a typical market basket of related stocks, and a beta of 1.2. We then enter this information into the following formula to arrive at the cost of equity capital:

$$\text{Cost of equity capital} = \text{Risk-free return} + \text{Beta (Average stock return} - \text{risk-free return)}$$
$$\text{Cost of equity capital} = 6\% + 1.2\,(12\% - 6\%)$$
$$\text{Cost of equity capital} = \underline{13.2\%}$$

Now that we know the cost of each type of funding, it is a simple matter to construct a table such as the one shown in Exhibit 2.6 that lists the amount of each type of funding and its related cost, which we can quickly sum to arrive at a weighted cost of capital.

When combined into the weighted average calculation shown in Exhibit 2.6, we see that the weighted cost of capital is 9.75 percent. Though there is some considerably less expensive debt on the books, the majority of the funding is comprised of more expensive common and preferred stock, which drives up the overall cost of capital.

2-10　WHEN SHOULD I USE THE INCREMENTAL COST OF CAPITAL?

The trouble with the existing weighted cost of capital is that it reflects the cost of debt and equity only at the time the company obtained it. For example, if a company obtained debt at a fixed interest rate during a period in the past when the prime rate offered by banks for new debt was very high, the resulting cost of capital, which still includes this debt, will be higher than the cost of capital if that debt had been retired and refunded by new debt that was obtained at current market rates, which are lower. The same issue applies to equity, for the cost of equity can change if the underlying return on risk-free debt has changed, which it does continually (just observe daily or monthly swings in the cost of U.S. government securities, which are considered to be risk-free). Similarly, a company's beta will change over time as its overall risk profile changes, possibly due to changes in its markets, or internal changes that alter its mix of business. Accordingly, a company may find that its carefully calculated weighted cost of capital does not bear even a slight resemblance to what the same cost would be if recalculated based on current market conditions.

Where does this disturbing news leave us? If there is no point in using the weighted cost of capital that is recorded on the books, there is no reason why we cannot calculate the incremental weighted cost of capital based on current market conditions, and use that as a hurdle rate instead. By doing so, a company recognizes that it will obtain funds at the current market rates, and use the cost of this blended rate to pay for new projects. For example, if a company intends to retain the same proportions of debt and equity, and finds that the new weighted cost of capital is 2 percent higher at current market rates than the old rates recorded on the company books, then the hurdle rate used for evaluating new projects should use the new, higher rate.

It is also important to determine management's intentions in regard to the new blend of debt and equity, for changes in the proportions of the two will alter the weighted cost of capital. If a significant alteration in the current mix is anticipated, the new proportion should be factored into the weighted cost of capital calculation. For example, management may be forced by creditors or owners to alter the existing proportion of debt and equity. This is most common when a company is closely held, and the owners do not want to invest any more equity in the company, thereby forcing it to resort to debt financing. Alternatively, if the debt-to-equity ratio is very high, lenders may force the addition of more equity in order to reduce the risk of default, which goes up when there is a large amount of interest and principal to pay out of current cash flow. In short, the incremental cost of capital is the most relevant hurdle rate figure when using new funds to pay for new projects.

The concept of incremental funds costs can be taken too far, however. If a company is initiating only one project in the upcoming year and needs to borrow funds at a specific rate to pay for it, then a good case can be made for designating the cost of that funding as the hurdle rate for the single project under consideration, since the two are inextricably intertwined. However, such a direct relationship is rarely the case. Instead, there are many projects being implemented, which are spread out over a long time frame, with funds being acquired at intervals that do not necessarily match those of the funds requirements of individual projects. For example, a company may hold off on an equity offering in the public markets until there is a significant upswing in the stock market, or borrow funds a few months early if it can obtain a favorably low, long-term fixed rate. When this happens, there is no way to tie a specific funding cost to a specific project, so it is better to calculate the blended cost of capital for the period and apply it as a hurdle rate to all of the projects currently under consideration.

All this discussion of the incremental cost of capital does not mean that the cost of capital that is derived from the book cost of existing funding is totally irrelevant—far from it. Many companies finance all new projects out of their existing cash flow, and have no reason to go to outside lenders or equity markets to obtain new funding. For these organizations, the true cost of debt is indeed the same as the amount recorded on their books, since they are obligated to pay that exact amount of debt, irrespective of what current market interest rates may be. However, the weighted cost of capital does not just include debt; it also includes equity, and this cost *does* change over time. Even if a company has no need for additional equity, the cost of its existing equity will change, because the earnings expectations of investors will change over time, as well as the company's beta. For example, the underlying risk-free interest rate can and will change as the inflation rate varies, so there is some return to investors that exceeds the rate of inflation. Similarly, the average market rate of return on equity will change over time as investor expectations change. Further, the mix of businesses and markets in which a company is involved will inevitably lead to variation in its beta over time, as the variability of its cash flows becomes greater or lower. Consequently, the book cost of debt is still a valid part of the weighted cost of capital as long as no new debt is added, whereas the cost of equity *will* change as the expectation for higher or lower returns by investors changes, which results in a weighted cost of capital that can blend the book and market costs of funding in some situations.

2-11 HOW DO I USE NET PRESENT VALUE IN CAPITAL BUDGETING?

The typical capital investment is composed of a string of cash flows, both in and out, that will continue until the investment is eventually liquidated at some point in the future. These cash flows are comprised of many things: the initial payment for equipment, continuing maintenance costs, salvage value of the equipment when it is eventually sold, tax payments, receipts from product sold, and so on. The trouble is, since the cash flows are coming in and going out over a period of many years, how do we make them comparable for an analysis that is done in the present? This requires the use of a discount rate (usually based on the cost of capital) to reduce the value of a future cash flow into what it would be worth right now. By applying the discount rate to each anticipated cash flow, we can reduce and then add them together, which yields a single combined figure that represents the current value of the entire proposed capital investment. This is known as its *net present value*.

For an example of how net present value works, Exhibit 2.7 lists the cash flows, both in and out, for a capital investment that is expected to last for five years. The year is listed in the first column, the amount of the cash flow in the second column, and the discount rate in the third column. The final column multiplies the cash flow

Exhibit 2.7   Simplified Net Present Value Example

Year	Cash Flow	Discount Factor[*]	Present Value
0	−$100,000	1.000	−$100,000
1	+25,000	.9259	+23,148
2	+25,000	.8573	+21,433
3	+25,000	.7938	+19,845
4	+30,000	.7350	+22,050
5	+30,000	.6806	+20,418
		Net Present Value	+$6,894

* *Note:* Discount factor is 8%.

from the second column by the discount rate in the third column to yield the present value of each cash flow. The grand total cash flow is listed in the lower-right corner of the table.

Notice that the discount factor in Exhibit 2.7 becomes progressively smaller in later years, since cash flows further in the future are worth less than those that will be received sooner. The discount factor is published in present value tables, which are listed in many accounting and finance textbooks. They are also a standard feature in midrange hand-held calculators. Another variation is to use the following formula to manually compute a present value:

$$\text{Present value of a future cash flow} = \frac{(\text{Future cash flow})}{(1 + \text{Discount rate})^{(\text{squared by the number of periods of discounting})}}$$

Using the above formula, if we expect to receive $75,000 in one year, and the discount rate is 15 percent, then the calculation is:

$$\text{Present value} = \frac{\$75,000}{(1 + .15)^1}$$
$$\text{Present value} = \$65,217.39$$

Here are the most common cash flow line items to include in a net present value analysis:

- *Cash inflows from sales.* If a capital investment results in added sales, then all gross margins attributable to that investment must be included in the analysis.
- *Cash inflows and outflows for equipment purchases and sales.* There should be a cash outflow when a product is purchased, as well as a cash inflow when the equipment is no longer needed and is sold off.
- *Cash inflows and outflows for working capital.* When a capital investment occurs, it normally involves the use of some additional inventory. If there are added sales, then there will probably be additional accounts receivable. In either case, these are additional investments that must be included in the analysis as cash outflows. Also, if the investment is ever terminated, then the inventory will presumably be sold off and the accounts receivable collected, so there should be line items in the analysis, located at the end of the project timeline, showing the cash inflows from the liquidation of working capital.
- *Cash outflows for maintenance.* If there is production equipment involved, then there will be periodic maintenance needed to ensure that it runs properly.
- *Cash outflows for taxes.* If there is a profit from new sales that are attributable to the capital investment, then the incremental income tax that can be traced to those incremental sales must be included in the analysis. Also, if there is a significant

quantity of production equipment involved, the annual personal property taxes
that can be traced to that equipment should also be included.

* *Cash inflows for the tax effect of depreciation.* Depreciation is an allowable tax
deduction. Accordingly, the depreciation created by the purchase of capital
equipment should be offset against the cash outflow caused by income taxes.
Though depreciation is really just an accrual, it does have a net cash flow impact
caused by a reduction in taxes, and so should be included in the net present value
calculation.

The net present value approach is the best way to see if a proposed capital
investment has a sufficient rate of return to justify the use of any required funds.
Also, because it reveals the amount of cash created in excess of the cost of capital,
it allows management to rank projects by the amount of cash they can potentially
spin off.

2-12 WHAT PROPOSAL FORM SHOULD I REQUIRE FOR A CASH FLOW ANALYSIS?

Department managers are responsible for assembling all the cash flow information needed for the accountant to create a net present value analysis. They should
use a standard application form, such as the one shown in Exhibit 2.8, so that the
same types of information are consistently used to arrive at net present value
results.

The form shown in Exhibit 2.8 is divided into several key pieces. The first is the
identification section, in which we insert the name of the project sponsor, the date
on which the proposal was submitted, and the description of the project. For a
company that deals with a multitude of capital projects, it may also be useful to
include a specific identifying code for each one. The next section is the most
important one—it lists all cash inflows and outflows, in summary form, for each
year. The sample form has room for just five years of cash flows, but this can be
increased for companies with longer-term investments. Cash outflows are listed as
negative numbers, and inflows as positive ones. The annual depreciation figure
goes into the box in the "Tax Effect of Annual Depreciation" column. The column
of tax deductions listed directly below the depreciation box are automatic
calculations that determine the tax deduction, based on the tax rate noted in
the far-right column. All of the cash flows for each year are then summarized in the
far-right column. A series of calculations are listed directly below this "Total"
column, which itemize the payback period and net present value. This can be
considered a risky project, since the net present value is negative and the number of
years needed to pay back the initial investment is quite lengthy. The next section of
the form is for the type of project. The purpose of this section is to identify those
investments that *must* be completed, irrespective of the rate of return; these are

Capital Investment Proposal Form

Name of Project Sponsor:	*H. Henderson*	**Submission Date:**	*3/5/2007*

Investment Description:
Additional press for newsprint.

Cash Flows:

Year	Equipment	Working Capital	Maintenance	Tax Effect of Annual Depreciation	Salvage Value	Revenue	Taxes	Total
0	–5,000,000	–400,000		800,000				–5,400,000
1			–100,000	320,000		1,650,000	– 700,000	1,170,000
2			–100,000	320,000		1,650,000	–700,000	1,170,000
3			–100,000	320,000		1,650,000	–700,000	1,170,000
4			–100,000	320,000		1,650,000	–700,000	1,170,000
5		400,000	–100,000	320,000	1,000,000	1,650,000	–700,000	2,570,000
Totals	–5,000,000	0	–500,000	2,400,000	1,000,000	8,250,000		1,850,000

	Tax Rate:	**40%**
	Hurdle Rate:	**10%**
	Payback Period:	4.28
	Net Present Value:	(86,809)

Type of Project (check one):

Legal requirement	
New product-related	
Old product extension	Yes
Repair/replacement	
Safety issue	

Approvals:

Amount	Approver	Signature
<$5,000	Supervisor	
$5–19,999	General Mgr.	
$20– 49,999	President	
$50,000+	Board	

Exhibit 2.8 Capital Investment Proposal Form

usually due to legal or safety issues. Also, if a project is for a new product, management may consider it to be especially risky, and so will require a higher hurdle rate. This section identifies those projects. The last section is for approvals by managers. It lists the level of manager who can sign off on various investment dollar amounts, and ensures that the correct number of managers have reviewed each investment. This format is comprehensive enough to give an accountant sufficient information to conduct a rapid analysis of most projects.

2-13 SHOULD I USE THE PAYBACK PERIOD IN CAPITAL BUDGETING?

The net present value method shown earlier misses one important element, which is that it does not fully explain investment risk, which is the chance that the initial investment will not be earned back, or that the rate of return target will not be met. Discounting can be used to identify or weed out such projects, simply by increasing the hurdle rate. For example, if a project is perceived to be risky, an increase in the hurdle rate will reduce its net present value, which makes the investment less likely to be approved by management. However, management may not be comfortable dealing with discounted cash flow methods when looking at a risky investment; they just want to know how long it will take until they get their invested funds back—the payback period.

There are two ways to calculate the payback period. The first method is the easiest to use, but can yield a skewed result. That calculation is to divide the capital investment by the average annual cash flow from operations. For example, in Exhibit 2.9 we have a stream of cash flows over five years that is heavily weighted toward the time periods that are furthest in the future. The sum of those cash flows is $8,750,000, which is an average of $1,750,000 per year. We will also assume that the initial capital investment was $6,000,000. Based on this information, the payback period is $6,000,000 divided by $1,750,000, which is 3.4 years. However, if we review the stream of cash flows in Exhibit 2.9, it is evident that the cash inflow did not cover the investment at the 3.4-year mark. In fact, the actual cash inflow did not exceed $6,000,000 until shortly after the end of the fourth year. What happened? The stream of cash flows in the example was so skewed toward future periods that the annual *average* cash flow was not representative of the annual actual cash flow. Thus, we can use the averaging method only if the stream of future cash flows is relatively even from year to year.

The most accurate way to calculate the payback period is to do so manually. This means that we deduct the total expected cash inflow from the invested balance, year by year, until we arrive at the correct period. For example, we have recreated the stream

Exhibit 2.9   Stream of Cash Flows for a Payback Calculation

Year	Cash Flow
1	$1,000,000
2	1,250,000
3	1,500,000
4	2,000,000
5	3,000,000

Exhibit 2.10   Stream of Cash Flows for a Manual Payback Calculation

Year	Cash Flow	Net Investment Remaining
0	0	$6,000,000
1	$1,000,000	5,000,000
2	1,250,000	3,750,000
3	1,500,000	2,250,000
4	2,000,000	250,000
5	3,000,000	—

of cash flows from Exhibit 2.9 in Exhibit 2.10, but now with an extra column that shows the net capital investment remaining at the end of each year. We can use this format to reach the end of year 4; we know that the cash flows will pay back the investment sometime during year 5, but we do not have a month-by-month cash flow that tells us precisely when. Instead, we can assume an average stream of cash flows during that period, which works out to $250,000 per month ($3,000,000 cash inflow for the year, divided by 12 months). Since there was only $250,000 of net investment remaining at the end of the fourth year, and this is the same monthly amount of cash flow in the fifth year, we can assume that the payback period is 4.1 years.

2-14 HOW CAN A POST-COMPLETION ANALYSIS HELP ME?

The greatest failing in most capital review systems is not in the initial analysis phase, but in the post-completion phase, because there isn't one. The accountant usually puts a great deal of effort into compiling a capital investment proposal form, educating managers about how to use it, and then setting up control points around the system to ensure that all capital requestors make use of the approval system. However, if there is no methodology for verifying that managers enter accurate information into the approval forms, which is done by comparing actual results to them, then managers will eventually figure out that they can alter the numbers in the approval forms in order to beat the corporate hurdle rates, even if this information is incorrect. However, if managers know that their original estimates will be carefully reviewed and critiqued for some time into the future, then they will be much more careful in completing their initial capital requests. Thus, analysis at the back end of a capital project will lead to greater accuracy at the front end.

Analysis of actual expenditures can begin before a capital investment is fully paid for or installed. The accountant can subtotal the payments made by the end of each month and compare them with the total projected by the project manager. A total that significantly exceeds the approved expenditure would then be grounds for an immediate review by top management. This approach works best for the largest capital expenditures, where reviewing payment data in detail is worth the extra effort by the accounting staff if it can prevent large overpayments. It is also worthwhile when capital expenditures cover long periods of time, so that a series of monthly reviews can be made.

Once a project is completed, there may be cash inflows that result from it. If so, a quarterly comparison of actual with projected cash inflows is the most frequent comparison to be made, with an annual review being sufficient in many cases. Such a review keeps management apprised of the performance of all capital projects, and lets the project sponsors know that their estimates will be the subject of considerable scrutiny for as far into the future as they had originally projected. For those companies that survive based on the efficiency of capital usage, it may even be reasonable to tie manager pay reviews to the accuracy of their capital investment request forms.

An example of a post-completion project analysis is shown in Exhibit 2.11. In this example, the top of the report compares actual with budgeted cash outflows, while the middle compares all actual cash outflows with the budget. Note that the cash outflows section is complete, since these were all incurred at the beginning of the project, whereas the inflows section is not yet complete, because the project has completed only the third year of a five-year plan. To cover the remaining two years of activity, there is a column for estimated cash inflows, which projects them for the remaining years of the investment, using the last year in which there is actual data available. This projected information can be used to determine the net present value. We compare the actual and projected net present values at the bottom of the report, so that management can see if there are any problems worthy of correction. In this case, the initial costs of the project, both in terms of capital items and working capital, were so far over budget that the actual net present value is solidly in the red. In this case, management

Exhibit 2.11   Comparison of Actual to Projected Capital Investment Cash Flows

Description	Actual	Projected Actual	Budget	Actual Present Value[*]	Budget Present Value[*]
Cash Outflows					
Capital Items	$1,250,000	—	$1,100,000	$1,250,000	$1,100,000
Working Capital	750,000	—	500,000	750,000	500,000
Total Outflows	$2,000,000	—	$1,600,000	$2,000,000	$1,600,000
Cash Inflows					
Year 1	250,000		$250,000	$229,350	$229,350
Year 2	375,000		400,000	315,638	336,680
Year 3	450,000		500,000	347,490	386,100
Year 4		450,000	500,000	318,780	354,200
Year 5		450,000	500,000	292,455	324,950
Total Inflows	$1,075,000	$900,000	$2,150,000	$1,503,713	$1,631,280
Net Present Value	—	—	—	−$496,287	+$31,280

[*] *Note:* Uses discount rate of 9%.

should take a hard look at reducing the working capital, since this is the single largest cash drain in excess of the budget, while also seeing whether cash inflow can be increased to match the budgeted annual amounts for the last two years of the investment.

2-15 WHAT FACTORS SHOULD I CONSIDER FOR A SITE SELECTION?

The analysis of a capital request for a site selection is entirely different from the analysis process for any other type of capital expenditure. Rather than a strict analysis of constraints or discounted cash flows, this analysis involves the consideration of a multitude of additional factors, which include the following items:

- *Local labor force*. If the proposed facility requires a great deal of skilled labor, then the presence of a local university may be a key consideration. Alternatively, if the facility requires low-cost labor, then this will mandate a location in an economically depressed area or perhaps in another country with the needed characteristics. Also, if the sheer quantity of available labor is a factor, then locating near a population center will be important.

- *Infrastructure*. If the facility requires the transport of extremely bulky or heavy items, this may mandate a location near a rail siding. In most cases, it will at least call for locating next to a well-graded road with close access to a highway system or airfield. The required infrastructure may also call for access to a broadband communications network.

- *Suppliers*. If the new facility is to be operated on a just-in-time basis, or if supply chain management is crucial to its success, the company may be forced to locate near its key suppliers, or alternatively convince them to create facilities near the new location. The result may be a facility that is equidistant from all key suppliers.

- *Weather.* The type of business operated by a company may only be possible under certain weather conditions, such as theme parks that must be open all year.

- *Local incentives*. Local governments may offer a broad array of incentives in exchange for locating within their jurisdictions. Typical incentives are training credits, free utility installations, free land, low-interest loans, and inclusions in economic development zones.

- *Local tax rates*. Irrespective of other incentives offered by local governments, long-term tax rates may differ so dramatically in some areas that they will have a significant impact on the expected return from a site location.

Clearly, a vast array of factors must be considered in a site selection—many of them such a mix of quantitative and qualitative factors that a site selection cannot be entirely determined through the use of financial analysis. Instead, use some of the quantitative factors outlined here to select a set of finalists, from which management can pick the winning site based on additional, nonquantitative factors.

One alternative that is generally overlooked is finding extra space in existing facilities, rather than obtaining entirely new facilities. It is frequently worthwhile to review existing sites to see how much space can be consolidated, or whether some items can be shipped off to lower-cost long-term storage. In some cases, it may also be possible to have employees work from home and use generally available office space only when they need to be in the office. By using any of these options, the potential savings could be dramatic.

Chapter 3

Credit and Collection Decisions

The accountant is usually in charge of granting credit to customers, as well as collecting funds from them. These basic responsibilities give rise to a number of fundamental credit management questions, such as how to create a credit policy, where to obtain financial information about customers, how to create a credit granting system, and when to review existing credit levels. Once credit is granted, the accountant must then determine the best ways to create and deliver invoices in a manner that will be most likely to ensure payment, as well as develop a system for keeping track of overdue invoices and ongoing contacts with customers. Finally, it is necessary to collect on overdue invoices, which calls for the appropriate use of the sales staff in making collections, handling customer deductions, optimizing the use of the collections staff, and involving legal assistance when necessary.

This chapter provides answers to all of these key questions. The following table itemizes the section number in which the answers to each question can be found:

Section	Decison
3-1	How do I create and maintain a credit policy?
3-2	When should I require a credit application?
3-3	How do I obtain financial information about customers?
3-4	How does a credit granting system work?
3-5	What payment terms should I offer customers?
3-6	When should I review customer credit levels?
3-7	How can I adjust the invoice content and layout to improve collections?
3-8	How can I adjust billing delivery to improve collections?
3-9	How do I accelerate cash collections?
3-10	Should I offer early payment discounts?
3-11	How do I optimize customer contacts?
3-12	How do I manage customer contact information?
3-13	How do I involve the sales staff in collections?
3-14	How do I handle payment deductions?
3-15	How do I collect overdue payments?
3-16	When should I take legal action to collect from a customer?

3-1 HOW DO I CREATE AND MAINTAIN A CREDIT POLICY?

One of the chief causes of confusion not only within the credit department but also between the credit and sales departments is the lack of consistency in dealing with customer credit issues. This includes who is responsible for credit tasks, what logical structure is used to evaluate and assign credit, what terms of sale are used, and what milestones are established for the collection process. Without consistent application of these items, customers never know what credit levels they are likely to be assigned, collection activities tend to jolt from one step to the next in no predetermined order, and no one knows who is responsible for what activities.

Establishment of a reasonably detailed credit policy goes a long way toward resolving these issues. The policy should clearly state the mission and goals of the credit department, exactly which positions are responsible for the most critical credit and collection tasks, what formula shall be used for assigning credit levels, and what steps shall be followed in the collection process. Further comments are as follows:

- *Mission.* The mission statement should outline the general concept of how the credit department does business: Does it provide a loose credit policy to maximize sales, or work toward high-quality receivables (implying reduced sales), or manage credit at some point in between? A loose credit policy might result in this mission: "The credit department shall offer credit to all customers except those where the risk of loss is probable."

- *Goals.* This can be quite specific, describing the exact performance measurements against which the credit staff will be judged. For example, "The department goals are to operate with no more than one collections person per 1,000 customers, while attaining a bad debt percentage no higher than 2 percent of sales, and annual days sales outstanding of no higher than 42 days."

- *Responsibilities.* This is perhaps the most critical part of the policy, based on the number of quarrels it can avert. It should firmly state who has final authority over the granting of credit and the assignment of credit hold status. This is normally the credit manager, but the policy can also state the order volume level at which someone else, such as the CFO or treasurer, can be called upon to render final judgment.

- *Credit level assignment.* This section may be of extreme interest to the sales staff, the size of whose sales (and commissions) is based on it. The policy should at least state the sources of information to be used in the calculation of a credit limit, such as credit reports or financial statements, and can also include the minimum credit level automatically extended to all customers, as well as the criteria used to grant larger limits.

- *Collections methodology.* The policy can itemize what collection steps shall be followed, such as initial calls, customer visits, e-mails, notification of the sales staff, credit holds, and forwarding to a collections agency. This section can be written in too much detail, itemizing exactly what steps are to be taken after a certain number of days. This can constrain an active collections staff from taking unique steps to achieve a collection, so a certain degree of vagueness is acceptable here.

- *Terms of sale.* If there are few product lines in a single industry, it is useful to clearly state a standard payment term, such as a 1 percent discount if paid in 10 days; otherwise full payment is expected in 30 days. An override policy can be included, noting a sign-off by the controller or CFO. By doing so, the sales staff will be less inclined to attempt to gain better terms on behalf of customers. However, where there are multiple industries served with different customary credit terms, it may be too complicated to include this verbiage in the credit policy.

Company management can experience significant losses if it loosens the credit policy without a good knowledge of the margins it earns on its products. For example, if it earns only a 10 percent profit on a product that sells for $10 and extends credit for one unit on that product to a customer who defaults, it has just incurred a loss of $9 that will require the sale of nine more units to offset the loss. On the other hand, if the same product had a profit of 50 percent, it would require the sale of only one more unit to offset the loss on a bad debt. Thus, loosening or tightening the credit policy can have a dramatic impact on profits when product margins are low. Consequently, always review product margins before altering the credit policy.

When economic conditions within an industry worsen, a company whose credit policy has not changed from a more expansive period will likely find itself granting more credit than it should, resulting in more bad debts. Similarly, a restrictive credit policy during a boom period will result in lost sales that go to competitors. This latter approach is particularly galling over the long term, since customers may permanently convert to a competitor and not come back, resulting in lost market share. To prevent these problems, schedule a periodic review of the credit policy to see when it should be changed to match economic conditions. A scheduled quarterly review is generally sufficient for this purpose. To prepare for the meeting, assemble a list of leading indicators for the industry, tracked on a trend line, that show where the business cycle is most likely to be heading. This information is most relevant for the company's industry, rather than the economy as a whole, since the conditions within some industries can vary substantially from the general economy. If a company has international operations, then the credit policy can be tailored to suit the business cycles of specific countries.

If a company's products are subject to rapid obsolescence, a tight credit policy can result in limited product sales that leave excess quantities on hand that will be scrapped. In such cases, loosen the credit policy on those inventory items most likely to become obsolete in the near term. The logic is that, even if inventory is sold to customers with a questionable ability to pay for the goods, this at least presents higher odds of obtaining payment than if the company throws away the goods. To implement this approach, keep the credit department informed of the obsolescence status of inventory items, usually by having the sales, marketing, and logistics staffs flag potentially obsolete items in the inventory database and giving the credit department online access to this information. When customers send in orders, the credit staff accesses this information, verifies the obsolescence status of the items ordered, and modifies the credit policy as needed.

3-2 WHEN SHOULD I REQUIRE A CREDIT APPLICATION?

The credit application function can be a hit-or-miss affair, with some uncertainty regarding the order volume at which an application is required. This is a particular problem when a customer places a large number of small orders, none of which individually are cause for concern, but which in total can represent a serious credit risk. If the credit department is overwhelmed with work, it may not have the time to delve into the need for applications, and will be content to let many seemingly smaller orders pass by with no credit review. A solution for some situations is to require a completed credit application from all customers, irrespective of order size. This at least generates all paperwork needed to initiate a credit review, even if the credit staff does not choose to pursue a complete investigation. This is not a valid best practice when order sizes are small, since the extra hassle may drive away small customers. Also, it is not useful when the credit staff is so small that it has no chance of ever reviewing all the applications.

If a customer has not placed an order recently, its financial situation may have changed considerably, rendering its previously assigned credit level no longer valid. This is a particular problem when the customer may be shopping through an industry to see who will accept an order, and is forced back to the company when no other suppliers are willing to deal with it anymore. If the company's credit department simply dusts off the old credit review and allows the same credit limit, there could be a bad debt lurking in the immediate future. A solution is to require customers to complete a new credit application after a preset interval has passed, such as two years. This represents a significant additional work load for the credit staff, so require it only if the old credit level was a sufficiently high one to represent a noticeable potential bad debt loss. Though the computer system can be designed to flag these customers for a credit review when new orders arrive, an alternative is to simply purge from the accounting database all customers with whom there has been no business in the past two years. Then, when an order arrives and the accounting system shows no customer record, the credit staff knows it needs to get involved.

When customers are delinquent in paying, it is common to see their receivable balances exceed their credit limits, especially when a company has a tight credit policy and grants only moderate credit limits. In these cases, the collections staff must constantly contact customers to hound them about payments. The usual threat is that all new orders will be held until the customers pay enough to bring the outstanding balance sufficiently below the credit limit for them to place more orders. This is a time-consuming and repetitive process. A simple alternative is a standard mailing to customers having exceeded the credit limit, telling them of the overage problem, and that they now have to fill out a new credit application in order to have the chance of obtaining a new, higher credit limit. If the attached credit application is sufficiently bulky, customers may very well choose to make a payment rather than go through the ordeal of another credit application. In order to accelerate this process, consider converting the credit application into PDF format and e-mailing it to the customer.

3-3 HOW DO I OBTAIN FINANCIAL INFORMATION ABOUT CUSTOMERS?

When a customer calls to ask for a delivery on credit, the credit department is operating from a clean slate—it has no idea whether the information the customer enters into a credit application is correct. Though a painstaking amount of labor can eventually verify this information, there is a large time penalty required to do so. Meanwhile, customers must wait for the application to be completed, which may take days, sending frustrated customers elsewhere. One solution is to purchase credit reports on customers. These reports list company locations, names, officer information, credit histories, legal problems, banking relations, financial information, and other data of great use to the credit department. The largest purveyor of these reports is Dun &Bradstreet (www.dnb.com), followed by Equifax (www.equifax.com). Report prices range from $40 to $125 for reports with varying amounts of information, with reduced pricing if one agrees to purchase a monthly subscription. Low-cost reports include only basic customer information, such as corporate names, locations, ownership, and corporate history, while the more expensive reports include a variety of financial and payment information. Equifax reports present information more graphically, but the two report providers issue essentially the same information. Both companies provide credit reports over the Internet.

It is substantially easier to obtain financial information about publicly held customers. By going to the www.sec.gov Web site, one can easily call up all of the most recent financial filings submitted by these entities. The best source of information is the 10-Q report, which details and discusses a company's quarterly results. Though a shorter report than the annual 10-K report, it contains much more current information, and so is of more use to the credit department.

Another source of information is an industry credit group. These groups exchange information about specific customers, such as recent problems with not-sufficient-funds (NSF) checks, bankruptcies, accounts being sent to collections, and other financial difficulties, so the credit department can take quick action to tighten credit where necessary. The National Association of Credit Management (NACM), which can be reached at www.nacm.org, maintains a listing of national credit management groups, including the following:

National agricultural credit conference

National Christian suppliers

National electronics and communications

National fundraising manufacturers

National garage door and operating devices

National home centers credit group

National housewares/consumer products manufacturers

National lawn and garden suppliers

National leisure living manufacturers

National metal building and components

National metal producers

National musical instrument

National paper packaging credit group

National coated paper and film manufacturing

National professional apparel manufacturers

National seed distributors

National steel mill

National suppliers to window manufacturers credit group

National tool and accessories

National truck, trailer, and equipment credit group

National vinyl fence credit group

National water products manufacturers

National waterway carriers/suppliers

The NACM lists meeting intervals and contact information for each group's administrator.

3-4 HOW DOES A CREDIT GRANTING SYSTEM WORK?

The credit staff should have a procedure for granting credit that uses a single set of rules that are not to be violated. The exact procedure will vary by credit department and the experience of the credit manager. As an example, a credit person can obtain a credit report for a prospective customer and use this as a source of baseline information for deriving a credit level. A credit report is an excellent source upon which to create a standard credit level, for the information contained in it is collected in a similar manner for all companies, resulting in a standardized and highly comparable basis of information. Credit reports show the high, low, and median sales levels granted to a customer by other companies, giving the credit manager some idea of what other organizations consider to be an appropriate credit range for the customer. However, just using existing sales levels is not sufficient, since one must also consider the number of extra days beyond terms that a customer takes to pay its suppliers. This information is a good indicator of creditworthiness and is also contained in the credit report.

An example of how the "payment" information can be included in the calculation of a credit level is to take the median credit level other companies granted as a starting point and then subtract 5 percent of this amount for every day that a customer pays its suppliers later than standard payment terms. For example, if the median credit level is $10,000 and a customer pays an average of 10 days late, 50 percent of the median credit level is taken away, resulting in a revised credit level of $5,000. The exact system a company uses will be highly dependent on its willingness to incur credit losses and expend extra effort on collections. A company willing to obtain more marginal sales will adopt the highest credit level shown in the credit report and not discount the impact of late payments at all, whereas a risk-averse company may be inclined to use the lowest reported credit level and further discount it heavily for the impact of any late payments by the potential customer.

Another example is to set up a system whereby the amount of credit granted is a percentage of the customer's reported level of equity. The percentage is calculated by creating a credit score based on a variety of factors, such as the perceived riskiness of the country in which the customer is located, the presence of a clean audit report, positive cash flow, no family members in senior management positions, the possibility of significant repeat business with the customer, and so on. The exact set of criteria used will depend upon the industry in which the company is located and fine-tuning of the system by the credit manager, who maintains it.

Another possibility is to create and consistently use a credit decision table. This is a simple Yes/No decision matrix based on a few key credit issues. Here is an example of how a decision table might work:

1. Is the initial order less than $1,000? If so, grant credit without review.
2. Is the initial order more than $1,000 but less than $10,000? Require a completed credit application. Grant a credit limit of 10 percent of the customer's net worth.
3. Is the initial order more than $10,000? Require a completed credit application and financial statements. If a profitable customer, grant a credit limit of 10 percent of the customer's net worth. Reduce the credit limit by 10 percent for every percent of customer loss reported.
4. Does an existing customer's order exceed its credit limit by less than 20 percent and there is no history of payment problems? If so, grant the increase.
5. Does an existing customer order exceed its credit limit by more than 20 percent or there is a history of payment problems? If so, forward to the credit manager for review. Use the same credit granting process listed in step 3.
6. Does an existing customer have any invoices at least 60 days past due? If so, freeze all orders.

While this approach does not completely eliminate variability from the credit granting process, it sets up clear decision points governing what actions to take for the majority of situations, leaving only the more difficult customer accounts for additional review.

Many companies do not have the resources to create an in-house credit scoring system for their customers. An alternative is to use the Dun & Bradstreet credit scoring model, called the "Credit eValuator Report." This report contains both a conservative and aggressive credit limit, a customer's payment performance trend, basic company details, and legal filings information. The report costs $35 per customer, with a discount if one purchases a subscription service with Dun & Bradstreet. This is a good, low-cost approach for determining an approximate credit score, but it does not include variables that may be of considerable importance in a specific industry. Also, though the cost per report is low, this is not a sufficiently cost-effective scoring approach for very small customer accounts.

3-5 WHAT PAYMENT TERMS SHOULD I OFFER TO CUSTOMERS?

The baseline payment terms that a company should consider offering to its customers is the standard terms offered in the industry, which may range from immediate payment to 60-day terms. The key issue is to give the appearance of offering competitive terms, so that prospective customers will not be turned away. However, it is quite acceptable to modify these baseline terms considerably if a customer appears to present a credit risk.

One solution is to shorten the terms of sale. For example, a customer may plan to place 10 orders for $3,000 each within the company's standard 30-day terms period, resulting in a required credit line of $30,000. Reducing payment terms to 15 days would mean that the customer should be able to purchase the same quantity of goods from the company on a credit line of just $15,000. This approach works only if a customer is placing many small orders rather than one large one, the orders are evenly spaced out, and the customer's own cash receipts cycle allows it to pay on such short terms.

Another possibility is to offer a leasing option to customers, which allows them to make a series of smaller payments over time. Though the company could offer this service itself and earn extra interest income on the sale, this still leaves the risk of collection with the company. An alternative is to engage the services of an outside leasing firm, so the company receives payment from the lessor as soon as payment is authorized by the customer, thereby eliminating the collection risk in the shortest possible time frame. A company can also earn a small interest percentage on the lease as part of its outsourcing agreement with the leasing company, usually in the range of ½ to 1 percent. This approach is most effective when the company and the leasing agency have come to a joint leasing agreement well in advance of a customer sale, so the sales staff can present the leasing option to the customer as part of the initial sale presentation. This frequently gives the company a distinct advantage in making the sale. Of course, a lease is a viable alternative only when the company is selling a fixed asset that the customer intends to retain.

Another approach is to leave the payment terms alone, but to have an individual with personal assets guarantee payment. The personal guarantee makes collection easier, since the signer knows that he or she is responsible for the amount of the receivable, and will make sure that this invoice is paid before other unsecured invoices. If possible, obtain a joint guarantee from the individual and his or her spouse. By doing so, the company can get around some state-level community property laws requiring collection only if the spouse also agrees to a guarantee.

Finally, consider leaving the payment terms alone, but obtaining credit insurance on the invoice. This is a guarantee by an insurance company against customer non-payment. Credit insurance is available for domestic credit, export credit, and coverage of custom products prior to delivery, in case customers cancel orders. If a credit insurance policy stipulates a maximum credit limit per customer, the insurance company must make the decision to increase the credit limit, or the company can take on the uninsured risk of granting extra credit. If a customer is considered by the insurance company to be high-risk, it will likely grant no insurance at all. Also, goods being exported to countries with a high perceived level of political risk will not be granted credit insurance. The cost of credit insurance can exceed ½ percent of the invoiced amount, which varies considerably by the perceived risk of each customer. The company does not have to absorb this cost; where possible, consider rebilling it to the customer, who may be willing to pay it in order to obtain a larger line of credit than would otherwise be the case.

3-6 WHEN SHOULD I REVIEW CUSTOMER CREDIT LEVELS?

Conducting a careful review of the credit levels of all customers can require a massive investment of time by the credit staff. This can include requesting and reviewing customer financial statements, pulling Dun & Bradstreet credit reports, visiting customer sites, reviewing payment histories, and having customers revise existing credit applications. With the burden of processing new credit applications tacked onto this considerable chore, the typical credit department will be completely buried in work.

A simple solution is to stratify the customer list by order volume over the past year, and review the credit of only that 20 percent of the list comprising 80 percent of the order volume. This approach drastically reduces the amount of credit analysis work while still ensuring a high level of review on those accounts that could have a serious bad debt impact on the company.

This approach can be further refined to exclude obviously creditworthy government entities, such as the federal government. Conversely, it may be necessary to set up an additional system for reviewing the credit of customers with smaller order histories whose orders are increasing in size, even if they fall outside the 20 percent review threshold. For example, if an existing customer increases its orders from $1,000 per month to $10,000 per month, this sudden jump may be sufficient cause for a credit review. However, these cases are exceptions that should not alter the credit review work load to a noticeable extent.

Another option is to review customer credit levels when a customer issues more than a single not-sufficient-funds (NSF) check within a predetermined time period. This option requires the use of NSF tracking by customer. To make this process easier, consider recording each NSF check returned by the bank in a separate general ledger account, with each journal entry clearly identifying the customer. One can then summarize this account to see which customers are repeat offenders.

When a customer gets into financial difficulty, a common ploy is to pay the smallest invoice first, or to ignore the largest invoice in a group of invoices that are all payable at the same time. By doing so, a company will at least receive *something* on the due date, which may keep it from pursuing collection of the unpaid invoices quite so aggressively as would normally be the case. Skipping payments is a clear sign that a customer is experiencing cash flow difficulty. As soon as the cash application staff sees this happening, they should notify the credit manager, who in turn should schedule the customer for an immediate credit review. This review cannot be delayed, since the financial condition of some customers may rapidly spiral down into bankruptcy.

When a customer stops taking cash discounts, it is possible that the customer's financial condition has declined to the point where it no longer has the cash to make an early payment. Thus, this is an excellent early warning of a decline in a customer's financial condition. If the cash application staff notices this change, they should notify the credit manager at once, who can reevaluate the customer's credit limit.

3-7 HOW CAN I ADJUST THE INVOICE CONTENT AND LAYOUT TO IMPROVE COLLECTIONS?

Most invoices contain nearly all of the information a customer needs to make a payment, but the layout may be so poor that they must hunt for the information. In other cases, adding information will reduce payment problems. This section describes a number of invoice layout changes that can help improve collections.

When a customer receives an invoice and has a question about it, whom does he call? The invoice usually includes only the company's mailing address, and may show only a post office box where the corporate lockbox is located. The solution is to clearly state contact information on the invoice. This should be delineated by a box and possibly noted in bold or colored print. If the billing staff is large, it may not be practical to put a specific contact name on the invoice, but at least list a central contact phone number. If a company has chosen to assign specific customers to individuals in the collections department, it may be possible to list the name of the assigned collections person in the computer file of the customers for whom they are responsible, so the names of assigned people appear on invoices.

Some customers prefer to pay for invoices with a credit card, rather than a check. If so, they call the general number for the company, ask to be routed to the accounting department, and leave credit card information with the first "live" person they contact. This person is frequently not trained in the types of credit card information to collect (writing down the name on the credit card, card number, expiration date, billing address, and need for a receipt can be overwhelming for some), so inadequate information is eventually forwarded to the person trained in processing credit card payments. This person must call back the customer (who may not have left a return phone number!) to obtain the required information. A better approach is to list the credit card contact number on the invoice. A refinement of the concept is to list on the invoice the types of credit cards accepted by the company, which may prevent customers from making unnecessary calls if they do not have the right types of cards.

The standard invoice presentation shows the invoice date in one of the upper corners, and the payment terms (such as "Net 30") somewhere in the header bar, just above the detailed billing information. For the customer to calculate the proper payment date, she must locate the invoice date, add to it the payment terms, and enter this payment date in her computer system. The reality is more complex. The typical accounting computer system automatically defaults the invoice date to the current date (invariably later than the invoice date), and adds to it a default payment-terms date that is stored in the customer file. Thus, there are two ways for a customer to delay payment: (1) be lazy and accept the current date as the invoice date, and (2) always use the preset payment terms. The result is chronically late payments. The solution is to take the payment date calculation chore away from the customer and clearly state the invoice payment date on the invoice, preferably in bold and located in a box. To make matters as simple as possible, it may make sense to even eliminate all mention of payment terms, so the customer does not try to second guess the company on the proper payment date.

If there is too much clutter on an invoice, customers will have a difficult time locating key information. For example, some information used by the accounting staff but not by the customer is included in the header bar, such as the initials of the customer's salesperson (usually for commission calculation purposes) and the job number. At a particularly high level of obscurity, some accounting systems label the invoice number as something else, such as the "document number." The end result is more time spent by the customer wading through an invoice to find the relevant information, and a greater risk that the wrong or incorrect information will be transferred from the invoice to the customer's accounts payable system. The solution is to strip out unnecessary information or clarify the labeling of needed items. All but the most primitive accounting computer systems contain report writers that should allow one to make these changes to the invoice template.

There may be cases where customers demand proof of their receipt of a delivery from the company before they will pay its invoice. One way to provide this information is to use either FedEx or United Parcel Service to make deliveries, since both organizations post receipt signatures on their Web sites. One can then copy the signature images out of the Web sites and paste them directly into an invoice, thereby providing proof of receipt to the customer on the invoice. If necessary, the billing staff can also add the delivery reference number used by either United Parcel Service or FedEx to the invoice. Either the customer or the company can then go straight to the Web site of either package delivery company to obtain further evidence of the time and place of delivery of the package in question. This approach has the distinct advantage of consolidating both the billing and receiving information for a delivery on one piece of paper. The downside is that the invoice cannot be issued until the delivery has been received by the customer, rather than being sent when the package leaves the company's premises.

3-8 HOW CAN I ADJUST BILLING DELIVERY TO IMPROVE COLLECTIONS?

An excellent way to increase the speed of invoice delivery, as well as to enhance the process flow of customer approvals, is to use Adobe's Acrobat software to create a perfect electronic copy of an invoice. This copy is then attached to an e-mail and forwarded straight to a customer's accounting department where it can be opened, printed, and paid. Implementing the conversion of invoices into the Acrobat format is quite simple. First, go to the Adobe Web site (www.adobe.com) to order the Acrobat software, and purchase a copy for $249. Once installed, go to your accounting software package and prepare to print an invoice. When the printing screen appears, change the assigned printer to Adobe PDF, which will appear as one of the available printers. The software will ask where to store the resulting file and what to name it. After a few seconds, the conversion of the invoice into a picture-perfect PDF file will be complete. This is a significant, inexpensive, and operationally elegant way to accelerate cash flow.

There are many situations in which a company knows the exact amount of a customer billing well before the date on which the invoice is to be sent, such as for a recurring subscription. In these cases, it makes sense to create the invoice and deliver it to the customer one or two weeks in advance of the date when it is actually due. By doing so, the invoice has more time to be routed through the receiving organization, passing through the mail room, accounting staff, authorized signatory, and back to the accounts payable staff for payment. This makes it much more likely that the invoice will be paid on time, which improves cash flow and reduces a company's investment in accounts receivable. The main difficulty with advance billings is that the date of the invoice should be shifted forward to the accounting period in which the invoice is supposed to be billed.

When an accounting department issues an invoice containing a large number of line items, it is more likely that the recipient with have an issue with one or more of the line items, and will hold payment on the entire invoice while those line items are resolved. Though this may not be a significant issue when an invoice is relatively small, it is a large issue indeed when the invoice has a large-dollar total, and holding the entire invoice will have a serious impact on the amount of accounts receivable outstanding. To avoid this problem, split apart large invoices into separate ones, with each invoice containing just one line item. By doing so, it is more likely that some invoices will be paid at once, while other ones over which there are issues will be delayed. This can have a significant positive impact on a company's investment in accounts receivable. The only complaint arising from this approach is that customers can be buried under quite a large pile of invoices. This can be ameliorated by clustering all of the invoices in a single envelope, rather than sending a dozen separately mailed invoices on the same day. Also, it may be prudent to cluster small-dollar line items on the same invoice, since this will cut down on the number of invoices issued, while not having a significant impact on the overall receivable balance if these invoices are put on hold.

Some customers with extremely large payment volumes create payments only on certain days of the month in order to yield the greatest level of efficiency in processing what may be thousands of checks. If a company does not send an invoice early enough to be included in the next check processing run, it may have to wait a number of additional weeks before the next check run occurs, resulting in a late payment. The solution is to ask customers when they process checks, and make sure that the company issues invoices well in advance of these dates in order to be paid as early as possible. If customers are unwilling to divulge this information, it should be possible to guess at the check printing dates after a few months by tracking the dates when payments are received.

3-9 HOW DO I ACCELERATE CASH COLLECTIONS?

The acceleration of cash movement from the customer to the company is a constant problem for the accountant. The classic solution is to have them sent to a lockbox, which is a mailbox maintained by the company's bank. The bank opens all incoming envelopes, cashes all checks contained therein, and forwards copies of the checks to a single individual at the company. The advantage of this approach is that if all customers are properly notified of the address, all checks will unerringly go to one location, where they are deposited and then consolidated into a single packet and forwarded to the cash application person at the company. There are two disadvantages to be considered. One is the one-day delay in routing checks through a lockbox, which translates into a one-day delay in applying the cash (though it has already been deposited by the bank). This problem can be overcome by using lockboxes operated only by banks that scan the incoming checks and post the images on secure Web sites. This approach allows the collections staff to access check images immediately after checks arrive at the lockbox. The other problem is that all customers must be notified of the change to the lockbox address, which usually requires several follow-up contacts with a few customers who continue to send their payments to the wrong address.

Lockbox locations will become out of date as customer locations change. For example, if a company with its accounting headquarters in Kansas City sets up a lockbox on the west coast to service the bulk of its customers, this does little good when a geographical expansion to the east coast results in all the east coast checks being sent to the west coast lockbox, thereby lengthening the mail float before the company receives its cash. The solution is a periodic review of lockbox locations. A company can conduct a simple lockbox review by comparing customer locations with the nearest lockbox locations. However, the periodic change of lockbox locations will require ongoing contacts with customers to inform them of the address changes, inevitably resulting in a large number of repeat contacts before all customers are mailing payments to the new addresses. Given the effort required for this last item, it is unwise to change lockbox locations more than once a year.

Another way to accelerate cash receipts is to accept credit card payments, preferably from every major credit card company. By doing so, a company can frequently persuade the customer to place payment for smaller amounts on either a corporate or personal credit card, and have the money appear in the corporate bank account in one or two business days. The maximum amount customers can charge will vary according to internal customer credit card policy, though somewhere in the range of $1,000 to $2,500 is common. One downside is the credit card servicing fee charged by the bank, typically resulting in a deduction of 2 to 3 percent. However, consider this to be the same as offering an early payment discount; it is equivalent to a 2 to 3 percent discount in exchange for nearly immediate cash.

Another option is to use lockbox truncation. This is the process of converting a paper check into an electronic deposit. The basic process is to scan a check into a check reader, which scans the magnetic ink characters on the check into a vendor-supplied software package. The software sends this information to a third-party ACH processor, which typically clears payment in one or two days. The system has the additional benefit of eliminating deposit slips and the per-transaction deposit fees usually charged by banks. Also, not-sufficient-funds (NSF) fees are lower than if a regular check payment had been made, while NSFs can be redeposited at once. Another use of lockbox truncation is to enter into the system check information given to the company over the phone or fax by a customer. Rather than use the check scanner, one can manually punch in the information. This approach avoids the age-old check-is-in-the-mail excuse.

3-10 SHOULD I OFFER EARLY PAYMENT DISCOUNTS?

Only a company having severe cash flow problems should offer early payment discounts to its customers. The problem is that the effective interest rate the company is offering to its customers is extremely high. For example, allowing customers to take a 2 percent discount if they pay in 10 days, versus the usual 30, means that the company is offering a 2 percent discount in order to obtain cash 20 days earlier than normal. The annualized interest rate of 2 percent for 20 days is about 36 percent. All but the most debt-burdened companies can borrow funds at rates far lower than that!

Furthermore, many customers will not pay within the 10-day discount period, but will still take the discount. This can lead to a great deal of difficulty in obtaining payment of the withheld discount. In addition, the collection staff may have difficulty in applying the cash to open receivables if it is not clear on which invoice a customer is paying a discounted amount.

3-11 HOW DO I OPTIMIZE CUSTOMER CONTACTS?

The prime calling hours for most business customers are in the early to mid-morning hours, before they have been called away for meetings or other activities. If customers are concentrated in a single time zone, this can mean that the time period available for calls is extremely short, and is a particular problem if the collections staff is not prepared to call customers during that time period. Also, if the customer base spans multiple time zones, a collections staff based in one time zone may be making calls to customers that are outside the customers' prime calling hours, resulting in few completed calls. Awareness of prime calling hours for individual customers is key. The accountant should avoid any meetings during prime calling hours, instead focusing on having the collections staff fully prepared to make calls, with all required information close at hand. In addition, the accountant should require a collections workday that is built around prime calling hours. For example, if the collections staff is based on the west coast but most of its customer contacts are on the east coast, its workday should begin very early in order to make up for the three-hour time difference.

The typical list of overdue invoices is so long that the existing collections staff cannot possibly contact all customers about all invoices on a sufficiently frequent basis. This problem results in many invoices not being collected for an inordinately long time. A good solution is to utilize collections call stratification. The concept behind this approach is to split up, or stratify, all of the overdue receivables and concentrate the bulk of the collections staff's time on the largest invoices. By doing so, a company can realize improved cash flow by collecting the largest dollar amounts sooner. The downside of this method is that smaller invoices will receive less attention and therefore take longer to collect, but this is a reasonable shortcoming if the overall cash flow from using stratified collections is improved. To implement it, perform a Pareto analysis of a typical accounts receivable listing and determine the cutoff point above which 20 percent of all invoices will constitute 80 percent of the total revenue. For example, a cutoff point of $1,000 means that any invoice of more than $1,000 is in the group of invoices representing the bulk of a company's revenue. When it is necessary to contact customers about collections issues, a much higher number of customer contacts can be assigned for the invoices over $1,000. For example, a collections staff can be required to contact customers about all high-dollar invoices once every three days, whereas low-dollar contacts can be limited to once every two weeks. By allocating the time of the collections staff in this manner, it is possible to collect overdue invoices more rapidly.

The typical assignment of overdue customer accounts to the collections staff is quite basic: Customer names beginning with A through D go to collector Smith, E through H to collector Jones, and so on. Though this may seem to be a fair and equitable approach to handing off work, what if the most difficult customers are all lumped into one cluster of collections assignments? When the distribution of difficult customers does not match the method of job assignment or (more commonly) the skill level of collectors does not match the customers to whom they are assigned, a company will find that its collections are not overly efficient. One solution is to measure the collections staff's performance to determine which ones are the top performers, and then assign them the most difficult customers. By doing so, the company orients its collections resources in the most targeted manner to achieve the highest possible collections percentage.

3-12 HOW DO I MANAGE CUSTOMER CONTACT INFORMATION?

A poorly organized collections group is one that does not know which customers to call, what customers said during previous calls, and how frequently contacts should be made in the future. The result of this level of disorganization is overdue payments being ignored for long periods, other customers being contacted so frequently that they become annoyed, and continually duplicated efforts. To a large extent, these problems can be overcome by using a collections call database. The basic concept of a collections call database is to keep a record of all contacts with the customer, as well as when to contact the customer next and what other actions to take. The first part of the database, the key contact list, should contain the following information:

- Customer name
- Key contact name
- Secondary contact name
- Internal salesperson's name with account responsibility
- Phone numbers of all contacts
- Fax numbers of all contacts
- E-mail addresses of all contacts

The contact log comprises the second part of the database and should contain:

- Date of contact
- Name of person contacted
- Topics discussed
- Action items

The information noted is easily kept in a notebook if there is a single collections person, but may require a more complex, centralized database if there are many collections personnel. However, a notebook-based database can be set up in a few hours with minimal effort, whereas a computerized database, especially one closely linked to the accounting records for each account receivable, may be a major undertaking.

For those who prefer to install a complete customer contact database on a rapid time schedule, consider purchasing a software package such as GetPAID, which can be reviewed at the www.getpaid.com Web site. This product is linked to a company's legacy accounting system (specifically, the open accounts receivable and customer files) by customized interfaces, so there is either a continual or batched flow of information into it. A key feature it offers is the assignment of each customer to a specific collections person, so that each person can call up a subset of the overdue invoices for which he or she is responsible. Within this subset, the software will also categorize accounts in different sort sequences, such as placing those at the top that have missed their promised payment dates. Also, the software will present on a single screen all of the contact information related to each customer, including the promises made by customers, open issues, and contact information. The system will also allow the user to enter information for a fax, and then route it directly to the recipient without requiring the collections person to ever leave his chair. It can also be linked to an auto-dialer, so the collections staff spends less time attempting to establish connections with overdue customers. To further increase the efficiency of the collections staff, it will even determine the time zone in which each customer is located, and prioritize the recommended list of calls, so that only those customers in time zones that are currently in the midst of standard business hours will be called.

As can be the case in a long marriage, a company's collections staff and a customer's accounts payable department can grow tired of each other, resulting in the same old collections procedures that the customer gradually begins to ignore. One solution is to maintain a special database of emergency customer contacts. This list should never include an accounts payable person, focusing instead on someone a level or more higher in the customer's organization. There should be a personal link with any person on the list, such as a prior meeting with a salesperson or a counterpart within the company, so the individual will be more likely to assist the collections staff with an occasional request. Once created, do not use it too much. People outside the accounts payable area do not enjoy being pestered, and will not appreciate a flood of requests. Instead, call emergency contacts only when an overdue receivable is a large one or there is considerable trouble obtaining collection through normal channels.

3-13 HOW DO I INVOLVE THE SALES STAFF IN COLLECTIONS?

The sales staff and credit and collections employees must sometimes wonder if they work for the same company. The sales staff sees itself as trying to bring in new orders to bolster company revenues and market share, while the credit and collections people do not like the burden of having to collect on overdue invoices from some of the less creditworthy customers brought in by the sales staff. Thus, it is not uncommon to see a considerable amount of bad feeling between these groups. Though some tension is always likely to exist between the sales and credit organizations, one can at least try to make the two groups see each others' viewpoints by fostering regular communications, which can take a variety of forms. One is to have representatives of each department make presentations to or at least attend the regular meetings of their counterparts. Another option, especially useful for wide-ranging sales forces, is to include the credit staff in periodic conference calls with the sales staff. Any of these approaches are especially useful when the company has a change in credit policy, so the staff will be aware of its impact on them as soon as possible. Other potential topics of conversation include descriptions of the credit and collections procedures used, whom to contact within each department about a variety of issues, and having open discussions about prospective changes within each department that may impact the other group.

The sales staff tends to focus only on the commission resulting from the sale and not on the excessive work required by the collections staff to bring in the payment, not to mention the much higher bad debt allowance needed to offset uncollectible accounts. To avoid this problem, change the commission system so that salespeople are paid a commission only on the cash received from customers. This change will instantly turn the entire sales force into a secondary collections agency, since they will be very interested in bringing in cash on time. They will also be more concerned about the creditworthiness of their customers, since they will spend less time selling to customers that have little realistic chance of paying. However, this approach requires salespeople to wait longer before they are paid a commission, so they are markedly unwilling to change to this new system. A tougher variation is to not pay commissions at all if invoices go over 90 days old, on the grounds that the commission system should push the sales staff to collect as soon as possible. This variation is least effective when commissions are quite small in comparison to the base pay of the sales staff, and most effective when commissions make up a large proportion of a salesperson's pay.

Another possibility is to periodically e-mail the accounts receivable aging report directly to the sales staff, so they can quickly ascertain the payment status of their customers. This is easily done in most commercially available accounting software packages by converting the aging report to Excel, sorting the report by salesperson, and issuing the file as an e-mail attachment. Since most salespeople have Excel on their computers, they can easily call up the report, spot impending late payment situations, and take action before accounts become so old that collection becomes problematic.

A negative way to involve the sales staff in collections is to periodically issue a report listing bad debts by salesperson. Since many sales should never have been made except at the insistence of the sales staff, and many collections are never made due to their nonresponsiveness in assisting in the collections effort, this report serves as a report card. The bad debt report must be issued with considerable caution, for it shows only the bad side of a sales staff that may in other respects be highly productive. Further, considering the potential level of conflict this report can engender, it is best to present it to the sales manager during a face-to-face meeting, and not to spray it all over the company with an e-mail distribution.

3-14 HOW DO I HANDLE PAYMENT DEDUCTIONS?

An annoying problem with deductions is how they are passed from person to person within the company without ever reaching resolution. The usual problem is that the initial reviewer passes it along to the person who initially appears to be most likely to resolve the problem, and then forgets that the deduction exists, having merely achieved the short-term goal of removing it from her desk. Then the recipient either passes the issue along to a third person or requests a response from the customer, promptly forgetting about the issue. This constant transfer of responsibility inevitably results in very long deduction resolution periods, annoyed customers, and slow cash flow. The solution is to centrally manage the deductions resolution process. A single person should be assigned responsibility for the deductions of a small group of customers and monitor the status of each open deduction on a daily basis, no matter which person within the company is currently handling resolution issues. By doing so, one can apply constant pressure to deduction resolution, thereby shrinking the number of receivable days outstanding.

An accountant may inherit a large deductions problem where there are hundreds of deductions sitting on the accounts receivable aging. The solution is to resolve deductions for the largest-dollar items first, and then work down through the deductions list in declining dollar order. This approach is initially designed to take out of the accounts receivable list the largest deductions; but more importantly, it allows the collections staff to research the reasons why the largest deductions are occurring, and to put a stop to them. As the staff gradually fixes these issues and moves down to small deductions, it can address relatively smaller underlying deduction issues. Thus, this approach is designed to use deduction dollar volume as the criterion for determining the relative importance of fixes needed to resolve problems causing deductions. This approach may have the initial reverse result of actually *increasing* the number of unresolved deductions on the books, since the collections staff is now focusing on the largest and therefore most time-consuming deduction problems. Though a likely outcome, the underlying problem resolutions implemented by the collections team should gradually eliminate source problems, which will dry up the flood of incoming deductions, so the situation will improve a number of months into the future.

As just noted, delving into the reasons why deductions occur is the key to reducing the overall number of deductions. To attack the core problems causing deductions, have the collections staff summarize all deductions on a regular basis and forward this information to management. The management team can then review the data to see what problems are causing the deductions, and correct them. The summary report can be sorted a number of ways: by customer, by dollar volume, by product, by date, and so on. It may be best to issue the report sorted in several formats, since problems hidden within one reporting format are more visible in others. This approach calls for the use of a central deductions database, which can be as simple as an electronic spreadsheet for smaller organizations or a database comprising part of a larger enterprise resources planning system, as is used in large companies.

Deductions management works even better when coupled with a deductions handling procedure. The procedure tends to follow a tiered approach, where very small deductions are not worth the effort of even a single customer contact, and are immediately written off. For larger deductions, a company may require immediate follow-up or only follow-up after the second deduction, or an immediate rebilling— the choice is up to the individual company. The procedure should include such basic steps as:

1. Ensuring that the customer has provided adequate documentation of the problem
2. Collection of data needed to substantiate or refute the claim
3. Contacting the customer to obtain missing information
4. Once collected, reviewing all information to determine a recommended course of action
5. Depending on the size of the deduction, obtaining necessary approvals
6. Contacting the customer with resolution information
7. If approved, entering credit information into the accounting system to clear debit balances representing valid deductions

The main point is to be consistent. The collections staff must be drilled in the use of this procedure, so there is absolutely no question about how to handle a deduction. This will favorably increase departmental efficiency and require less management time to pass judgment on individual deductions problems.

3-15 HOW DO I COLLECT OVERDUE PAYMENTS?

There are a multitude of methods for collecting payments from customers. In this section, we progress from several milder contact methods into significantly more aggressive collections techniques.

Most collections departments do not start contacting customers until a number of days after an invoice due date, either on the assumption that the Postal Service takes a mighty long time to make deliveries or that a customer's payment process may be interfering with timely payment. Whatever the reason, customers with an interest in delaying payment have an almost guaranteed extra week before a collections person even begins to think about contacting them. Instead, begin calling immediately after the invoice due date has passed. If the invoice is due in 30 days, this means contacting the customer after 31 days. Though some checks will indeed be in the mail at this time, rendering some calls unnecessary, the vast majority of calls made will be to companies who have not paid. By taking this approach, the company instills in its customers the idea that payment terms are to be taken seriously, and the company absolutely expects payment on the stated date.

The best way to collect small overdue balances is to restrict collections activities to the use of dunning letters. This is the least expensive way to contact customers, and is to be preferred over more labor-intensive activities such as direct personal contact or phone calls. Though only one collections method is advised in this situation, one can certainly mix up the methods and timing of delivery in order to gain the customer's attention. Instead of the traditional mailing, try sending the letter by fax or e-mail, and distribute it to different people within the customer's organization in hopes of jarring loose a response. An easy technological twist to this method is to send the dunning letters by e-mail. Not only is transmission instantaneous, but recipients also tend to forward the messages straight to the party who is best able to handle payment. Further, an e-mail response is likely for a high percentage of these issuances, especially when dunning messages are custom-written.

A series of dunning letters may not force a delinquent customer into paying for an overdue invoice. The next step should be to issue an attorney letter. This is a letter issued on an attorney's letterhead and supposedly written by the attorney, threatening legal action if payment is not made. The implication is that the customer is now much closer to a lawsuit, which sometimes brings about a rapid settlement of the outstanding balance. Attorney letters are expensive if custom-written by the attorney. To reduce the cost, write the letter for the attorney and just ask him to print it on his letterhead. To further reduce costs, state in the letter that all customer responses be made back to the company, not the attorney. This has the double purpose of keeping the attorney from being buried by phone calls and keeping down billed hours.

Customers do not normally like to pay for an invoice until all disputes related to it have been resolved, thereby allowing them to pay the full amount, staple the remittance advice to the complete packet of resolution documentation, and file it away. This approach is also used by customers not willing to pay at all; they create a dispute over a small item and refuse payment on the entire invoice, resulting in very long waits for payment. The solution is to insist on payment of undisputed balances right away. This is especially appropriate on multiline invoices where only a few items are being debated. If a customer has a history of withholding payment based on a disputed item, act quickly and insist on immediate payment of the undisputed balance until the customer figures out that this ploy will no longer work.

Customers like to promise payment by a certain date, wait for the date to pass, and then dispute the details of their promise with the collections staff. Even if a collector has properly documented the last customer contact, the customer can get into the "he said, she said" game and claim that the collector did not write down the details correctly. Besides being frustrating, this game also delays payment. The best solution is to write down the promised payment information in a letter or e-mail and send it to the customer. This confirmation approach ensures that customers see the collector's version of the earlier conversation as soon as possible, and have an opportunity to dispute it at that time. By the time the promised payment date arrives, the customer should have few excuses left for not paying. If a customer has agreed to a repetitive series of payments, use this approach to both thank him for the most recent payment and remind him of the amount and due date of the next payment. Though this may call for the issuance of quite a few letters, customers will be very aware that the company is keeping a close eye on the arrival dates of their payments.

There are a few cases where a shipped product is still on hand and untouched by the customer, making it possible to accept a merchandise return. This possibility exists in seasonal businesses, where customers may not have been able to sell off all their goods during the peak season, and now have no way to clear out their inventories. Another possibility is to review the latest customer financial statements and see if its inventory turnover is very slow; if so, the customer's overstocking practices may mean that the company's goods are still untouched in the customer's warehouse. Even if a customer has used up most of the company's goods, there may still be a few units on hand that can be sent back in partial settlement of the outstanding debt.

When a customer does not pay the balance of an overdue invoice, one option is to shift it over to cash-on-delivery (COD) payment terms. If the customer has no other source for goods and so must buy from the company, add the entire open balance or a portion of it to the COD amount, thereby enforcing payment if the customer ever wants to see any additional goods delivered.

A common approach when no other collections method works is to shift selected invoices to a collections agency for more aggressive follow-up. In exchange, the agency requires a percentage of each collected invoice (typically one-third) as payment for its services. Despite the common perception that collections agencies only go after larger outstanding invoices, a few specialize in the more difficult types of collections, such as discounts for pricing discrepancies, damaged goods, promotional allowances, quality problems, quantity-delivered variances, unearned cash discounts, and the like. Though collections agencies charge high fees for these specialized services to compensate them for the extra effort required, this may still be better than a complete write-off of the deductions.

3-16 WHEN SHOULD I TAKE LEGAL ACTION TO COLLECT FROM A CUSTOMER?

Initiating legal action against a customer is an enormously expensive and prolonged undertaking that is almost never worth the effort. The only party that is assured to come out ahead on the situation is the lawyer. Even if the court awards a substantial settlement, the customer may go to great lengths to hide its assets, so the company never collects a dime. The solution is to always prescreen a customer's debts prior to initiating a legal action. This should at least involve purchasing a credit report on the customer to determine the number of judgments and tax liens already filed against it, as well as other types of outstanding debt. This type of investigation may very well reveal that the customer has so many calls upon its assets already that an investment in legal action is completely uneconomical.

A low-cost legal technique that may rattle an intransigent customer is the threat of a small claims court filing. Even if the company has no real intent to take an issue to court, just obtain the complaint documentation from the appropriate court, fill it out, and send a copy to the customer, with a note attached stating when the cash has to be in the company's hands or else the paperwork will be filed with the court. It helps to build up a reference library of small claims court forms, which vary by state (and sometimes by county), thereby making the filing process faster. Claims of this type are generally filed in the county where the customer resides, so a great many forms may be required to cover the locations of the entire customer base.

If the previously noted attempt to obtain payment by sending a small claims complaint to a customer does not work, the next step is to actually file the complaint with a small claims court. This is usually in the county where the customer resides, but can also be where the action over which a complaint is filed took place. In either case, check with the court to verify the maximum amount of money they will address. If the amount being claimed is higher, waive the difference in order to fit under the court's maximum cap. Also, pull a credit report on the customer to verify its official legal name and corporate status, so this information can be correctly listed on the complaint form. Finally, locate a collections attorney located near the small claims court and request representation at the court for a modest fee and percentage of any proceeds. These steps are not difficult, and the cost of continuing the process into small claims court is typically far less than the amount of the debt. Also, since a local attorney represents the company in court, the collections staff does not waste time traveling to court. To make the process even more efficient, create a procedure for this process and maintain a list of local attorneys to contact for representation in court. With these steps in place, collecting through small claims court becomes a mechanical and efficient process.

Even if a court issues a judgment against a customer and in favor of the company, the customer may illegally attempt to dispose of corporate assets, so there is nothing left for the company to attach. Thus, after all the time and expense of court proceedings, a company still receives nothing for its efforts. Consider having the court issue a restraining notice to the customer. This is a document stating that the customer cannot dispose of any assets. It is especially effective when used to freeze the customer's bank account, since the receiving bank will block all account access at once. This approach is useful only after a legal judgment has been obtained, so a customer will have already had plenty of time (possibly years) to fraudulently dispose of assets.

Though the average lawyer can be counted on to have training and expertise in the general conduct of a lawsuit, this does not mean that she has any idea of how to collect the money judgment in the event of a successful lawsuit. Collection requires tracking down the location of assets (possibly through a court-ordered interrogatory), filing the correct paperwork to attach them, and assisting in asset liquidation. Few lawyers have taken the time to acquire this level of expertise. Clearly, finding a lawyer with money judgment collection expertise is of paramount importance if a company regularly finds itself with money judgments but no way to collect. Though one can find the right lawyer through references from other attorneys or collections agencies, this can involve a long process of trying out a succession of lawyers until a productive one is found.

Chapter 4

Control System Decisions

The proper use of controls has become an increasingly important part of the accountant's role, given the highly publicized abuse of company assets that have been reported in the press in recent years. The accountant needs to be concerned with control usage in many processes throughout the company, including order entry, purchasing, payables, inventory management, billings, cash receipts, and payroll. In all of these areas, the potential exists for significant asset losses.

This chapter provides detailed answers to questions about which controls to install over each of these areas, and more. The following table itemizes the section number in which the answers to each question can be found:

Section	Decision
4-1	Why do I need controls?
4-2	How do I control order entry?
4-3	How do I control credit management?
4-4	How do I control purchasing?
4-5	How do I control procurement cards?
4-6	How do I control payables?
4-7	How do I control inventory?
4-8	How do I control billings?
4-9	How do I control cash receipts?
4-10	How do I control payroll?
4-11	How do I control fixed assets?

4-1 WHY DO I NEED CONTROLS?

Any company operates under a complex set of policies and procedures that in total comprise a set of processes that ultimately generate revenues and profits. These processes are subject to breakdown at a variety of failure points, either inadvertently or intentionally, through fraud. We install controls to identify or forestall process failures.

A control can itself break down through inattention, lack of formal training or procedures, or intentionally, through fraud. To mitigate these issues, some processes involving especially high levels of asset loss are more likely to require two controls to attain a single control objective, thereby reducing the risk that the control objective will not be attained. However, double controls are not recommended in most situations, especially if the controls are not automated, since they can increase the cost and duration of the processes they are designed to safeguard.

All areas of a company contain some control weaknesses, while some harbor key risk areas, especially the diversion of company assets or misrepresentation of financial results. Of primary concern are those areas where these two issues coincide. A major risk area is revenue recognition, for there are a variety of ways to manipulate it to improperly accelerate revenues, thereby reporting excessively profitable financial results. Other areas of significant risk are the capitalization of assets and the valuation of such reserves as bad debts, warranty claims, or product returns. Several other high-risk areas are also unrelated to basic process flows: the valuation of acquired assets, related-party transactions, contingent liabilities, and special-purpose entities. Thus, even with in-depth and comprehensive controls over such key processes as purchasing, billings, and cash receipts, there are still significant areas lying outside the traditional control systems that can be easily circumvented.

4-2 HOW DO I CONTROL ORDER ENTRY?

Order entry is the initial point at which a customer order enters a company. It is not only the creation of a sales order for distribution throughout the company, but also a number of additional steps: verifying the existence of the customer, ensuring that there is sufficient inventory on-hand to fill the order, and verifying pricing and related order terms.

One significant control for order entry is verifying that the person placing the order is an approved buyer. This control is not frequently used for small orders, since the chances of a control problem are relatively slight in most cases. However, it may be useful when the size of the order being placed is extremely large.

Also, review the on-hand status of any inventory being ordered, in case the company would otherwise be committing to an order it cannot ship. If the order entry computer system is linked to the current inventory balance, then the system should warn the order entry staff if there is not a sufficient quantity in stock to fulfill an order, and will predict the standard lead time required to obtain additional inventory. A more advanced level of automation results in the computer system presenting the order entry staff with similar products that are currently in stock, which the staff can present to customers as alternative purchases.

One of the best control improvements that a computer system brings to the order entry process is the ability to automatically set up product prices based on the standard corporate price book. If the information in the price book varies from the price listed on the purchase order, then the order entry staff must either obtain a supervisory override to use the alternative price, or discuss the situation with the customer.

If the order entry staff still fills out a sales order based on the customer order, rather than entering this information into the computer for automatic distribution throughout the company, then an additional control is to compare the information on the sales order and originating customer purchase order, to ensure that the order information was transcribed correctly.

Finally, when products are returned by customers, it is possible that an error in the order entry or shipment processes caused the return. To investigate this potential problem, compare the return documents with the customer purchase order and sales order.

4-3 HOW DO I CONTROL CREDIT MANAGEMENT?

The credit management function involves an examination of the finances of customers, to ensure that they are financially capable of paying for any orders that the company ships to them. There is a considerable risk that orders may be shipped in circumvention of the credit management process, so the controls noted below should be considered essential.

A mandatory control is to require that all sales orders be sent to the credit department for approval before any shipment is made. It is customary to bypass the credit approval process for small orders, repair and maintenance orders, and when customers have established credit lines with the company.

If the order entry system has a workflow management capability, then any orders entered by the order entry staff will be routed to the credit department as soon as the orders are entered. This control not only speeds up the credit review process, but also ensures that every order entered will be routed to the credit department. This control is typically modified, so that orders falling below a minimum threshold are automatically approved.

It is possible for sales orders to be fraudulently routed around the credit department, so create an approval stamp to be used on each sales order. This approval stamp should include space for the signature of the credit manager, and for the date when the approval was granted. The shipping manager should not ship from any sales order that does not contain this signed approval stamp. Also, the credit approval stamp should be locked up when not in use.

If an enterprisewide computer system is in use, then the credit department can issue an online approval of a customer order, which the computer system then routes to the shipping department for fulfillment. The beauty of this control is that the shipping staff never sees the customer order until it has been approved, so there is minimal risk of an unapproved order inadvertently being shipped.

A serious control problem arises when there is no formal definition of how to calculate a credit limit. This results in widely varying credit levels being granted. To resolve this problem, create and consistently apply a standardized credit policy to all customers.

Finally, the financial condition of customers will inevitably change over time, thereby rendering the original credit review obsolete. A useful control is to build several flags into the computer system that highlight those customers whose ordering or payment habits indicate a change in their financial condition. These flags should trigger a credit review. Examples of possible flags are customer checks being returned due to insufficient funds in their bank accounts, recurring evidence of payments being skipped, and early payment discounts no longer being taken. In addition, a regularly scheduled credit review of the largest customers may spot incipient credit problems.

4-4 HOW DO I CONTROL PURCHASING?

The purchasing process can result in considerable losses if a few key controls are not implemented. These losses can be considerable, since the bulk of all corporate expenditures flow through the purchasing department. Further, if a company uses automated check signing, rather than a review by a manager before any checks are manually signed, then the purchasing process is the only point at which improper payments can be spotted.

The first necessary control is a policy that a purchase order must be issued for every purchase made by the company. This means that the purchasing staff must also forward a copy of each purchase order to the receiving dock, where it is used to verify the purchasing authorization for each item received.

As a continuation of the last control, the receiving staff must reject any incoming deliveries for which there is no authorizing purchase order. This control can be quite time-consuming for the receiving department, which must research purchase order information for every delivery. To ease their workload, suppliers should be asked to prominently tag their deliveries with the authorizing purchase order number.

Also, if the purchasing department uses paper-based purchase orders, then it must restrict access to the purchase orders by locking them in a storage cabinet when not in use. Otherwise, blank forms could be used by unauthorized parties to order goods. In addition, the purchasing manager can more easily determine if blank forms have been removed by prenumbering all purchase orders, keeping track of the numbers used, and investigating any missing numbers.

If the purchasing department creates all of its purchase orders through a computer database, then it must restrict access to that database to guard against the unauthorized creation of purchase orders. Typical controls include password protection, regular password changes, access being limited to a small number of purchasing staff, and a human resources check-off list for departing employees that calls for the immediate cancellation of their database access privileges.

Finally, a detective control is to compare payments with authorizing purchase orders, in order to spot payments made without a supporting purchase order. This constitutes evidence of a breach of the corporate policy to require a purchase order for all expenditures.

4-5 HOW DO I CONTROL PROCUREMENT CARDS?

Procurement cards are essentially credit cards that are used by designated employees to purchase small-dollar items without any prior authorization. Their use greatly reduces the labor of the purchasing department, which can instead focus its purchasing efforts on large-dollar items. However, because the use of procurement cards falls completely outside the normal set of controls used for the procurement cycle, an entirely different set of controls are needed.

The first key control for procurement cards is for users to enter their receipt information into a procurement card transaction log. When employees use procurement cards, there is a danger that they will purchase a multitude of items, and not remember all of them when it comes time to approve the monthly purchases statement. By maintaining a log of purchases, the card user can tell which statement line items should be rejected. A sample transaction log is shown in Exhibit 4.1.

Another key control is to reconcile the transaction log with the monthly card statement. Each card holder must review his or her monthly purchases, as itemized by the card issuer on the monthly card statement. A sample of the statement of account used for this reconciliation is shown in Exhibit 4.2, where it is assumed that the company obtains an electronic feed of all procurement card transactions from the card provider, and dumps this information into individualized reports for each card user. This approach provides each user with a convenient checklist of reconciliation activities within the statement of account, but the same result can be obtained by stapling a reconciliation activity checklist to a copy of the bank statement.

Each card user must also fill out a missing receipt form. This form itemizes each line item on the statement of account for which there is no receipt. The department manager must review and approve this document, thereby ensuring that all purchases made are appropriate. A sample missing receipt form is shown in Exhibit 4.3.

In addition, there must be an organized mechanism for card holders to reject line items on the statement of account. A good approach is to use a procurement

Exhibit 4.1   Procurement Card Transaction Log

Trans. No.	Date	Supplier Name	Purchased Item Description	Total Price	Comments
1	5/1/07	Acme Electric Supply	200w floodlights	$829.00	
2	5/2/07	Wiley Wire Supply	Breaker panels	741.32	
3	5/5/07	Coyote Electrical	12-gauge cable	58.81	Returned for credit
4	5/7/07	Roadrunner Electric	Foot light trim	940.14	

Procurement Card Statement of Account
[Company Name]

A

Statement Date:	May 2006	**Statement Reference Number:** 12345678

Cardholder: Mary Follett
123 Sunny Lane
Anywhere, USA 01234

B

	Single Purchase	Monthly Purchase Total	Authorizations Allowed per Day
Spending Limits:	$2,500	$25,000	10

C

Transaction Detail:

Transaction Date	Reference Number	Supplier	SIC Code	Account Number	Amount
5/1/06	1234567AB043	Acme Electric Supply	7312	-	$829.00
5/2/06	2345678CD054	Wiley Wire Supply	7312	-	741.32
5/5/06	3456789DE065	Coyote Electrical	7312	*040-1720*	58.81
5/7/06	4567890EF076	Roadrunner Electric	7312	-	940.14
				Total	$2,569.27

D

Reconciliation Checklist:

☐ I have reconciled this statement of account

☐ I have attached all receipts to this statement of account

☐ I have completed and attached the Procurement Card Missing Receipt form for all line items for which I have no receipts

☐ I have entered account numbers in the "Account Number" column for those line items that vary from the default expense account number

☐ I have circled any items currently under dispute with suppliers

☐ I have signed and dated this statement of account

☐ I have retained a copy and understand that it must be retained for three years

Cardholder Signature: _____   Date: _____

Exhibit 4.2   Monthly Procurement Card Account Statement

Procurement Card Missing Receipt Form
[Company Name]

A

Your Contact Information:

Name: _____   Address Line 1: _____

Phone Number: _____   Address Line 2: _____

Fax Number: _____

B

Account Statement Information:

Statement Month/Year: _____/_____

Statement Reference Number: _____

Line Item Number	Line Item Date	Line Item Amount	Supplier Name	Description

C

I certify that the above expenditures were legitimate business expenditures on behalf of the company.

Card Holder
Signature: _____   Date: _____

Department Manager
Signature: _____   Date: _____

Form PUR-196

Exhibit 4.3   Procurement Card Missing Receipt Form

card line item rejection form, as shown in Exhibit 4.4, which users can send directly to the card issuer.

Finally, there must be a third-party review of all purchases made with procurement cards. An effective control is to hand this task to the person having budgetary responsibility for the department in which the card holder works. By doing so, the

---

Missing Procurement Card Form
[Company Name]

A

Your Contact Information:
Name: _____   Address Line 1: _____

Phone Number: _____   Address Line 2: _____

Fax Number: _____

B

Loss Information:
☐ Card was stolen

☐ Card was lost

☐ Other (describe): _____

C

Procurement Card Number:

☐☐☐☐ - ☐☐☐☐ - ☐☐☐☐ - ☐☐☐☐

☐ I do not have a record of the procurement card number.

D

Bank Notification Information:

Name of person contacted at bank: _____

Date of contact: _____   Time of contact: _____

E

Card Replacement Information:

☐ Send me a replacement card by regular mail.

☐ Send me a replacement card by overnight delivery.

My FedEx account number is: _____

F

Card Holder
Signature: _____   Date: _____

Form PUR-197

Exhibit 4.4   Procurement Card Line Item Rejection Form

reviewer is more likely to conduct a detailed review of purchases that will be charged against his or her budget.

4-6 HOW DO I CONTROL PAYABLES?

The accounts payable process is among the most complex and difficult to control of all company processes, because it is the recipient of a blizzard of paperwork from all over the company—supplier invoices, receiving documents, purchase orders, and expense reports. The key to controlling payables is to install iron-clad controls in just a few control points, where incoming information can be properly sorted, identified, and scheduled for payment.

The first control is locating authorization of payment for every supplier invoice. The complex variation on this control is the three-way match, whereby the supplier invoice is matched against both the authorizing purchase order and receiving documentation. This is a tedious, error-prone, and inefficient control, and so should be used only for the most expensive purchases.

Also, if supplier invoices are being stored in an accounting database, have the software automatically conduct a duplicate invoice number review. This results in the automatic rejection of duplicate invoices.

Having multiple supplier records for the same supplier presents a problem when attempting to locate duplicate supplier invoices, since the same invoice may have been charged multiple times to different supplier records. One of the best ways to address this problem is to adopt a standard naming convention for all new supplier names, so that it will be readily apparent if a supplier name already exists. For example, the file name might be the first seven letters of the supplier name, followed by a sequential number. Under this sample convention, the file name for Smith Brothers would be recorded as SMITHBR001.

A lesser control is that payments may be made to suppliers too early or too late, either depriving the company of interest income (in the first place) or causing it to incur supplier ill-will or late charges (in the latter case). If the payables system is paper-based, the proper control for this is to store payables by their due dates, and then pay based on this filing system. If the system is computer-based, the best control is to not only set up payment terms in the vendor master file, but also to periodically compare supplier invoices against this file, to see whether any payment terms have changed.

An employee with access to the vendor master file could alter a supplier's remit-to address, process checks having a revised address that routes the checks to the employee, and then alter the vendor master record again, back to the supplier's remit-to address. If this person can also intercept the cashed check copy when it is returned by the bank, there is essentially no way to detect this type of fraud. The solution is to run a report listing all changes to the vendor master record, which includes the name of the person making changes.

The payment part of the payables process calls for several additional controls. First, always keep unused check stock in a locked storage cabinet. In addition, the range of check numbers used should be stored in a separate location, and cross-checked against the check numbers on the stored checks, to verify that no checks have been removed from the locked location. Also, the check signer must compare the backup information attached to each check against the check itself, verifying the payee name, amount to be paid, and the due date. This review is intended to spot unauthorized purchases, payments to the wrong parties, or payments being made either too early or too late. This is a major control point for companies not using purchase orders, since the check signer represents the only supervisory-level review of purchases.

In addition, if there are many check signers, it is possible that unsigned checks will be routed to the person least likely to conduct a thorough review of the accompanying voucher package, thereby rendering this control point invalid. Consequently, it is best to have only two check signers: one designated as the primary signer to whom all checks are routed, and a backup who is used only when the primary check signer is not available for a lengthy period of time.

Finally, always perforate the voucher package with the word "Paid," or some other word that clearly indicates the status of the voucher package. Otherwise, the voucher package could be reused as the basis for an additional payment.

4-7 HOW DO I CONTROL INVENTORY?

A company's investment in inventory may be considerable, so maintaining proper controls over both the quantity and the valuations assigned to it may be paramount. Controls in this area cover both the storage of inventory and its movement within the company's premises.

Inventory is nearly impossible to store if employees are allowed into the storage area, since they may move it within the warehouse or remove it entirely. Accordingly, a necessary control is to fence in the storage area, and allow only authorized warehouse staff into the storage area. Also, all storage locations within the warehouse must be tagged in an orderly and logical manner, so that inventory can be more easily located by its storage identification numbers.

Additionally, qualified employees who are highly knowledgeable in inventory identification should label each inventory item with the correct part number and unit of measure, so that inventory is not lost through misidentification.

Furthermore, all received inventory should be put away at once and its identification and storage information entered into an inventory database immediately. Otherwise, there will be no record of received inventory, so it can be neither used nor counted.

Another control that may be of considerable use to companies handling customer inventory is to physically segregate such inventory, so that it is not commingled with company-owned inventory. Commingled assets will likely result in an incorrect overstatement of on-hand inventory.

When inventory is moved from the warehouse to the production or shipping areas, there is a chance that the picking information will be inaccurate, especially if it has been copied from a source document. To avoid the possibility of transcription errors, always use a copy of the source document, such as the sales order or the customer's original purchase order, to ensure that the correct items are picked. Also, always record inventory movements on move tickets that can then be used to enter the changes into the inventory database (or better yet, scan the information on-site with a bar-code scanner). Otherwise, the warehouse staff will quickly lose track of its move transactions, resulting in the complete corruption of the inventory database. These move tickets should also be prenumbered, so that all missing move tickets can be periodically investigated.

Inventory valuation will be more accurate if it is supported by several controls. First, if the company's computer system has a bill of materials, periodically review the file change log to determine what changes have been made, and by whom. This log contains evidence of alterations that could significantly change the inventory valuation. Another way to achieve the same result is to compare the unextended product cost on a per-unit basis with the same cost in previous periods, to spot any changes. The inventory valuation may also be affected by journal entries made to the inventory or cost-of-goods-sold account. Accordingly, part of the standard month-end closing procedure should include the investigation of all journal entries made to these accounts.

Inventory valuation may also be affected by the application of the lower-of-cost-or-market (LCM) rule, whereby inventory can be valued no higher than its market price as of the measurement date. To ensure that the company is not surprised by such changes, always schedule an LCM review as part of the closing process.

Another issue impacting inventory valuation is obsolete inventory, which must be written off once it has been identified. One control used to mitigate this expense is a policy requiring that impacted inventory be used up before an engineering change order that affects them is implemented. Also, items identified as obsolete should be segregated in a central area, where they can be more easily dispositioned.

Finally, the inventory valuation will be greatly assisted by the implementation of a cycle counting system, which is arguably the best inventory control of all. Under cycle counting, a small percentage of the inventory is counted by experienced warehouse personnel every day, with all variances being thoroughly investigated and resolved. The problem-resolution phase of cycle counting will likely locate a number of process-related problems that, if corrected, will lead to a much more accurate database and inventory valuation.

4-8 HOW DO I CONTROL BILLINGS?

The act of creating and delivering an invoice is central to a company's ability to collect cash from its customers, so several key controls are required to ensure that this process proceeds smoothly.

The first and most important control is to compare the shipping log to the invoice register to ensure that all shipments have been billed. If a company is in the service industry, then a similar comparison would be between the log of billed hours and the invoice register. The intent is to ensure that all products or services provided to customers are properly billed.

A form of control is to modify the physical layout of the invoice in order to make it as simple as possible for the recipient to understand and process for payment. This should include the clear presentation of the amount due, invoice number, and due date. Of equal importance, all information *not* relevant to the customer (such as the name of the salesperson, the job number, and the document number) should be removed from the invoice. Also, if there are continuing problems with the accuracy of issued invoices, then a good control is to include an accounting manager's phone number on the standard invoice form, and encourage customers to call if they have problems. Do not have customers call the person who created the invoice, since this person would be more likely to ignore or cover up the complaint.

Some invoices are so complex, involving the entry of purchase order numbers, many line items, price discounts and other credits, that it is difficult to create an error-free invoice. If so, customers reject the invoices, thereby delaying the payment process. To correct this problem, assign a second person to be the invoice proofreader. This person has not created the invoice, and so has an independent view of the situation and can provide a more objective view of invoice accuracy. However, due to the delay caused by proofreading, it may be unnecessary for small-dollar or simplified invoices.

Finally, the billing and collection functions should always be segregated. By doing so, it becomes much more difficult for a collections person to fraudulently access incoming customer payments and alter invoices and credit memos to hide the missing funds.

4-9 HOW DO I CONTROL CASH RECEIPTS?

Cash has historically been the most obvious asset to steal from a company. Accordingly, the handling of checks and cash has been burdened with the largest number of controls of all processes, even though the total amount of cash on hand at any time is usually much less than for other types of company assets. Accordingly, use only the minimum number of controls noted in this section to ensure a reasonable level of control over cash receipts; any additional controls will only increase the workload on an already inefficient process.

The best control over cash receipts is to not receive the cash at all—have customers send it to a lockbox instead. This approach eliminates many controls, since the cash is immediately deposited by the receiving bank. The next best control is to have the mailroom staff immediately reroute all incoming payments to the lockbox, thereby also avoiding the same controls.

If cash or checks must be received in-house, then the first control is to have the mailroom staff prepare a check prelist, which itemizes the amounts of all checks and cash received. Preferably, two people in the mailroom should open the mail together, to ensure that no cash is stolen at this point. This list can then be compared with the results of downstream processing operations to see if any payment information was subsequently modified. The mailroom staff also endorses all checks "for deposit only" and clearly specifies the account number into which they should be deposited, so that they cannot be cashed into some other account.

The cashier then enters the receipts into the cash receipts journal, prepares a daily bank deposit slip, and sends the checks and cash to the bank. A different person should then compare the check prelist against the deposit slip (even better, use the validated deposit slip that is returned by the bank) and cash receipts journal to see if the numbers match. Finally, another clerk should reconcile the month-end bank statement to the general ledger, to ensure that the company's cash receipt records match those of the bank.

If a company is primarily handling cash, rather than checks, then the control situation is somewhat different. When receiving cash from a customer, always give that person a receipt and retain a copy; this gives the customer a chance to spot an error on the receipt. Also, a different clerk from the one who initially entered the cash receipts should reconcile the on-hand cash to the receipt copies. Then, the cash should be transported to the bank in a locked container. Finally, the bank's deposit receipt should be reconciled to the company's receipt records.

A few additional cash-handling controls can enhance the cash control environment. First, give only one person access to a cash register during a work shift. This makes it easier to assign responsibility for any inaccuracies in the recording of cash receipts. A more obtrusive control is video surveillance of the cash registers.

Second, require supervisory approval of cash refunds. This is because an employee can steal cash by taking money from the cash register and recording a refund on the cash register tape. By requiring a supervisory password or key entry for every refund issued, the cash register operator has no opportunity to steal cash by this method.

The use of petty cash is not recommended, since it is too easy for anyone to pilfer the petty cash box, or to steal the entire box. Thus, the best control over petty cash is to eliminate it entirely. If this cannot be achieved, then always require a valid receipt as proof of expenditure whenever issuing petty cash, and also require a receipt signature on all payments. The signature requirement is especially important, since otherwise the petty cash custodian could manufacture receipts and directly pocket funds from the petty cash box. In addition, conduct unannounced audits of petty cash, looking for incomplete or suspicious receipts, missing receipt vouchers, or missing cash. Finally, install a petty cash contact alarm that will be triggered if the petty cash box is removed.

4-10 HOW DO I CONTROL PAYROLL?

In many companies, payroll comprises the largest expense, especially in the service industry. Accordingly, payroll controls must be especially stringent in order to avoid excessive expenditures.

An essential control is to verify that all timecards have been received, because it is entirely possible for an employee's timesheet to disappear during the accumulation of timesheet data, or to never be submitted. In either case, once payday comes and there is no check, impacted employees will want an immediate payment, which represents not only additional work for the payroll staff, but a sudden and unexpected additional cash outflow.

Supervisors should also review the time submitted by employees, and specifically approve all overtime hours worked. This is needed, because employees may pad their timesheets with extra hours, hoping to be paid for these amounts. Alternatively, they may have fellow employees clock them in and out on days when they are not working. Despite this control, such actions can be difficult to spot, especially when there are many employees for a supervisor to track, or if employees work in outlying locations.

A very important control is to obtain written approval of all pay rate changes, since these changes can cumulatively result in extremely large increases in expenditures. This approval should be from a person knowledgeable in the proposed rate of change in pay, and of what pay rate has been budgeted. It is also useful to have someone besides the payroll clerk compare the payroll register to the authorizing pay documents, to ensure that the correct pay rates are being used.

If the company uses an employee self-service portal, it is possible that employees will make erroneous changes to their employee records. To spot these problems, have the payroll system automatically send a confirming e-mail message detailing the change. This gives employees the opportunity to spot errors in their entries, while also notifying them if someone else has gained access to the payroll system using their access codes and has altered their payroll information.

When calculated manually, payroll is the single most error-prone function in the accounting area. To reduce the number of errors, have someone other than the payroll clerk review the wage and tax calculations for errors. This does not have to be a detailed duplication of all calculations made; a simple scan for reasonableness is likely to spot obvious errors.

The person who physically hands out paychecks to employees is sometimes called the paymaster. This person does not prepare the paychecks or sign them, and his sole responsibility in the payroll area is to hand out paychecks. If an employee is not available to accept a paycheck, then the paymaster retains that person's check in a secure location until the employee is personally available to receive it. This approach avoids the risk of giving the paycheck to a friend of the employee who might cash it, and also keeps the payroll staff from preparing a check and cashing it themselves.

It is quite useful to periodically give supervisors a list of paychecks issued to everyone in their departments, because they may be able to spot payments being made to employees who are no longer working there. This is a particular problem in larger companies, where any delay in processing termination paperwork can result in continuing payments to ex-employees. It is also a good control over any payroll clerk who may be trying to defraud the company by delaying termination paperwork and then pocketing the paychecks produced in the interim.

When the bank sends back copies of cashed checks as part of its monthly bank statement, consider reviewing the checks for double endorsements. If a payroll clerk has continued to issue checks to a terminated employee and is pocketing the check, then the cashed check should contain a forged signature for the departed employee, as well as a second signature for the account name into which the check is deposited.

4-11 HOW DO I CONTROL FIXED ASSETS?

Fixed assets can involve very large sums of cash, so controls are needed over their initial acquisition, as well as their subsequent tracking and ultimate disposition.

The first control over fixed asset acquisitions is to obtain funding approval through the annual budgeting process. This is an intensive review of overall company operations, as well as of how capital expenditures will be integrated into the company's strategic direction. Expenditure requests included in the approved budget should still be subjected to some additional approval at the point of actual expenditure, to ensure that they are still needed. However, expenditure requests *not* included in the approved budget should be subjected to a considerably higher level of analysis and approval, to ensure that there is a justifiable need for them.

Given the significant amount of funds usually needed to acquire a fixed asset, always require and review a completed capital investment approval form before issuing a purchase order. An example is shown in Exhibit 4.5. Depending on the size of the acquisition, a number of approval signatures may be required, extending up to the company president or even the chairperson of the board of directors.

A good detective control to ensure that all acquisitions have been properly authorized is to periodically reconcile all fixed asset additions to the file of approved capital expenditure authorizations. Any acquisitions for which there is no authorization paperwork are then flagged for additional review, typically including reporting of the control breach to management.

Compare fixed asset serial numbers with the existing serial number database. There is a possibility that employees are acquiring assets, selling them to the company, then stealing the assets and selling them to the company again. To spot this behavior, always enter the serial number of each acquired asset in the fixed asset master file, and then run a report comparing serial numbers for all assets to see if there are duplicate serial numbers on record.

There are a number of downstream errors that can arise when fixed asset information is incorrectly entered in the fixed asset master file. For example, an incorrect asset description can result in an incorrect asset classification, which in turn may result in an incorrect depreciation calculation. Similarly, an incorrect asset location code can result in the subsequent inability to locate the physical asset, which in turn may result in an improper asset disposal transaction. Further, an incorrect

Capital Request Form

Project name: _____

Name of project sponsor: _____

Submission date: _____ Project number: _____

	Approvals
☐ Constraint-Related Project	<u>Approvals</u>

Initial expenditure: $ _____

Additional annual expenditure: $ _____

Impact on throughput: $ _____

Impact on operating expenses: $ _____

Impact on ROI: $ _____

(Attach calculations)

All _____
Process Analyst

$100,000 _____
Supervisor

$100,001– _____
$1,000,000 President

$1,000,000+ _____
Board of Directors

☐ Risk-Related Project <u>Approvals</u>

Initial expenditure: $ _____

Additional annual expenditure: $ _____

Description of legal requirement fulfilled or
risk issue mitigated (attach description as needed):

_____

_____

< $50,000 {
_____
Corporate Attorney

_____
Chief Risk Officer

$50,001 + _____
President

$1,000,000+ _____
Board of Directors

☐ Non-Constraint-Related Project <u>Approvals</u>

Initial expenditure: $ _____

Additional annual expenditure: $ _____

☐ Improves sprint capacity?
Attach justification of sprint capacity increase

☐ Other request
Attach justification for other request type

All _____
Process Analyst

<$10,000 _____
Supervisor

$10,001– _____
$100,000 President

$100,000+ _____
Board of Directors

Exhibit 4.5 Capital Investment Approval Form

Capital Asset Disposition Form

Issuing Department Name: _____   **Department Manager Signature:** _____

Step 1: List all equipment being dispositioned in the following spaces:

Tag Number	Item Name	Model Number	Serial Number
1.			
2.			
3.			
4.			
5.			

Step 2: Check one of the action categories listed below (limit of one):

☐ **Return to Seller**	☐ **Lost/Stolen**
Supplier RMA Number: _____	Insurance Claim Number Filed: _____
Shipping Supervisor Signature: _____	Risk Manager Signature: _____
Date: _____	Date: _____
☐ **Transfer to Another Department**	☐ **Trade-In**
Department Name: _____	Purchase Order Number: _____
Receiving Manager Signature: _____	Shipping Supervisor Signature: _____
Date: _____	Date: _____
☐ **Cannibalize for Parts**	☐ **Disposal**
Purchasing Manager Signature: _____	Administrative Officer Signature: _____
Warehouse Manager Signature: _____	Warehouse Manager Signature: _____
Date: _____	Date: _____

Copies: to (1) Accounting, (2) Department Receiving the Assets, (3) Issuing Department

Exhibit 4.6   Capital Asset Disposition Form

acquisition price may result in an incorrect depreciation calculation. To mitigate the risk of all these errors, have a second person review all new entries to the fixed asset master file for accuracy.

If a company acquires assets that are not easily differentiated, then it is useful to affix an identification plate to each one to assist in later audits. The identification plate can be a metal tag if durability is an issue, or can be a laminated bar-code tag for easy scanning, or even a radio frequency identification tag. The person responsible for tagging should record the tag number and asset location in the fixed asset master file.

There is a significant risk that assets will not be carefully tracked through the company once they are acquired. To avoid this, formally assign responsibility for each asset to the department manager whose staff uses the asset, and send all managers a quarterly notification of what assets are under their control. Even better, persuade the human resources manager to include "asset control" as a line item in the formal performance review for all managers.

Fixed assets decline in value over time, so it is essential to conduct a regular review to determine whether any assets should be disposed of before they lose their resale value. This review should be conducted at least annually, and should include representatives from the accounting, purchasing, and user departments. An alternative approach is to create capacity utilization metrics (which are most easily obtained for production equipment), and report on utilization levels as part of the standard monthly management reporting package; this tends to result in more immediate decisions to eliminate unused equipment.

There is a risk that employees could sell off assets at below-market rates or disposition assets for which an alternative in-house use had been planned. Also, if assets are informally disposed of, the accounting staff will probably not be notified, and so will continue to depreciate an asset no longer owned by the company, rather than writing it off. To avoid these problems, require the completion of a signed capital asset disposition form such as the one shown in Exhibit 4.6.

If the company owns fixed assets that can be easily moved and have a significant resale value, then there is a risk that they will be stolen. If so, consider restricting access to the building during non-work hours, and hire a security staff to patrol the perimeter or at least the exits. An alternative is to affix a radio frequency identification (RFID) tag to each asset, and then install a transceiver near every building exit that will trigger an alarm if the RFID tag passes by the transceiver.

Chapter 5

Financial Analysis Decisions

The accountant is constantly asked to conduct a variety of financial analyses regarding key management decisions. These analyses usually require a knowledge of analysis techniques well beyond the typical transaction processing and accounting presentation skills learned in college. Instead, the accountant must understand breakeven analysis, product mix analysis, how to create a *what-if* analysis with an electronic spreadsheet, how to create a cost variance table, how to allocate funds, and how throughput analysis can assist with a number of major decisions.

This chapter provides answers to all of these issues and more. The following table itemizes the section number in which the answers to each question can be found:

Section	Decision
5-1	How do I calculate the breakeven point?
5-2	What is the impact of fixed costs on the breakeven point?
5-3	What is the impact of variable cost changes on the breakeven point?
5-4	How do pricing changes alter the breakeven point?
5-5	How can the product mix alter profitability?
5-6	How do I conduct a "what-if" analysis with a single variable?
5-7	How do I conduct a "what-if" analysis with double variables?
5-8	How do I calculate cost variances?
5-9	How do I conduct a profitability analysis for services?
5-10	How are profits affected by the number of days in a month?
5-11	How do I decide which research and development projects to fund?
5-12	How do I create a throughput analysis model?
5-13	How do I determine whether more volume at a lower price creates more profit?
5-14	Should I outsource production?
5-15	Should I add staff to the bottleneck operation?
5-16	Should I produce a new product?

5-1 HOW DO I CALCULATE THE BREAKEVEN POINT?

Breakeven analysis is the revenue level at which a company earns exactly no profit. It is also known as the cost-volume-profit relationship. To determine a breakeven point, add up all the fixed costs for the company or product being analyzed, and divide it by the associated gross margin percentage. This results in the sales level at which a company will neither lose nor make money—its breakeven point. The formula is shown in Exhibit 5.1.

Exhibit 5.1   The Breakeven Formula

Total fixed costs/Gross margin percentage = Breakeven sales level

---

For those who prefer a graphical layout to a mathematical formula, a breakeven chart can be quite informative. In the sample chart shown in Exhibit 5.2, we show a horizontal line across the chart that represents the fixed costs that must be covered by gross margins, irrespective of the sales level. The fixed cost level will fluctuate over time and in conjunction with extreme changes in sales volume, as noted in the next section, but we will assume no changes for the purposes of this simplified analysis. Also, there is an upward-sloping line that begins at the left end of the fixed cost line and extends to the right across the chart. This is the percentage of variable costs, such as direct labor and materials that are needed to create the product. The last major component of the breakeven chart is the sales line, which is based in the lower-left corner of the chart and extends to the upper-right corner. The amount of the sales volume in dollars is noted on the vertical axis, while the amount of production capacity used to create the sales volume is noted across the horizontal axis. Finally,

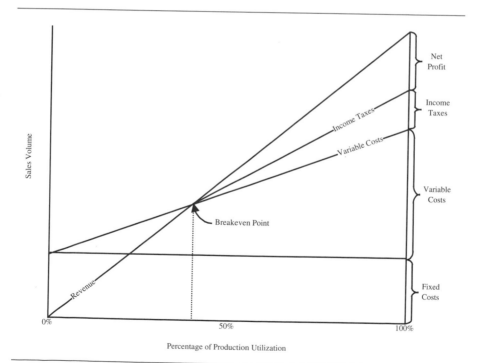

Exhibit 5.2   Breakeven Chart

there is a line that extends from the marked breakeven point to the right and that is always between the sales line and the variable cost line. This represents income tax costs. These are the main components of the breakeven chart.

It is also useful to look between the lines on the graph and understand what the volumes represent. For example, as noted in Exhibit 5.2, the area beneath the fixed costs line is the total fixed cost to be covered by product margins. The area between the fixed cost line and the variable cost line is the total variable cost at different volume levels. The area beneath the income line and above the variable cost line is the income tax expense at various sales levels. Finally, the area beneath the revenue line and above the income tax line is the amount of net profit to be expected at various sales levels.

5-2 WHAT IS THE IMPACT OF FIXED COSTS ON THE BREAKEVEN POINT?

A common alteration in fixed costs is when additional personnel or equipment are needed in order to support an increased level of sales activity. As noted in the

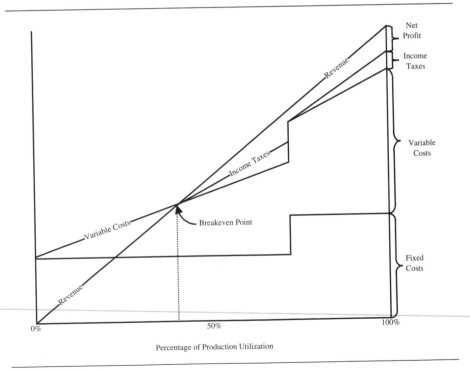

Exhibit 5.3 Breakeven Chart Including Impact of Step Costing

breakeven chart in Exhibit 5.3, the fixed cost will step up to a higher level (an occurrence known as step costing) when a certain capacity level is reached. An example of this situation is when a company has maximized the use of a single shift, and must add supervision and other overhead costs such as electricity and natural gas expenses in order to run an additional shift. Another example is when a new facility must be brought on line or an additional machine acquired. Whenever this happens, management must take a close look at the amount of fixed costs that will be incurred, because the net profit level may be less after the fixed costs are added, despite the extra sales volume. In Exhibit 5.3, the maximum amount of profit that a company can attain is at the sales level just *prior to* incurring extra fixed costs, because the increase in fixed costs is so high. Though step costing does not always involve such a large increase in costs as noted in Exhibit 5.3, this is certainly a major point to be aware of when increasing capacity to take on additional sales volume. In short, more sales do not necessarily lead to more profits.

5-3 WHAT IS THE IMPACT OF VARIABLE COST CHANGES ON THE BREAKEVEN POINT?

Though one would think that the variable cost is a simple percentage that is composed of labor and material costs, and which never varies, this is not the case. This percentage can vary considerably, and frequently drops as the sales volume increases. The reason for the change is that the purchasing department can cut better deals with suppliers when it orders in larger volumes. In addition, full truckload or railcar deliveries result in lower freight expenses than would be the case if only small quantities were purchased. The result is shown in Exhibit 5.4, where the variable cost percentage is at its highest when sales volume is at its lowest, and gradually decreases in concert with an increase in volume.

Because material and freight costs tend to drop as volume increases, it is apparent that profits will increase at an increasing rate as sales volume goes up, though there may be step costing problems at higher capacity levels, as is the case in Exhibit 5.4.

Another point is that the percentage of variable costs will not decline at a steady rate. Instead, and as noted in Exhibit 5.4, there will be specific volume levels at which costs will drop. This is because the purchasing staff can negotiate price reductions only at specific volume points. Once such a price reduction has been achieved, there will not be another opportunity to reduce prices further until a separate and distinct volume level is reached once again. In short, suppliers do not charge lower prices just because a customer's sales volume goes up incrementally by one unit—they only reduce prices when there are increases in the volume of purchases of thousands of units.

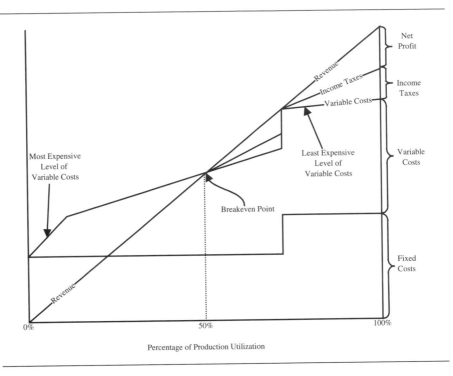

Exhibit 5.4   Breakeven Chart Including Impact of Volume Purchases

5-4 HOW DO PRICING CHANGES ALTER THE BREAKEVEN POINT?

A common problem impacting the volume line in the breakeven calculation is that unit prices do not remain the same when volume increases. Instead, a company finds that it can charge a high price early on, when the product is new and competes with few other products in a small niche market. Later, when management decides to go after larger unit volume, unit prices drop in order to secure sales to a larger array of customers, or to resellers who have a choice of competing products to resell. Thus, higher volume translates into lower unit prices. The result appears in Exhibit 5.5, where the revenue per unit gradually declines despite a continuing rise in unit volume, which causes a much slower increase in profits than would be the case if revenues rose in a straight, unaltered line.

The breakeven chart in Exhibit 5.5 may make management think twice before pursuing a high-volume sales strategy, since profits will not necessarily increase. The only way to be sure of the size of price discounts would be to begin negotiations with resellers or to sell the product in test markets at a range of lower prices to determine changes in volume. Otherwise, management is operating in a vacuum of relevant data. Also, in some cases the only way to survive is to keep cutting prices in pursuit of

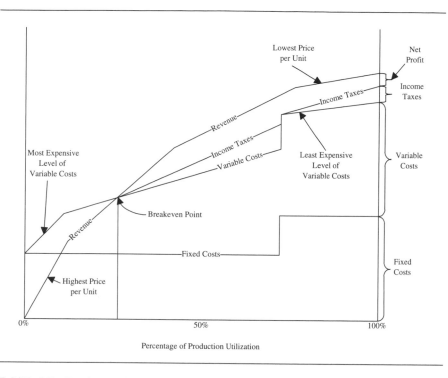

Exhibit 5.5 Breakeven Chart Including Impact of Variable Pricing Levels

greater volume, since there are no high-priced market niches in which to sell. For example, would anyone buy a flat panel color television set for more than a slight price premium? Of course not; this market is so intensely competitive that all competitors must continually pursue a strategy of selling at the smallest possible unit price.

The breakeven chart previously noted in Exhibit 5.5 is a good example of what the breakeven analysis really looks like in the marketplace. Fixed costs jump at different capacity levels, variable costs decline at various volume levels, and unit prices drop with increases in volume. Given the fluidity of the model, it is reasonable to periodically revisit it in light of continuing changes in the marketplace in order to update assumptions and make better calculations of breakeven points and projected profit levels.

5-5 HOW CAN THE PRODUCT MIX ALTER PROFITABILITY?

Product mix has an enormous impact on corporate profits, except for those very rare cases where all products happen to have the same profit margins. To determine how the change in mix will impact profits, it is best to construct a chart, such as the one

Exhibit 5.6   Calculation Table for Margin Changes Due to Product Mix

Product	Unit Sales	Margin %	Margin $
Flow meter	50,000	25%	$12,500
Water collector	12,000	32%	3,840
Ditch digger	51,000	45%	22,950
Evapo-Preventor	30,000	50%	15,000
Piping connector	17,000	15%	2,550
Totals	160,000	36%	$56,840

shown in Exhibit 5.6, that contains the number of units sold and the standard margin for each product or product line, and the resulting gross margin dollars. The resulting average margin will impact the denominator in the standard breakeven formula. For example, if the average mix for a month's sales results in a gross margin of 40 percent, and fixed costs for the period were $50,000, the breakeven point would be $50,000/40 percent, or $125,000. If the product mix for the following month were to result in a gross margin of 42 percent, the breakeven point would shift downward to $50,000/42 percent, or $119,048. Thus, changes in product mix will alter the breakeven point by changing the gross margin number that is part of the breakeven formula.

5-6 HOW DO I CONDUCT A "WHAT-IF" ANALYSIS WITH A SINGLE VARIABLE?

When the accountant must determine the answer to a formula where one element varies, the simplistic approach is to create a table containing all possible expected values of the variable, and calculate the answer for each one. Though workable, this approach is slow. Instead, consider using the table-fill function of Excel to more rapidly develop an answer. An example is shown in Exhibits 5.7 through 5.9. In Exhibit 5.7, we have set up a formula to determine the present value of a series of payments of $1,500 per payment, extending over eight periods. However, the interest rate could vary, so a results table has been created below the present value calculation, showing a range of possible interest rates in quarter-percent increments. Comment fields show the present value calculation in cell C8, and also show that the information appearing in cells B12 and C12 at the top of the results table are references from cells C4 and C8, respectively. All other interest rates shown in cells B13 to B32 are typed in. The main task remaining is to fill in the present value for each of the interest rates shown in the results table. We could recreate the present value calculation next to each of those interest rates, but there is an alternative approach.

The alternative method is to highlight the range of cells from B12 to C32, and then access the Data, Table command in Excel. This results in the screen shown in Exhibit 5.8, where a data entry pop-up screen asks where the input value comes from (the interest rate field in cell C4), and whether we want the results to appear vertically in a column, or horizontally in a row. Since we want the present value results to appear in a

	A	B	C	D	E	F
1						
2		**Present Value Calculation**				
3						
4		Interest rate	5%			
5		Number of periods	8			
6		Payment in each period	$ 1,500			
7						
8		Present value	$ 9,694.82	Present Value Formula: =-PV(C4,C5,C6)		
9						
10		**Results Table**		Cell Reference: C4		
11		Interest Rate	Present Value			
12		5.00%	$ 9,694.82	Cell Reference: C8		
13		5.25%				
14		5.50%				
15		5.75%				
16		6.00%				
17		6.25%				
18		6.50%				
19		6.75%				
20		7.00%				
21		7.25%				
22		7.50%				
23		7.75%				
24		8.00%				
25		8.25%				
26		8.50%				
27		8.75%				
28		9.00%				
29		9.25%				
30		9.50%				
31		9.75%				
32		10.00%				

Exhibit 5.7 Layout of a Single-Variable Table

column next to the interest rates that have already been entered in column B, we enter C4 in the "Column input cell" field in the pop-up screen, as shown in the exhibit.

The result is shown in Exhibit 5.9, where Excel has automatically filled in the present value for each of the interest rates in the results table, ranging from a present value of $9,694.82 for a 5 percent interest rate to $8,002.39 for a 10 percent interest rate.

	A	B	C	D	E	F	G	H
1								
2		**Present Value Calculation**						
3								
4		Interest rate	5%					
5		Number of periods	8					
6		Payment in each period	$ 1,500					
7								
8		Present value	$ 9,694.82					
9								
10		**Results Table**						
11		Interest Rate	Present Value					
12		5.00%	$ 9,694.82					
13		5.25%						
14		5.50%						
15		5.75%						
16		6.00%						
17		6.25%						
18		6.50%						
19		6.75%						
20		7.00%						
21		7.25%						
22		7.50%						
23		7.75%						
24		8.00%						
25		8.25%						
26		8.50%						
27		8.75%						
28		9.00%						
29		9.25%						
30		9.50%						
31		9.75%						
32		10.00%						

Table

Row input cell:

Column input cell: C4

OK   Cancel

Exhibit 5.8   Data Table Input for a Single-Variable Table

5-7 HOW DO I CONDUCT A "WHAT-IF" ANALYSIS WITH DOUBLE VARIABLES?

The problem becomes more difficult when there are two variables in the formula, since the range of possible answers becomes much greater. In this case, the use of automation tools becomes more helpful to the controller, since the alternative is to manually create a large number of formulas.

	A	B	C
1			
2		**Present Value Calculation**	
3			
4		Interest rate	5%
5		Number of periods	8
6		Payment in each period	$ 1,500
7			
8		Present value	$ 9,694.82
9			
10		**Results Table**	
11		Interest Rate	Present Value
12		5.00%	$ 9,694.82
13		5.25%	$ 9,597.59
14		5.50%	$ 9,501.85
15		5.75%	$ 9,407.56
16		6.00%	$ 9,314.69
17		6.25%	$ 9,223.22
18		6.50%	$ 9,133.13
19		6.75%	$ 9,044.38
20		7.00%	$ 8,956.95
21		7.25%	$ 8,870.82
22		7.50%	$ 8,785.96
23		7.75%	$ 8,702.34
24		8.00%	$ 8,619.96
25		8.25%	$ 8,538.78
26		8.50%	$ 8,458.77
27		8.75%	$ 8,379.93
28		9.00%	$ 8,302.23
29		9.25%	$ 8,225.64
30		9.50%	$ 8,150.15
31		9.75%	$ 8,075.74
32		10.00%	$ 8,002.39

Exhibit 5.9   Completed Single-Variable Table

	A	B	C	D	E	F	G
1							
2		**Present Value Calculation**					
3							
4		Interest rate	5%				
5		Number of periods	8				
6		Payment in each period	$ 1,500				
7				Present Value Formula:			
8		Present value	$9,694.82	=-PV(C4,C5,C6)			
9		Cell reference: C8					
10		**Results Table**					
11		Interest Rate	Number of Periods over which Cash is Received				
12		$9,694.82	6	7	8	9	10
13		5.00%					
14		5.25%					
15		5.50%					
16		5.75%					
17		6.00%					
18		6.25%					
19		6.50%					
20		6.75%					
21		7.00%					
22		7.25%					
23		7.50%					
24		7.75%					
25		8.00%					
26		8.25%					
27		8.50%					
28		8.75%					
29		9.00%					
30		9.25%					
31		9.50%					
32		9.75%					
33		10.00%					

Exhibit 5.10   Layout of a Double-Variable Table

We will continue with the present value example used for single-variable analysis to illustrate how double variables can be addressed. In Exhibit 5.10, we assume that both the interest rate and the duration of payments may vary, which yields a large number of possible present values that shall be contained within a grid covering cells C13 to G33. Possible interest rates are listed down the left side of this grid, as was the case for the single-variable calculation, while the number of possible periods is displayed in a row across the top of the grid.

For the double-variable calculation to function properly, the present value result cell must be placed in the top-left corner of the results table, where the column and row headings intersect. The point of this intersection is cell B12, which in turn references the present value result cell, which is located at cell C8.

The next step is to reformat cell B12 to identify it as "Interest Rate," even while the underlying formula is still present. To achieve this step, click on cell B12 and then access the Format, Cell commands in Excel. This will bring up the Format Cells screen, which is shown in Exhibit 5.11. As shown in the exhibit, click on the "Custom" field under the Category heading, then select the "General" option under the Type heading, and enter "Interest Rate" in the Type data entry field. The number in cell B12 will be replaced with the words "Interest Rate," though the underlying formula will still be present.

Next, highlight cells B12 through G33, which places cell B12 in the upper-left corner of the results table. This tells Excel the location of the present value calculation that it will replicate throughout the results table. Then access the Data, Table command in Excel. This creates a data entry pop-up screen, as shown in Exhibit 5.12, which asks for the source of the number of periods in the present value calculation (which is cell C5), as well as the source of the interest rates to be used in the same calculation (which is cell C4).

After completing the data entry pop-up screen and clicking on OK, Excel automatically populates the results table with a complete set of present values for all interest rates and periods listed in the table. The final result is shown in Exhibit 5.13.

5-8 HOW DO I CALCULATE COST VARIANCES?

There are many types of cost variance, which fall into the two general categories of price and efficiency variances. The *price variance* is the difference between the standard and actual price paid for anything, multiplied by the number of units of each item purchased. The derivations of price variances for materials, wages, variable overhead, and fixed overhead are as follows:

- *Materials price variance.* This is based on the actual price paid for materials used in the production process, minus their standard cost, multiplied by the number of units used. It is typically reported to the purchasing manager. This calculation is a bit more complicated than it at first seems, since the *actual* cost is probably either the LIFO, FIFO, or average cost of an item. Here are some additional areas to investigate if there is a materials price variance:
  - The standard price is based on a different purchase volume.
  - The standard price is incorrectly derived from a different component.

	A	B	C	D	E	F	G
1							
2		**Present Value Calculation**					
3							
4		Interest rate	5%				
5		Number of periods	8				
6		Payment in each period	$ 1,500				
7							
8		Present value	$9,694.82	Present Value Formula: =-PV(C4,C5,C6)			
9							
10		**Results Table**					
11		Interest Rate	Cell reference: C8	eriods over which Cash is Received			
12		$9,694.82			8	9	10
13		5.00%					
14		5.25%					
15		5.50%					
16		5.75%					
17		6.00%					
18		6.25%					
19		6.50%					
20		6.75%					
21		7.00%					
22		7.25%					
23		7.50%					
24		7.75%					
25		8.00%					
26		8.25%					
27		8.50%					
28		8.75%					
29		9.00%					
30		9.25%					
31		9.50%					
32		9.75%					
33		10.00%					

Format Cells dialog:

Number | Alignment | Font | Border | Patterns | Protection

Category:
General
Number
Currency
Accounting
Date
Time
Percentage
Fraction
Scientific
Text
Special
Custom

Sample
Interest Rate

Type:
"Interest Rate"

General
0
0.00
#,##0
#,##0.00
#,##0_);(#,##0)
#,##0_);[Red](#,##0)

Delete

Type the number format code, using one of the existing codes as a starting point.

OK | Cancel

Exhibit 5.11   Cell Reformatting in the Double-Variable Table

- ○ The materials were purchased on a rush basis.
- ○ The materials were purchased at a premium, due to a supply shortage.
- *Labor price variance.* This is based on the actual price paid for the direct labor used in the production process, minus its standard cost, multiplied by the number of units used. It is typically reported to the managers of both production and human resources—the production manager because this person is responsible

	A	B	C	D	E	F	G
1							
2		**Present Value Calculation**					
3							
4		Interest rate	5%				
5		Number of periods	8				
6		Payment in each period	$ 1,500				
7				Present Value Formula:			
8		Present value	$9,694.82	=-PV(C4,C5,C6)			
9							
10		**Results Table**					
11				Cell reference: C8	Periods over which Cash is Received		
12		Interest Rate			8	9	10
13		5.00%					
14		5.25%					
15		5.50%					
16		5.75%					
17		6.00%					
18		6.25%					
19		6.50%					
20		6.75%					
21		7.00%					
22		7.25%					
23		7.50%					
24		7.75%					
25		8.00%					
26		8.25%					
27		8.50%					
28		8.75%					
29		9.00%					
30		9.25%					
31		9.50%					
32		9.75%					
33		10.00%					

Table

Row input cell: C5

Column input cell: C4

OK   Cancel

Exhibit 5.12   Data Table Input for a Double-Variable Table

for staffing jobs with personnel at the correct wage rates, and the human resources manager because this person is responsible for setting the allowable wage rates that employees are paid. This tends to be a relatively small variance, as long as the standard labor rate is regularly revised to match actual labor rates in the production facility. Since most job categories tend to be clustered into relatively small pay ranges, there is not much chance that a labor price variance will

	A	B	C	D	E	F	G
1							
2		**Present Value Calculation**					
3							
4		Interest rate	5%				
5		Number of periods	8				
6		Payment in each period	$ 1,500				
7				Present Value Formula:			
8		Present value	$9,694.82	=-PW(C4,C5,C6)			
9							
10		**Results Table**					
11				Cell reference: C8	riods over which Cash is Received		
12		Interest Rate			8	9	10
13		5.00%	7,613.54	8,679.56	9,694.82	10,661.73	11,582.60
14		5.25%	7,553.04	8,601.47	9,597.59	10,544.03	11,443.26
15		5.50%	7,493.30	8,524.45	9,501.85	10,428.29	11,306.44
16		5.75%	7,434.28	8,448.49	9,407.56	10,314.47	11,172.08
17		6.00%	7,375.99	8,373.57	9,314.69	10,202.54	11,040.13
18		6.25%	7,318.40	8,299.67	9,223.22	10,092.44	10,910.54
19		6.50%	7,261.52	8,226.78	9,133.13	9,984.16	10,783.25
20		6.75%	7,205.33	8,154.87	9,044.38	9,877.64	10,658.21
21		7.00%	7,149.81	8,083.93	8,956.95	9,772.85	10,535.37
22		7.25%	7,094.96	8,013.95	8,870.82	9,669.76	10,414.69
23		7.50%	7,040.77	7,944.90	8,785.96	9,568.33	10,296.12
24		7.75%	6,987.23	7,876.78	8,702.34	9,468.53	10,179.61
25		8.00%	6,934.32	7,809.56	8,619.96	9,370.33	10,065.12
26		8.25%	6,882.04	7,743.22	8,538.78	9,273.70	9,952.61
27		8.50%	6,830.38	7,677.77	8,458.77	9,178.59	9,842.02
28		8.75%	6,779.33	7,613.18	8,379.93	9,085.00	9,733.33
29		9.00%	6,728.88	7,549.43	8,302.23	8,992.87	9,626.49
30		9.25%	6,679.02	7,486.51	8,225.64	8,902.19	9,521.46
31		9.50%	6,629.74	7,424.42	8,150.15	8,812.93	9,418.20
32		9.75%	6,581.03	7,363.13	8,075.74	8,725.05	9,316.67
33		10.00%	6,532.89	7,302.63	8,002.39	8,638.54	9,216.85

Exhibit 5.13   Results of Calculation in Double-Variable Table

become excessive. Here are some areas to investigate if there is a labor price variance:

- The standard labor rate has not been recently adjusted to reflect actual pay changes.
- The actual labor rate includes overtime or shift differentials that were not included in the standard.

○ The staffing of jobs is with employees whose pay levels are different from those used to develop standards for those jobs.

- *Variable overhead spending variance.* To calculate this variance, subtract the standard variable overhead cost per unit from the actual cost incurred, and multiply the remainder by the total unit quantity of output. This is very similar to the material and labor price variances, since there are some overhead costs that are directly related to the volume of production, as is the case for materials and labor. The detailed report on this variance is usually sent to the production manager, who is responsible for all overhead incurred in the production area. This variance can require considerable analysis, for there may be a number of costs that fall into this category, all of which may be hiding significant variances. Here are some areas to investigate if there is a variable overhead spending variance:

  ○ The cost of activities in any of the variable overhead accounts has been altered by the supplier.

  ○ The company has altered its purchasing methods for the variable overhead costs to or from the use of blanket purchase orders (which tend to result in lower prices due to higher purchase volumes).

  ○ Costs are being misclassified between the accounts, so that the spending variance appears too low in one account and too high in another.

- *Fixed overhead spending variance.* This is the total amount by which fixed overhead costs exceed their total standard cost for the reporting period. Notice that, unlike the preceding price variance definitions, this one is not multiplied by any type of production volume. There is no way to relate this price variance to volume, since it is not directly tied to any sort of activity volume. The detailed variance report on this topic may be distributed to a number of people, depending on who is responsible for each general ledger account number that it contains. Investigation of variances in this area generally centers on a period-to-period comparison of prices charged to suppliers, with particular attention to those experiencing recent price increases. It may be beneficial to link this investigation to a summary of all contractual agreements with suppliers, since these documents will reveal any allowable pricing changes; only those *not* allowed by such agreements will still require further investigation.

The *efficiency variance* is the difference between the actual and standard usage of a resource, multiplied by the standard price of that resource. The efficiency variance applies to materials, labor, and variable overhead. It does not apply to fixed overhead costs, since these costs are incurred independently from any resource usage. Here is a closer examination of the efficiency variance, as applied to each of these areas:

- *Materials yield variance.* Though its traditional name is slightly different, this is still an efficiency variance. It measures the ability of a company to manufacture a product using the exact amount of materials allowed by the standard. A variance will arise if the quantity of materials used differs from the preset standard. It is calculated by subtracting the total standard quantity of materials that are supposed to be used from the actual level of usage, and multiplying the remainder by the standard price per unit. This information is usually issued to the production manager. Here are some of the areas to investigate to correct the material yield variance:

- Excessive machine-related scrap rates
- Poor material quality levels
- Excessively tight tolerance for product rejections
- Improper machine setup
- Substitute materials that cause high reject rates

- *Labor efficiency variance.* This measures the ability of a company's direct labor staff to create products with the exact amount of labor set forth in the standard. A variance will arise if the quantity of labor used is different from the standard; note that this variance has nothing to do with the cost per unit of labor (which is the price variance), only the quantity of it that is consumed. It is calculated by subtracting the standard quantity of labor consumed from the actual amount, and multiplying the remainder times the standard labor rate per hour. As was the case for the material yield variance, it is most commonly reported to the production manager. Here are the likely causes of the labor efficiency variance:

  - Employees have poor work instructions.
  - Employees are not adequately trained.
  - Too many employees are staffing a workstation.
  - The wrong mix of employees is staffing a workstation.
  - The labor standard used as a comparison is incorrect.

- *Variable overhead efficiency variance.* This measures the quantity of variable overhead required to produce a unit of production. For example, if the machine used to run a batch of product requires extra time to produce each product, there will be an additional charge to the product's cost that is based on the price of the machine, multiplied by its cost per minute. This variance is not concerned with the machine's cost per minute (which would be examined through a price variance analysis), but with the number of minutes required for the production of each unit. It is calculated by subtracting the budgeted units of activity on which the variable overhead is charged from the actual units of activity, times the standard variable overhead cost per unit. Depending on the nature of the costs that make up the pool of variable overhead costs, this variance may be reported to several managers, particularly the production manager. The causes of this variance will be tied to the unit of activity on which it is based. For example,

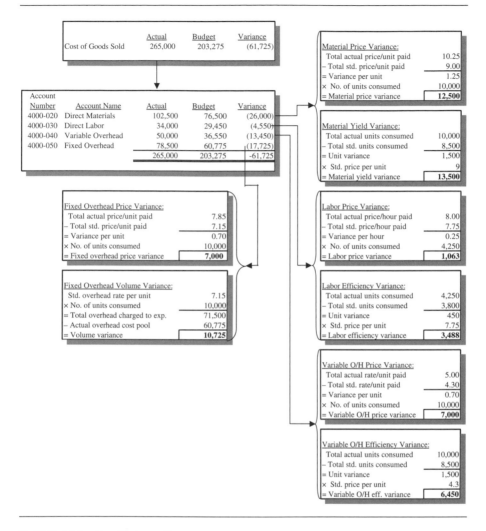

Cost of Goods Sold	Actual	Budget	Variance
	265,000	203,275	(61,725)

Account Number	Account Name	Actual	Budget	Variance
4000-020	Direct Materials	102,500	76,500	(26,000)
4000-030	Direct Labor	34,000	29,450	(4,550)
4000-040	Variable Overhead	50,000	36,550	(13,450)
4000-050	Fixed Overhead	78,500	60,775	(17,725)
		265,000	203,275	-61,725

Material Price Variance:
Total actual price/unit paid	10.25
– Total std. price/unit paid	9.00
= Variance per unit	1.25
× No. of units consumed	10,000
= Material price variance	**12,500**

Material Yield Variance:
Total actual units consumed	10,000
– Total std. units consumed	8,500
= Unit variance	1,500
× Std. price per unit	9
= Material yield variance	**13,500**

Fixed Overhead Price Variance:
Total actual price/unit paid	7.85
– Total std. price/unit paid	7.15
= Variance per unit	0.70
× No. of units consumed	10,000
= Fixed overhead price variance	**7,000**

Fixed Overhead Volume Variance:
Std. overhead rate per unit	7.15
× No. of units consumed	10,000
= Total overhead charged to exp.	71,500
– Actual overhead cost pool	60,775
= Volume variance	**10,725**

Labor Price Variance:
Total actual price/hour paid	8.00
– Total std. price/hour paid	7.75
= Variance per hour	0.25
× No. of units consumed	4,250
= Labor price variance	**1,063**

Labor Efficiency Variance:
Total actual units consumed	4,250
– Total std. units consumed	3,800
= Unit variance	450
× Std. price per unit	7.75
= Labor efficiency variance	**3,488**

Variable O/H Price Variance:
Total actual rate/unit paid	5.00
– Total std. rate/unit paid	4.30
= Variance per unit	0.70
× No. of units consumed	10,000
= Variable O/H price variance	**7,000**

Variable O/H Efficiency Variance:
Total actual units consumed	10,000
– Total std. units consumed	8,500
= Unit variance	1,500
× Std. price per unit	4.3
= Variable O/H eff. variance	**6,450**

Exhibit 5.14   Cost Variance Report

if the variable overhead rate varies directly with the quantity of machine time used, then the main causes will be any action that changes the rate of machine usage. If the basis is the amount of materials used, then the causes will be those just noted for the materials yield variance.

An example of a cost variance report is shown in Exhibit 5.14, where actual and budgeted costs are extracted from the general ledger and posted in the upper-left corner, with all variance calculations in the exhibit being derived from that information.

5-9 HOW DO I CONDUCT A PROFITABILITY ANALYSIS FOR SERVICES?

In the services industry, employee billable hours constitute the prime criterion for overall corporate profitability. Financial analysis should encompass the following three factors, which encompass the primary determinants of profitability in the services sector:

1. Percentage of time billed
2. Full labor cost per hour
3. Billing price per hour

The percentage of time billed can be easily tracked with a spreadsheet, such as the one shown in Exhibit 5.15, where billable employee time is listed by week, with a month-to-date billable percentage listed not only by employee, but also for the entire company. This approach easily highlights any staff who is not meeting minimum billable targets.

In the exhibit, note the "Workdays" row at the bottom, which indicates the number of standard working days in each week of the report, as well as the maximum number of hours that employees can bill during the month. The exhibit shows that more than 100 percent of possible employee hours were billed during the first week of February, due to the billable overtime hours worked by T. Chubby. However, J. Abrams later becomes unbillable, resulting in only a 46 percent billable percentage for that employee by the end of the month. In total, the group has an 82 percent billable percentage during the month.

The full labor cost per hour encompasses not only the hourly rate paid per employee, but also the hourly cost of payroll taxes, various types of insurance, and other benefits (net of deductions paid by employees). Exhibit 5.16 shows the calculation of the full labor cost per hour for several employees.

A key consideration is that, if the employees providing services are being paid on a salary basis, then any overtime hours worked by them that are billable to customers represent a pure profit increase, since there is no offsetting labor cost.

Exhibit 5.15   Billable Hours Report

		Week Ending				
Name	07 Feb.	14 Feb.	21 Feb.	28 Feb.	Hours	Billable %
Abrams, J.	40	30	0	0	70	**46%**
Barlow, M.	40	32	27	39	138	**91%**
Chubby, T.	48	32	42	43	165	**109%**
Totals	**128**	**94**	**69**	**82**	**373**	**82%**
Billable %	**107%**	**98%**	**58%**	**68%**	**82%**	
Workdays	**5**	**4**	**5**	**5**		

Exhibit 5.16 Full Labor Cost per Hour Calculation

Name	Labor Rate per Hour	Payroll Taxes	Pension Matching	Medical Insurance	Long-term Disability	Full Labor Cost/Hour
Abrams, J.	**$17.50**	$1.37	$0.05	$2.93	$0.04	**$21.89**
Barlow, M.	**29.32**	2.30	0.05	5.17	0.03	**36.87**
Chubby, T.	**41.07**	3.22	0.05	2.93	0.04	**47.31**

The price billed per hour means little unless it is compared with the full labor rate cost per hour, thereby arriving at the margin being earned on each hour worked. Otherwise, a high hourly cost could entirely offset an otherwise impressive billing rate, resulting in no profitability for the company. Exhibit 5.17 shows how the billing rate, full labor cost per hour, and billable percentage can be combined to reveal a complete picture of profitability for billable employees.

In the exhibit, the billable percentage for J. Abrams has dropped so low that the net billing rate per hour is less than that employee's fully burdened labor cost per hour; the solution is to either increase the billing rate, increase the billable percentage, reduce the employee's cost, or terminate the employee. The situation for the third employee on the list, T. Chubby, is somewhat different. We assume that Chubby does not receive extra overtime pay; if this were not the case, then the labor cost per hour in the exhibit would increase substantially to include the cost of an overtime premium.

The analysis in Exhibit 5.17 could also include a charge for a commission percentage, on the grounds that a salesperson is being paid a commission for having obtained the services contract under which the employee is now billable.

Another use for Exhibit 5.17 is to calculate the breakeven billable percentage for each employee, which management can then use as a minimum billable target. This information can be determined by shifting the information in the exhibit slightly and revising the calculation, as shown in Exhibit 5.18.

The analysis in Exhibit 5.18 reveals a different aspect of the situation; though J. Abrams is currently not profitable, a relatively low billing percentage of 49 percent will result in a profit. Conversely, though T. Chubby is currently profitable on an hourly basis, the breakeven analysis reveals that a much higher billable percentage is

Exhibit 5.17 Employee Profitability Analysis

Name	Billing Rate Per Hour	×	Billable Percentage	=	Net Billing Rate per Hour	−	Full Labor Cost/Hour	=	Gross Margin
Abrams, J.	$45.00		46%		$20.70		$21.89		($1.19)
Barlow, M.	55.00		91%		50.05		36.87		13.18
Chubby, T.	60.00		109%		65.40		47.31		18.09

Exhibit 5.18   Breakeven Billable Percentage Calculation

Name	Full Labor Cost/Hour	/	Billing Rate per Hour	=	Breakeven Billable %
Abrams, J.	$21.89		$45.00		49%
Barlow, M.	36.87		55.00		67%
Chubby, T.	47.31		60.00		79%

required to maintain this situation, because the margin on Chubby's services is lower than for the other two employees.

The analysis of profitability for services is nearly complete, and excludes only the consideration of corporate overhead. The gross margins noted for employees in Exhibit 5.17 must be extrapolated by the total number of hours worked in the reporting period to arrive at the grand total gross margin earned during the period. Overhead expenses are then compared with this figure to determine the profit or loss for the period, as shown in Exhibit 5.19. The exhibit reveals that the company must either pare overhead expenses drastically, obtain additional billable staff, or greatly increase the gross margin per hour of the existing employees in order to earn a profit.

5-10 HOW ARE PROFITS AFFECTED BY THE NUMBER OF DAYS IN A MONTH?

In a service-related business, the prime focus of conversation usually includes such factors as billable rates per hour and the percentage of billable time. However, a third factor is worth a considerable amount of attention, as well: the number of business days in the month. Using the standard number of federal holidays in the

Exhibit 5.19   Corporate Profitability Analysis

Name	Gross Margin per Hour	×	Hours Worked in Period	=	Total Gross Margin
Abrams, J.	($1.19)		70		($83.30)
Barlow, M.	13.18		138		1,818.84
Chubby, T.	18.09		165		2,984.85
			Total gross margin		$4,720.39
			Overhead expenses		($9,425.00)
			Net loss		($4,704.61)

United States, here are the number of months with different quantities of business days:

Number of Business Days per Month	Number of Months
23	1
22	2
21	1
20	6
19	1
Total Months	**12**

Figure out the number of business days it takes for the consulting or service business to break even. If it takes 21 business days, then the company will lose money in 7 months out of 12. If it takes 22 or 23 business days, then there is a real problem. If this appears to be an issue, calculate the expense reduction required to reduce the breakeven point by one incremental day. This is an excellent approach for monitoring how well the business is structured to make money throughout the year.

5-11 HOW DO I DECIDE WHICH RESEARCH AND DEVELOPMENT PROJECTS TO FUND?

The traditional approach is to require all R&D proposals to pass a minimum return-on-investment hurdle rate. However, when there is limited funding available and too many investments passing the hurdle rate to all be funded, managers tend to pick the projects most likely to succeed. This selection process usually results in the least risky projects being funded, which are typically extensions of existing product lines or other variations on existing products that will not achieve breakthrough profitability. An alternative that is more likely to achieve a higher return on R&D investment is to apportion investable funds into multiple categories: a large percentage that is only to be used for highly risky projects with associated high returns, and a separate pool of funds specifically designated for lower-risk projects with correspondingly lower levels of return. The exact proportions of funding allocated to each category will depend on management's capacity for risk, as well as the size and number of available projects in each category. This approach allows a company the opportunity to achieve a breakthrough product introduction that it would probably not have funded if a single hurdle rate had been used to evaluate new product proposals.

If this higher-risk approach to allocating funds is used, it is likely that a number of new product projects will be abandoned prior to their release into the market, on the grounds that they will not yield a sufficient return on investment or will not be technologically or commercially feasible. This is not a bad situation, since some projects are bound to fail if a sufficiently high level of project risk is acceptable to management. Conversely, if no projects fail, this is a clear sign that management is not investing in sufficiently risky investments. To measure the level of project failure, calculate R&D waste, which is the amount of unrealized product development spending (e.g., the total expenditure on canceled projects during the measurement period). Even better, divide the amount of R&D waste by the total R&D expenditure during the period to determine the proportion of expenses incurred on failed projects. Unfortunately, this measure can be easily manipulated by accelerating or withholding the declaration of project termination. Nonetheless, it does give a fair indication of project risk when aggregated over the long term.

Though funding may be allocated into broad investment categories, management must still use a reliable method for determining which projects will receive funding and which will not. The standard approach is to apply a discount rate to all possible projects, and then to select those having the highest net present value (NPV). However, the NPV calculation does not include several key variables found in the expected commercial value (ECV) formula, making the ECV the preferred method. The ECV formula requires one to multiply a prospective project's net present value by the probability of its commercial success, minus the commercialization cost, and then multiply the result by the probability of technical success, minus the development cost. Thus, the intent of using ECV is to include all major success factors into the decision to accept or reject a new product proposal. The formula is as follows:

$$(((\text{Project net present value} \times \text{Probability of commercial success})$$
$$- \text{Commercialization cost}) \times (\text{Probability of technical success}))$$
$$- \text{Product development cost}$$

As an example of the use of ECV, the Moravia Corporation collects the following information about a new project for a battery-powered lawn trimmer, where there is some technical risk that a sufficiently powerful battery cannot be developed for the product:

Project net present value	$4,000,000
Probability of commercial success	90%
Commercialization cost	$750,000
Probability of technical success	65%
Product development cost	$1,750,000

Based on this information, Moravia computes the following ECV for the lawn trimmer project:

$$(((\$4,000,000 \text{ Project net present value} \times 90\% \text{ Probability of commercial success})$$
$$- \$750,000 \text{ Commercialization cost}) \times (65\% \text{ Probability of technical success}))$$
$$- \$1,750,000 \text{ Product development cost}$$
$$\text{Expected commercial value} = \$102,500$$

Even if some projects are dropped after being run through the preceding valuation analysis, this does not mean that they should be canceled for good. On the contrary, these projects may become commercially viable over time, depending on changes in price points, costs, market conditions, and technical viability. Consequently, the R&D manager should conduct a periodic review of previously shelved projects to see whether any of the factors just noted have changed sufficiently to allow the company to reintroduce a project proposal for development.

5-12 HOW DO I CREATE A THROUGHPUT ANALYSIS MODEL?

The primary focus of throughput accounting is on how to force as many through-put dollars as possible through the capacity constraint. It does this by first determining the throughput dollars per minute of every production job scheduled to run through the capacity constraint, and rearranging the order of production priority so that the products with the highest throughput dollars per minute are completed first. The system is based on the supposition that only a certain amount of production can be squeezed through a bottleneck operation, so the production that yields the highest margin must come first in order of production scheduling priority, to ensure that profits are maximized. The concept is most easily demonstrated in the example shown in Exhibit 5.20.

In the example, we have four types of products that a company can sell. Each requires some machining time on the company's capacity constraint, which is the circuit board manufacturing process (CBMP). The first item is a 19″ color television, which requires four minutes of the CBMP's time. The television sells for $100.00, and has associated direct materials of $67.56, which gives it a throughput of $32.44 (the price and direct materials cost are not shown in the exhibit, merely inferred). We then divide the throughput of $32.44 by the four minutes of processing time per unit on the capacity constraint to arrive at the throughput dollars per minute of $8.11 that is shown in the second column of the exhibit. We then calculate the throughput per minute for the other three products, and sort them in high–low order, based on which ones contribute the most throughput per minute. This leaves the 19″ color television at the top of the list. Next, we multiply the scheduled production for each item by the time required to move it through the constrained resource. We do this for all four products, and verify that the total planned time required for the constraint operation is equal to or less than the actual time available at the constraint, as shown in the "Total planned constraint time" row. In the exhibit, the maximum available constraint time is listed in bold as 8,000 minutes, which is the approximate usage level for an eight-hour day in a 21-day month of business days, assuming 80 percent efficiency. This number will vary dramatically, depending on the number of shifts used, scrap levels, and the efficiency of operation of the constrained resource.

A key concept is that the maximum number of units of the highest throughput-per-minute item (in this case, the 19″ color television) is to be sold, as well as the

Exhibit 5.20   The Throughput Model

Product Name	Throughput $$/min. of Constraint	Required Constraint Usage (min.)	Units of Scheduled Production	Constraint Utilization (minutes)	Throughput per Product
1. 19″ Color television	$8.11	4	500/500	2,000	$16,220
2. 32″ LCD television	7.50	6	350/350	2,100	15,750
3. 50″ High-definition TV	6.21	10	150/150	1,500	9,315
4. 42″ Plasma television	5.00	12	180/400	2,160	10,800
		Total planned constraint time		**7,760**	—
		Maximum constraint time		**8,000**	—
			Throughput total		**$52,085**
			Operating expense total		47,900
			Profit		$4,185
			Profit percentage		8.0%
			Investment		$320,000
			Return on investment*		15.7%

*Annualized.

maximum volume for each product listed below it. Only the production volume of the product listed at the bottom of the table (in this case, the 42″ plasma television) will be reduced in order to meet the limitations of the constrained resource. The amount of planned production as well as the amount of potential sales are shown in the "Units of Scheduled Production" column of the throughput model. For example, "500/500" is shown in this column for the 19″ color television, which means that there are 500 units of potential sales for this product, and the company plans to produce all 500 units. Only for the last product in the table, the 42″ plasma television, do the units of production not match the potential sales (180 units are being produced instead of the 400 units of potential sales). By doing so, a company can maximize throughput.

Then, by multiplying the throughput per minute by the number of minutes for each product, and then multiplying the result by the total number of units produced, we arrive at the total throughput for each product, as shown in the final column, as well as for the entire production process for the one-month period, which is $52,085. However, we are not done yet. We must still subtract from the total throughput the sum of all operating expenses for the facility, which is $47,900 in the exhibit. After they are subtracted from the total throughput, we find that we have achieved a profit of 8.0 percent and a return on investment (annualized, since the results of the model are only for a one-month period) of 15.7 percent.

This is the basic throughput financial analysis model, incorporating all the key throughput analysis elements of throughput dollars, operating expenses, and return on investment. It will be used as the foundation for several additional financial analysis scenarios later in this chapter. When reviewing a proposal with this model, one must review the impact of the decision on the incremental change in net profit caused by a change in throughput minus operating expenses, divided by the change in investment. If there is an incremental improvement in the model, then the proposed decision should be accepted. The model makes it easy to determine the exact amount of system improvement (or degradation) occurring by incrementally changing one element of the production system.

5-13 HOW DO I DETERMINE WHETHER MORE VOLUME AT A LOWER PRICE CREATES MORE PROFIT?

What happens when a customer indicates that a very large order is about to be issued—but only if the company grants a significant price reduction? The typical analysis is for the accountants to determine the fully burdened cost of the product in question, compare it with the low requested price, and then reject the proposal out of hand because they state that the company cannot cover its overhead costs at such a low price point. Conversely, the sales manager will ram through approval of the proposal, on the grounds that "we will make up the loss with higher volume." Which is right? Based on their logic, neither one, because they are not considering the net impact of this proposal on total system throughput. Perhaps the following example will clarify the situation.

The sales manager of the electronics company in our previous example runs into the corporate headquarters, flush from a meeting with the company's largest account, Electro-Geek Stores (EGS). He has just agreed to a deal that drops the price of the 32" LCD television by 20 percent, but which guarantees a doubling in the quantity of EGS orders for this product for the upcoming year. The sales manager points out that the company may have to hold off on a few of the smaller-volume production runs of other products, but it's no problem—the company is bound to earn more money on the extra volume. To test this assumption, the accountant pulls up the throughput model on his computer, shifts the LCD TV to the top of the priority list, adjusts the throughput to reflect the lower price, and obtains the results shown in Exhibit 5.21.

Exhibit 5.21   The Low Price, High Volume Decision

Product Name	Throughput $$/min. of Constraint	Required Constraint Usage (min.)	Units of Scheduled Production	Constraint Utilization (minutes)	Throughput per Product
1. 32″ LCD television	$4.36	6	700/700	4,200	$18,312
2. 19″ Color television	8.11	4	500/500	2,000	16,220
3. 50″ High-definition TV	6.21	10	150/150	1,500	9,315
4. 42″ Plasma television	5.00	12	25/400	300	1,500
		Total planned constraint time		**8,000**	—
		Maximum constraint time		**8,000**	—
			Throughput total		**$45,347**
			Operating expense total		47,900
			Profit		$(2,553)
			Profit percentage		(5.6%)
			Investment		$320,000
			Return on investment*		(9.6%)

*Annualized.

To be brief, the sales manager just skewered the company. By dropping the price of the LCD television by 20 percent, much of the product's throughput was eliminated, while so much of the capacity constraint was used up that there was little room for the production of any other products that might generate enough added throughput to save the company. Specifically, because of its low level of throughput dollars per minute, the planned production of the 42″ plasma television had to be dropped from 180 units to just 25, nearly eliminating the throughput of this product.

This example clearly shows that one must carefully consider the impact on the capacity constraint when debating whether to accept a high-volume sales deal. This is a particularly dangerous area in which to ignore throughput accounting, for the acceptance of a really large-volume deal can demand all of the time of the capacity constraint, eliminating any chance for the company to manufacture other products, and thereby eliminating any chance of offering a wide product mix to the general marketplace.

5-14 SHOULD I OUTSOURCE PRODUCTION?

A common decision to consider is whether to outsource production. The usual analysis will focus on the reduced margin that the company will earn, since the supplier will likely charge a higher price than the company can achieve if it keeps the work in-house. However, the correct view of the situation is whether the company can earn more throughput on a combination of the outsourced production and the additional new production that will now be available through the constrained resource.

For example, one of the company's key suppliers has offered to take over the entire production of the 50″ high-definition television, package it in the company's boxes, and drop ship the completed goods directly to the company's customers. The catch is that the company's throughput per unit will decrease from its current $62.10 to $30.00. The cost accounting staff would likely reject this deal, on the grounds that profits would be reduced. To see if this is a good deal, we turn once again to the throughput model, which is reproduced in Exhibit 5.22. In this exhibit, we have removed the number from the "Units of Scheduled Production" column for the high-definition television, since it can now be produced without the use of the capacity constraint. However, we are still able to put a cumulative throughput dollar figure into the final column for this product, since there is some margin to be made by outsourcing it through the supplier. By removing the high-definition television's usage of the capacity constraint, we are now able to produce more of the next product in line, which is the plasma television set. This additional production allows the company to increase the amount of throughput dollars, thereby creating $3,885 more profits than was the case before the outsourcing deal.

The traditional cost accounting approach would have stated that profits would be lowered by accepting an outsourcing deal that clearly cost more than the product's internal cost. However, by using this deal to release some capacity at the bottleneck, the company is able to earn more money on the production of other products.

5-15 SHOULD I ADD STAFF TO THE BOTTLENECK OPERATION?

When a company starts using constraint management as its guiding principle in managing throughput, an early area of decision making will be how to increase the output of the constrained resource. An obvious first step is to add staff to it, with the intent of achieving faster equipment setup time, less equipment downtime, more operational efficiency per machine, and so on. As long as the incremental increase in throughput exceeds the cost of each staff person added to the constraint, this should be a logical step to take. However, traditional accounting analysis will likely find that the additional labor assigned to the constrained resource will not be needed at all times and would therefore have a low level of efficiency, and would reject the proposal.

For example, the company realizes that it can vastly reduce job setup time by adding an employee to the constrained resource, thereby increasing the maximum

Exhibit 5.22   The Outsourced Production Decision

Product Name	Throughput $$/min. of Constraint	Required Constraint Usage (min.)	Units of Scheduled Production	Constraint Utilization (minutes)	Throughput per Product
1. 19″ Color television	$8.11	4	500/500	2,000	$16,220
2. 32″ LCD television	7.50	6	350/350	2,100	15,750
3. 50″ High-definition TV	3.00	10			4,500
4. 42″ Plasma television	5.00	12	325/400	3,900	19,500
		Total planned constraint time		**8,000**	—
		Maximum constraint time		**8,000**	—
			Throughput total		**$55,970**
			Operating expense total		47,900
			Profit		$8,070
			Profit percentage		14.4%
			Investment		$320,000
			Return on investment*		30.3%

*Annualized.

constraint time from 8,000 minutes per month to 8,800 minutes. Due to scheduling issues, the employee must be assigned to the constrained resource for an entire eight-hour day, even though she is only needed for a total of one hour per day. Her cost is $25 per hour, or $4,200 per month ($25/hour × 8 hours × 21 business days). The result of this change is shown in Exhibit 5.23.

The exhibit reveals that the company can use the extra capacity to build more units of the 42″ plasma television, resulting in $5,160 of additional throughput that, even when offset against the $4,200 additional labor cost (which has been added to the operating expense line item), still results in an incremental profit improvement of $960. The main problem is that the employee will be working on the constrained resource for only one hour out of eight, which is a 12.5 percent utilization percentage that will certainly draw the attention of the accounting staff. Consequently, low

Exhibit 5.23 The Increased Constraint Staffing Decision

Product Name	Throughput $$/min. of Constraint	Required Constraint Usage (min.)	Units of Scheduled Production	Constraint Utilization (minutes)	Throughput per Product
1. 19" Color television	$8.11	4	500/500	2,000	$16,220
2. 32" LCD television	7.50	6	350/350	2,100	15,750
3. 50" High-definition TV	6.21	10	150/150	1,500	9,315
4. 42" Plasma television	5.00	12	266/400	3,192	15,960
		Total planned constraint time		**8,792**	—
		Maximum constraint time		**8,800**	—
			Throughput total		**$57,245**
			Operating expense total		52,100
			Profit		$5,145
			Profit percentage		9.0%
			Investment		$320,000
			Return on investment*		19.3%

*Annualized.

incremental labor efficiency on the constrained resource can make sense if the resulting incremental throughput exceeds the cost of the labor.

5-16 SHOULD I PRODUCE A NEW PRODUCT?

When adding a new product that requires use of the constrained resource, management may be startled to find that profits actually decline as a result of the introduction, because the new product eliminated an old product that yielded more throughput per minute. The traditional cost accounting system will not spot this problem, because it focuses on the profitability of a product, rather than the amount of the constrained resource needed to produce it.

Exhibit 5.24 Comparison of Old and New Television Models

	32″ LCD Television (New)	32″ LCD Television (Old)
Price	$400	$400
Totally variable costs	$340	$355
Throughput	$60	$45
Overhead allocation	$35	$35
Profit	$25	$10
Required constraint usage	10 minutes	6 minutes
Throughput per minute of constraint	$6.00	$7.50

Exhibit 5.25 The New Product Addition Decision (Lower Cost)

Product Name	Throughput $$/min. of Constraint	Required Constraint Usage (min.)	Units of Scheduled Production	Constraint Utilization (minutes)	Throughput per Product
1. 19″ Color television	$8.11	4	500/500	2,000	$16,220
2. 50″ High-definition TV	6.21	10	150/150	1,500	9,315
3. 32″ LCD television (new)	6.00	10	350/350	3,500	21,000
4. 42″ Plasma television	5.00	12	83/400	996	4,980
		Total planned constraint time		**7,996**	—
		Maximum constraint time		**8,000**	—
		Throughput total			**$51,515**
		Operating expense total			47,900
		Profit			$3,615
		Profit percentage			8.0%
		Investment			$320,000
		Return on investment*			13.6%

*Annualized.

For example, the company's engineers have designed a new, lower-cost 32″ LCD television to replace the existing model. The two products are compared in Exhibit 5.24.

The traditional accountant would review this comparative exhibit and conclude that the new model is clearly better, since it costs less to build, resulting in a profit $15 greater than the old model. However, the new model achieves less throughput per minute, because its larger throughput is being spread over a substantial increase in the required amount of time on the constrained resource. By replacing the old model with the new model, we arrive at the results shown in Exhibit 5.25.

The model shows that profits have declined by $570, because the new model has used up so much constraint time that the company is no longer able to produce as many of the 42″ plasma televisions. Furthermore, the throughput per minute on the new product has declined so much that it is now ranked as the third most profitable product,

Exhibit 5.26   The New Product Addition Decision (Higher Throughput/Minute)

Product Name	Throughput $$/min. of Constraint	Required Constraint Usage (min.)	Units of Scheduled Production	Constraint Utilization (minutes)	Throughput per Product
1. 19″ Color television	$8.11	4	500/500	2,000	$16,220
2. 32″ LCD television **(new)**	8.00	5	350/350	1,750	14,000
3. 50″ High-definition TV	6.21	10	150/150	1,500	9,315
4. 42″ Plasma television	5.00	12	229/400	2,748	13,740
		Total planned constraint time		**7,998**	—
		Maximum constraint time		**8,000**	—
			Throughput total		**$53,275**
			Operating expense total		47,900
			Profit		$5,375
			Profit percentage		10.1%
			Investment		$320,000
			Return on investment*		20.2%

*Annualized.

instead of occupying the new number-two position, as was the case for its predecessor product.

Let us now modify the analysis so that the company's product engineers have spent their time reducing the required amount of constraint time for the 32″ LCD television, rather than in reducing its cost. In fact, let us assume that they *increase* the product's cost by $5 while *reducing* the amount of required constraint time from six minutes to five minutes, which increases its throughput per minute to $8.00. The result is shown in Exhibit 5.26, where the company's total throughput has increased because more time is now available at the constrained resource for additional production of the plasma television. However, this new product introduction would almost certainly have been canceled by the accountants because the cost per unit would have increased.

Chapter 6

Payroll Decisions

The payroll function has traditionally been highly labor-intensive, but available technology now makes it possible to automate almost every aspect of the process, leaving the payroll staff with only an oversight role, reviewing transactions for errors.

To see how simplification can be achieved, it is easiest to first break down the payroll function into three categories: inputs, processing, and outputs. In the inputs category, the payroll staff is usually burdened with manual rekeying of employee timecards, which can now be eliminated through the use of computerized time clocks, Web-based timekeeping systems, and data entry by phone. In the processing category, the payroll staff usually spends its time processing payroll deductions, issuing and receiving forms, and calculating payments. These tasks can now be automated with self-service portals, deduction management, and the outsourcing of payroll processing. The final category is outputs, or payments to employees, where the payroll staff traditionally creates and distributes checks. Instead, it is now possible not only to pay employees by several electronic methods, but also to post their remittance information on the Internet, rather than mailing it to them.

This chapter clarifies how all of these payroll simplification techniques work. The following table itemizes the section number in which the answers to each question can be found:

Section	Decision
6-1	How can I automate time clock data collection?
6-2	How do I collect time information by telephone?
6-3	How can I simplify payroll deductions?
6-4	How do employees enter their own payroll changes?
6-5	How do I automate payroll form distribution?
6-6	Should I pay employees via direct deposit?
6-7	How do paycards compare with payments by direct deposit?
6-8	What issues should I consider when setting up a paycard program?
6-9	How do I make electronic child support payments?
6-10	How do I automate payroll remittances?
6-11	Should I outsource payroll?
6-12	Can I outsource employment verifications?
6-13	Can I outsource benefits administration?
6-14	How many payroll cycles should I have?
6-15	How can I reduce the number of employee payroll–related inquiries?

6-1 HOW CAN I AUTOMATE TIME CLOCK DATA COLLECTION?

The most labor-intensive task in the payroll area is calculating hours worked for hourly employees. To do so, a payroll clerk must collect all of the employee timecards for the most recently completed payroll period, manually accumulate the hours listed on the cards, and discuss missing or excessive hours with supervisors. This is a lengthy process with a high error rate, due to the large percentage of missing start or stop times on timecards. Any errors are usually found by employees as soon as they are paid, resulting in possibly confrontational visits to the payroll staff, demanding an immediate adjustment to their pay with a manual check. These changes disrupt the payroll department and introduce additional inefficiencies to the process.

The solution is to install a computerized time clock. This clock requires an employee to swipe a uniquely identified card through a reader on its side. The card is encoded with either a magnetic strip or a bar code that contains the employee's identification number. Once the swipe occurs, the clock automatically stores the date and time, and downloads this information upon request to the payroll department's computer, where special software automatically calculates the hours worked and also highlights any problems for additional research (such as missed card swipes). Many of these clocks can be installed through a large facility or at outlying locations so that employees can conveniently record their time, no matter where they may be. More advanced clocks also track the time periods when employees are supposed to arrive and leave, and require a supervisor's password for card swipes outside of that time period; this feature allows for greater control over employee work hours. Many of these systems also issue absence reports, so that supervisors can tell who has not shown up for work. Thus, an automated time clock eliminates much low-end clerical work while at the same time providing new management tools for supervisors.

Before purchasing such a clock, be aware of its limitations. The most important one is cost. This type of clock costs $2,000 to $3,000 each, or can be leased for several hundred dollars per month. If several clocks are needed, this can add up to a substantial investment. In addition, outlying time clocks that must download their information to a computer at a distant location may require their own phone line. There may also be a fee for using the software on the central computer that summarizes all the incoming payroll information. Given these costs, it is most common for bar-coded time clocks to be used only in those situations where there are so many hourly employees that there is a significant savings in the payroll department resulting from their installation.

One problem with the computerized time clock is that it suffers from an integrity flaw—employees can use each other's badges to enter and exit from the payroll system. This means that some employees may be paid for hours when they were never really on-site at all. The biometric time clock resolves this problem by requiring an employee to place his or her hand on a sensor, which matches its size and shape to the dimensions already recorded for that person in a central database. The time entered into the terminal will then be recorded against the payroll file of the person whose hand was just measured. Thus, only employees who are on-site can have payroll hours credited to them. These systems have a secondary benefit, which is that no one needs an employee badge or passkey; these tend to be lost or damaged over time and so represent a minor headache for the accounting or human resources staffs, who must track them. In a biometric monitoring environment, all an employee needs is a hand.

Though the use of bar-coded or biometric time clocks certainly solves a variety of timekeeping problems in environments where many employees are clustered together, the approach does not work well where employees are scattered over a wide area. It is not efficient for these employees to travel long distances to the time clocks to record their time, and the clocks are too expensive to multiply into every possible employee location. In these cases, consider setting up a Web-based time-keeping system. Under this approach, employees call up a Web page that simulates a timecard, and use it to enter their hours worked. By doing so, the payroll staff has no keypunching duties at all, the online system can warn employees of obvious key-punching errors on the spot, and timekeeping data is available much more quickly to management.

Web-based timekeeping systems are becoming widely available through the larger payroll outsourcing suppliers. These products include ADP's ezLaborManager product, Cignify Corporation's PeopleNet product, and TALX Corporation's Fast-Time product. These products allow employees to charge time against a wide range of labor accounts. Using one of these outsourced solutions is particularly appealing if the payroll processing function is already outsourced, since the supplier can automatically port the input data directly into its payroll application, resulting in even less payroll processing work by the payroll department.

An alternative is to construct an in-house Web-based system, which may be more useful in companies that have closely integrated their timekeeping systems to a job billing system. Under this more customized approach, a logical configuration is to have employees enter time not only against a job number, but also to a labor code that translates into a specific billable hourly rate. The resulting reports should specify exactly who worked on a customer project during what time period, how many hours they worked, their billable rate, and the total charge being invoiced to the customer. Though this type of system requires considerable programming effort, the result is excellent automation not only of the timekeeping process, but of the billing process as well.

6-2 HOW DO I COLLECT TIME INFORMATION BY TELEPHONE?

The initial entry of timekeeping data remains a problem for many companies. They can either install computerized timekeeping units on the company premises, or require employees to log onto a Web-based system. The first solution requires a capital investment of up to $2,000 per unit and keeping track of employee badges, while the second solution requires everyone to have access to a computer. Until recently, the only other solution was having employees fill out paper timesheets, which the payroll staff would have to manually enter into the computer system (with the usual data entry errors).

An interesting alternative is the telephone. Under this approach, the company buys a rack-mounted server that contains an interactive voice response (IVR) system, and links it to their phone system. Employees then call into the IVR system to enter their time in response to a series of prompts. The capacity of the system ranges from one employee to over 100,000.

An online demonstration IVR system has been set up by Telliris, Inc. To use it, call 203-924-7000, extension 5000 and enter partner code 0000. Then use employee number 00001 to enter a variety of transactions, such as clocking in and out, reporting sick time, vacation time, bereavement, jury duty, and family illness.

A timekeeping IVR system requires a reduced investment, since it takes advantages of existing phones. Also, the system is so intuitive that employee training is almost completely unnecessary. Furthermore, the system has built-in validation, to avoid initial data entry errors by employees. It is even possible to limit phone calls to specific telephone numbers (presumably originating from fixed phone locations), so that employees can call in only from where they are supposed to be. This is a very good solution for mobile employees, such as those involved with equipment servicing, facilities maintenance, and health care. It is also useful for temporary employees, since the company would otherwise have to issue them an employee badge in order to use any in-house timekeeping systems.

In addition to Telliris, timekeeping IVR systems are also offered by TimeLink and TALX (though TALX's FastTime solution is offered only to companies having more than 3,500 employees).

6-3 HOW CAN I SIMPLIFY PAYROLL DEDUCTIONS?

A company can offer a large number of benefits to its employees, many of which require some sort of deduction from payroll. For example, a company can set up deductions for employee medical, dental, life, and supplemental life insurance, as well as flexible spending account deductions for medical insurance or child care payments, as well as 401(k) deductions and 401(k) loan deductions. If there are many employees and many deduction types, the payroll staff can be snowed under at payroll processing time by the volume of changes continually occurring in this area. Also, whenever there is a change in the underlying cost of insurance provided to the company, the company commonly passes along some portion of these costs to the employees, resulting in a massive updating of deductions for all employees who take that particular type of insurance. This not only takes time away from other, more value-added payroll tasks, but also is subject to error, so that adjustments must later be made to correct the errors, which requires even more staff time.

There are several ways to address this problem. One is to eliminate the employee-paid portion of some types of insurance. For example, if the cost to the company for monthly dental insurance is $20 per employee and the related deduction is only $2 per person, management can elect to pay for the entire cost, rather than burden the payroll staff with the tracking of this trivial sum. Another alternative is to eliminate certain types of benefits, such as supplemental life insurance or 401(k) loans, in order to eliminate the related deductions. Yet another alternative is to create a policy that limits employee changes to any benefit plans, so they can only make a small number of changes per year. This eliminates the continual changing of deduction amounts in favor of just a few large bursts of activity at prescheduled times during the year. A very good alternative is to create a benefit package for all employees that requires a single deduction of the same amount for everyone, or for a group (such as one deduction for single employees and another for employees with families); employees can then pick and choose the exact amount of each type of benefit they want within the boundaries of each benefit package, without altering the amount of the underlying deduction. This last alternative has the unique advantage of consolidating all deductions into a single item, which is much simpler to administer. Any of these approaches to the problem will reduce the number or timing of deduction changes, thereby reducing the workload of the payroll staff.

6-4 HOW DO EMPLOYEES ENTER THEIR OWN PAYROLL CHANGES?

Employees always have some sort of data change they want to make in the payroll system, such as changes to their direct deposit, withholding, address, name, and marital status information. The payroll staff must make all of these changes, as well as the inevitable corrections caused by errors in data entry. For example, when an employee first wants to set up direct deposit, she forwards this information to the payroll staff, which inputs it into whatever payroll software is in use. If the employee forwards incorrect information or it is incorrectly keypunched into the system, it is rejected and must be dealt with again during the next payroll cycle. In addition, employees may switch bank accounts or want to split deposits into multiple accounts, all of which require additional work by the payroll staff. Depending on the number of employees, these types of changes can represent a significant ongoing effort.

The latest advance in the area of self-service is for payroll outsourcing companies to manage self-service Web sites on behalf of their clients, who merely provide a link to these sites from their intranet sites. A typical self-service site allows the payroll manager to upload a variety of employee-centric documents, such as the employee manual, company phone directory, payroll forms, and news releases. In addition to these basic functions, the site also allows employees to access their pay statements and W-2 forms, view their earnings history, check their remaining vacation time, see performance reviews, view their 401(k) plan balances, and verify their benefits elections.

An alternative is to construct this type of portal for an in-house legacy payroll system, but the programming effort required is so substantial that a company must have a considerable number of employees to make it worthwhile. An alternative would be to install a self-service module if a company uses commercial off-the-shelf payroll software that already provides this functionality.

Self-service portals can also be constructed for managers, who can input a different set of information into the payroll system. This includes the setup and deletion of employees from the payroll database, as well as the recording of payroll events, such as employee pay raises, transfers, and employee leave situations. Though a few outsourcing payroll suppliers offer manager portals, they are still rare. Consequently, it may be necessary to construct a custom portal for managers. If so, consider the following issues before constructing the system:

- *Install data limit checkers.* Managers may inadvertently enter incorrect information that is patently false, such as a $1,000,000 salary, by not entering a decimal place. The data entry system can include a number of data limit checkers that will automatically reject data unless it falls within a tight parameter range.

- *Require transaction-specific approvals.* If a manager wants to give an employee an inordinately large pay raise, the system should bring this raise to the attention of the payroll staff or an upper-level manager, who must approve it before the payroll database is updated with the new information.

- *Issue warnings to affected departments.* When a manager enters an employee termination into the computer system, this should trigger a message to the human resources department, which may want to conduct an exit interview. Similarly, the 401(k) plan administrator needs to know about the termination in order to send plan termination documents to the former employee; the same goes for the health plan administrator, who must mail out a packet of COBRA information. A number of similar notifications are needed at the point of initial hire.

Thus, the manager self-service portal requires complex interfaces. It must review input data, issue notifications and warnings, and generally take over the role of an experienced payroll clerk to ensure that employee transition data is correctly handled throughout the company. Given the complexity of this portal, it is generally best to roll out only one function at a time, to ensure that sufficient system testing is conducted.

6-5 HOW DO I AUTOMATE PAYROLL FORM DISTRIBUTION?

Employees frequently come to the payroll department to ask for any of the variety of forms required for changes to their payroll status, such as the IRS's W-4 form, address changes, flexible spending account sign-up or change forms, and so on.

These constant interruptions interfere with the orderly flow of payroll work, especially when the department runs out of a form and must scramble to replenish its supplies.

This problem is neatly solved by converting all forms to Adobe Acrobat's PDF format and posting them on a company intranet site for downloading by all employees. By using this approach, no one ever has to approach the payroll staff for the latest copy of a form. Also, employees can download the required form from anywhere, rather than having to wait until they are near the payroll location to physically pick one up. Further, the payroll staff can regularly update the PDF forms on the intranet site, so there is no risk of someone using an old and outmoded form.

Converting a regular form to PDF format is simple. First, purchase the Acrobat software from Adobe's Web site and install it. Then access a form in whatever software package it was originally constructed, and print it to "PDF Acrobat," which will now appear on the list of printers. There are no other steps—your PDF format is complete! The IRS also uses the PDF format for its forms, which can be downloaded from the www.irs.gov site and posted to the company intranet site.

6-6 SHOULD I PAY EMPLOYEES VIA DIRECT DEPOSIT?

A major task for the payroll staff is to issue paychecks to employees. This task can be subdivided into several steps. First, the checks must be printed; though it seems easy, it is all too common for the check run to fail, resulting in the manual cancellation of the first batch of checks, followed by a new print run. Next, the checks must be signed by an authorized check signer, who may have questions about payment amounts that may require additional investigation. After that, the checks must be stuffed into envelopes and then sorted by supervisor (since supervisors generally hand out paychecks to their employees). The checks are then distributed, usually with the exception of a few checks that will be held for those employees who are not currently on-site for later pickup. If checks are stolen or lost, the payroll staff must cancel them and manually issue replacements. Finally, the person in charge of the bank reconciliation must track those checks that have not been cashed and follow up with employees to get them to cash their checks—there are usually a few employees who prefer to cash checks only when they need the money, surprising though this may seem. In short, there are a startlingly large number of steps involved in issuing payroll checks to employees. How can we eliminate this work?

We can eliminate the printing and distribution of paychecks by using direct deposit, which involves issuing payments directly to employee bank accounts. Besides avoiding some of the steps involved with issuing paychecks, it carries the additional advantage of putting money in employee bank accounts at once, so that those employees who are off-site on payday do not have to worry about how they will receive their money—it will appear in their checking accounts automatically, with no effort on their part. Also, there is no longer a problem with asking employees to cash their checks, since it is done automatically. Further, there is no longer any need to have an elaborate set of controls designed to store and track unused checks.

It can be difficult to get employees to switch over to direct deposit. Though the benefits to employees may seem obvious, there will be some portion of employees who prefer to cash their own checks or who do not have bank accounts. To get around this problem, an organization can either force all employees to accept direct deposit, or do so only with new employees (while existing employees are allowed to continue taking paychecks). If employees are forced to accept direct deposit, the company can either arrange with a local bank to give them bank accounts, or issue the funds to a debit card). Some companies also use raffles and other promotional devices to reward those employees who switch to direct deposit.

Another problem is the cost of this service. A typical charge by the bank is $0.50 for each transfer made, which can add up to a considerable amount if there are many employees and/or many pay periods per year. However, banks also charge a fee to process checks, so the net cost of processing a direct deposit instead of a check is relatively low. Also, this problem can be reduced by shrinking the number of pay periods per year. Also, one must factor in the time lost when employees go to the bank to deposit their checks; this factor alone makes the switch to direct deposit a cost-effective one.

Implementing direct deposit requires the transfer of payment information to the company's bank in the correct direct deposit format, which the bank uses to shift money to employee bank accounts. This information transfer can be accomplished either by purchasing an add-on to a company's in-house payroll software, or by paying extra to a payroll outsourcing company to provide the service; either way, there is an expense associated with starting up the service. If there is some trouble with finding an intermediary to make direct deposits, this can also be done through a Web site that specializes in direct deposits. For example, www.directdeposit.com provides this service, and even has upload links from a number of popular accounting packages, such as ACCPAC, DacEasy, and Great Plains.

Also, some paper-based form of notification should still be sent to employees, so that they know the details of what they have been paid. This means that using direct deposit will not eliminate the steps of printing a deposit advice, stuffing it in an envelope, and distributing it. An alternative is to send remittance information to employees in an electronic format, which is dealt with later in this chapter in Section 6–10 ("How do I automate payroll remittances?").

6-7 HOW DO PAYCARDS COMPARE WITH PAYMENTS BY DIRECT DEPOSIT?

A paycard is a debit card into which employee pay is deposited. The original reason for payroll cards was to provide funds for unbanked employees. This is not a small group, numbering about 30 million in the United States alone, but it does not apply to many employers who have few unbanked employees, and who are probably already paying their employees via direct deposit. However, payroll card features have gradually expanded, making them more competitive with direct deposit. Payroll cards are superior to direct deposit in the following respects:

- *First payment is electronic.* When paying an employee through direct deposit, the first payment to a new employee is with a check, since the bank wants to prenote the first direct deposit transaction. This is not the case for a payroll card, where the first payment can be issued electronically.

- *Data collection.* Direct deposit requires the employer to collect bank routing and account number information from employees, which may be incorrect or difficult to obtain. This is not needed for payroll cards, since the employer creates each account.

- *Account lockdown.* Employees sometimes shut down their bank accounts and forget to inform the company that direct deposit payments must now be sent to a new location. Since the employer controls the payroll card account, employees cannot shut down the account.

- *Termination pay.* Terminated employees can be paid within one day through a payroll card, and there is no need for them to come back to the office to pick up a final check.

- *Information security.* Unlike direct deposit, an employer does not need to retain personal banking information for payroll cards, since it is setting up all accounts.

- *Additional cards.* Some card providers will issue extra payroll cards to other family members, which allows them to withdraw funds in other cities; this keeps the wage earner from paying wire transfer fees to send money to other family members.

- *Pay routing.* Some card providers now allow card users to automatically route incoming funds to personal bank accounts, though there is a one-day delay in the funds transfer.

Payroll cards have the following additional benefits over paychecks:

- *Check cashing time and cost.* There is no need to wait in a bank line, since funds are sent electronically and can be withdrawn at any ATM. There is also no check cashing fee, though there may be an ATM fee.

- *Unclaimed property.* Since there is no check that an employee might not cash, there is no unclaimed property to track.

Do these benefits mean that it is time to convert to payroll cards? Most employees will probably stay with direct deposit, because they are accustomed to this payment approach. However, look for payroll cards to gradually encroach on the direct deposit and paycheck turf over the next few years.

6-8 WHAT ISSUES SHOULD I CONSIDER WHEN SETTING UP A PAYCARD PROGRAM?

Here are some considerations regarding the setup of a paycard program:

- *Withdrawal fees.* Employees should not have to pay a withdrawal fee when they extract funds from an ATM (in some states, it is illegal to require employees to pay such a fee as part of their payroll payments). Accordingly, either have the company pay the ATM fee, or have the paycard supplier specify in its contract which ATMs will offer free services to employees. It is also possible to set up an on-site company-owned ATM, which ensures that ATM fees will be free.

- *Card fees.* Paycard issuers can impose a blizzard of fees, such as fees for an excessive number of paycard transactions, card replacements, a "load fee" (when a card is funded), and a monthly fee. First, be sure than none of these fees are charged to employees, only the company. Second, write limitations into the contract on increases in these fees, as well as the exclusion of as-yet unspecified fees. Also, it is helpful to model the full cost of all fees, using reasonable estimates of card usage, in order to determine which paycard program is the most economical.

- *Bank insurance.* Some paycard issuers are not banks, so funds issued to paycards maintained by them could be lost if the issuer goes out of business. Instead, provide your employees with some extra security by using only paycards issued by a bank, which carries FDIC insurance on funds deposited with it.

6-9 HOW DO I MAKE ELECTRONIC CHILD SUPPORT PAYMENTS?

A larger company likely has been served with a large number of court orders, requiring it to deduct child support payments from the pay of those employees who have been unable or unwilling to make these payments on their own. Though most states still allow these payments to be made by check, an increasing number are requiring electronic payments. The U.S. Department of Health and Human Services maintains a Web page at the following address that itemizes the child support payment status for each state: http://www.acf.hhs.gov/programs/cse/newhire/employer/contacts/eftedi_statecontacts.htm.

Currently, California, Florida, Illinois, Indiana, and Massachusetts require that electronic payments be made, though the trigger point depends on either the size of the business or the number of remittances that it makes each month. The use of electronic payments is expanding, so rather than viewing this requirement as yet another payment exception that will increase the amount of work in the payroll department, consider attempting to install it for all states (except South Carolina, which does not yet accept electronic payments). By going fully electronic, it is much easier to make automated, recurring support payments in a timely manner.

To learn more about the process of setting up recurring electronic child support payments, the National Automated Clearing House Association has posted an excellent "User Guide for Electronic Child Support Payments" online, which is located at http://ecsp.nacha.org/resources.html. The guide provides an overview of how these payments work and why they are required, as well as explaining exactly how to set up the data contents of the Payment Order/Remittance Advice Transaction Set (820) for an electronic data interchange payment.

6-10 HOW DO I AUTOMATE PAYROLL REMITTANCES?

A company may go to a great deal of trouble to install a direct deposit option in order to avoid sending checks to employees, only to find that it must still send a remittance advice, which lists the amounts paid and incidental data such as vacation or sick time earned. Because a company must send its employees some evidence of payment, it is difficult to avoid this distribution step.

If a company has outsourced its payroll processing, it is possible that the supplier offers an Internet-based delivery solution, whereby it notifies employees by e-mail that remittances are available on the supplier's Web site. Employees then use a password to access images of their remittances, which they can print as needed.

If a company processes its payroll in-house, then the solution is the same but becomes more difficult to implement. The payroll system must compile a set of electronic messages after each payroll run, which are then loaded into the company's e-mail system for distribution to employees. Further, the company must post the remittance information on an intranet site, and do so with sufficient security to reasonably ensure that personal information cannot be accessed by an unauthorized person.

A variation on e-mail notifications is to post a schedule of remittance posting dates in the employee manual, so that employees know when to access their accounts on those dates to ascertain pay information. This eliminates the need for an e-mail notification step.

6-11 SHOULD I OUTSOURCE PAYROLL?

A typical in-house payroll department has many concerns. Besides the task of issuing paychecks, it may have to do so for many company locations, where tax rates differ, employees are paid on different dates, and tax deposits must be made to state governments by different means (e.g., direct deposit, bank deposit, or mail) and W-2 forms must be issued to all employees at the beginning of each year. Of all these issues, the one carrying the heaviest price for failure is a government tax deposit— missing such a payment by a single day can carry a large penalty that rapidly accumulates in size. All of these problems and costs can be avoided by handing over some or all portions of the payroll function to an outside supplier. Here are additional reasons for outsourcing payroll:

- *Tax remittances.* A supplier pays all payroll taxes without troubling the company. The savings from avoiding government penalties for late tax payments will in some cases pay for the cost of the payroll supplier!

- *Multilocation processing.* The supplier can usually process payroll for all company locations; several suppliers are based in all major cities, so they can handle paycheck deliveries to nearly any location. Other smaller suppliers get around not having multiple locations by sending checks via overnight delivery services—either approach works very well.

- *Direct deposit.* Suppliers can deposit payments directly into employee bank accounts, which is something that many in-house payroll systems, especially the smaller ones, are incapable of doing.

- *Check stuffing.* The time-consuming task of stuffing checks into envelopes is one that many suppliers will handle, thereby freeing up the internal staff for less mundane work.

- *Reporting.* Suppliers also provide a wide array of reports, usually including a report-writing package that can address any special reporting needs. Once again, many smaller in-house payroll systems lack a report-writing package, so this can be a real benefit.

- *New hire reporting.* Most states require a company to report to them whenever a new employee is hired, so they can determine if that person can be garnished for some outstanding court claim. Suppliers sometimes provide this service for free, since they can easily batch all new hires for all their customers and forward this information electronically to the state governments.

- *Expert staff.* Suppliers are staffed with a large team of experts who know all about the intricacies of the payroll process. They can answer payroll questions over the phone, provide specialized or standard training classes, or come out to company locations for hands-on consulting.

- *Cost.* A study commissioned by ADP and independently conducted by Price-WaterhouseCoopers shows that the total cost of outsourcing can be 30 percent less than the cost of having in-house payroll processing. The wide array of benefits has convinced thousands of companies to switch to an outsourced payroll solution.

- *Backups.* Though not usually considered a significant reason to outsource, suppliers back up their payroll systems at least daily, so there is minimal risk of lost payroll data.

- *Other services.* Some suppliers offer additional services, especially in the areas of benefits administration, 401(k) plans, and unemployment compensation management, that allow a company to outsource not only much of its payroll work, but also a great deal of its human resources functions as well.

Suppliers offering some or all of the functionality just noted include ADP, Inc.; Ceridian; Paychex, Inc.; and PayMaxx, Inc.

However, before jumping on the outsourcing bandwagon, consider a few reasons for *not* using a payroll supplier. One is that outsourcing can be more expensive than an in-house solution in some situations (despite the finding of the ADP study noted above), because the supplier must spend funds to market its services as well as make a profit—two items that an in-house payroll department does not include in its budget. A supplier will usually sell its services to a company by offering an apparently inexpensive deal with a small set of baseline services, and then charge high fees for add-on services, such as direct deposit, check stuffing, early check deliveries, report-writing software, and extra human resources functionality. As long as a company is well aware of these extra fees and budgets them into its initial cost-benefit calculations, there should be no surprises later on, as more supplier services are added and fees continue to mount.

The other main problem with outsourcing is that the payroll database cannot be linked to a company's other computer systems. Since its payroll data is usually located in a mainframe computer at an off-site supplier location, it is difficult to create an interface that will allow for electronic user access to payroll data. The best alternative (though a poor one) is to either keypunch the most important data in a company payroll database from payroll reports printed by the supplier or to download data from the supplier's computer. Because of this missing database linkage, a number of larger companies prefer to keep their payroll-processing work in-house.

In short, there are many good reasons for a company to outsource its payroll function to a qualified supplier. The only companies that should not do so are those that are either highly sensitive to the cost of payroll processing or those that must link their payroll data to other company databases.

6-12 CAN I OUTSOURCE EMPLOYMENT VERIFICATIONS?

Companies with a large number of employees will find that their payroll departments are constantly burdened with employment verification requests for both current and previous employees. This can be a considerable chore, and one that cannot wait, since employees need these verifications in order to qualify for car loans, mortgages, apartment leases, and so on.

A solution to this labor-intensive activity is to have a third party handle all employment verifications with both automated voice response and Internet access. The largest provider of this service is The Work Number, which is a service of the TALX Corporation. Using this service, employers send employee information to The Work Number's central database in either flat file or XML format. Then, when an outside party wants to verify employment information, they enter the employee's Social Security number and the 5-digit employer code (which is accessible on The Work Number's Web site at www.theworknumber.com). If they also want salary information, then the employee must use his PIN number to create a Salary Key Code (either through the Web site or over the phone), which is good for a one-time access of his salary information.

If the outside party is a low-volume user of The Work Number, they will pay $13 for each employment verification and $16 for each salary verification, while a higher-volume user will pay $11 and $14, respectively.

Fees to the employer are remarkably inexpensive. The Work Number charges the employer $0.25 per active employee per year, as well as a fee of between $4 and $5 for each social services verification.

The Work Number gives employers access to webManager, which is an online site on which they can see metrics for verification information, including verifications by the Web versus the phone, and for verifications of active versus inactive employee records.

By taking this approach, employers can eliminate all employment verification work, while also speeding up the verification process for their employees and ensuring that the information provided is as accurate as possible.

6-13 CAN I OUTSOURCE BENEFITS ADMINISTRATION?

Though benefits are normally administered through a separate human resources department, the payroll staff can become involved in two ways: first, the company is so small that both functions are combined into the payroll department; second, the payroll staff must handle benefit-related deductions and the disposition of the deducted funds. The latter situation occurs in nearly all companies, since a growing trend is to shift a greater proportion of benefit costs to employees through deductions. If there are a large number of different benefit providers, this can result in more time being spent on deduction tracking than on timekeeping!

Outsourcing benefits administration to the same company that provides a company's payroll services is an ideal way to improve the situation. For example, by shifting 401(k) withholding to the payroll supplier, the payroll staff no longer has to track the amount of 401(k) funds to transfer to the third-party plan administrator, since this is now done automatically by the payroll supplier. The same approach applies to flexible spending accounts (FSAs), which can be administered by the payroll supplier. An added benefit here is that a company can eliminate a bank account, which is usually kept separately to track withheld FSA funds. Further, employees can usually manage changes to their benefit packages online by accessing Web portals maintained by the payroll supplier, thereby removing benefits data entry from the payroll staff's list of responsibilities. Payroll suppliers that provide benefits services include ADP, Inc.; Ceridian; and PayMaxx, Inc.

Outsourcing benefits administration tends to be a better approach than acquiring software that conducts the same functions. The reason is that one can pay for only those aspects of a benefits outsourcing program that are most necessary, whereas acquiring a commercial software program will result in the acquisition and payment of ongoing maintenance on *all* the functionality of that software, which likely contains a great deal more than is needed.

If there is a downside to the consolidation of many services with a single supplier, it is the company's dependence on that organization for a long period of time, since it can be quite difficult (or at least inconvenient) to shift services away from a supplier once they have been consolidated. Consequently, it is useful to closely examine the payroll and benefits administration supplier's financial status, local operations staff, and operating procedures to ensure that there is a close fit that will likely result in a comfortable long-term relationship.

6-14 HOW MANY PAYROLL CYCLES SHOULD I HAVE?

Many payroll departments are fully occupied with processing some kind of payroll every week, and possibly even several times in one week. The latter situation occurs when different groups of employees are paid for different time periods. For example, hourly employees may be paid every week, while salaried employees may be paid twice a month. Processing multiple payroll cycles eats up most of the free time of the payroll staff, leaving it with little room for cleaning up paperwork or researching improvements to its basic operations.

All of the various payroll cycles should be consolidated into a single, company-wide payroll cycle. By doing so, the payroll staff no longer has to spend extra time on additional payroll processing, nor does it have to worry about the different pay rules that may apply to each processing period—instead, everyone is treated exactly the same. To make payroll processing even more efficient, it is useful to lengthen the payroll cycles. For example, a payroll department that processes weekly payrolls must run the payroll 52 times a year, whereas one that processes monthly payrolls only does so 12 times per year, which eliminates 75 percent of the processing that the first department must handle. These changes represent an enormous reduction in the payroll-processing time the payroll staff requires.

Any changes to the payroll cycles may be met with opposition by the organization's employees. The primary complaint is that the employees have structured their spending habits around the timing of the old pay system and that any change will not give them enough cash to continue those habits. For example, employees who currently receive a paycheck every week may have a great deal of difficulty in adjusting their spending to a paycheck that arrives only once a month. If a company were to switch from a short to a longer pay cycle, it is extremely likely that the payroll staff will be deluged with requests for pay advances well before the next paycheck is due for release, which will require a large amount of payroll staff time to handle. To overcome this problem, consider increasing pay cycles incrementally, perhaps to twice a month or once every two weeks, and also tell employees that pay advances will be granted for a limited transition period. By making these incremental changes, one can reduce the associated amount of employee discontent.

Review the prospective change with the rest of the management team to make sure that it is acceptable to them. They must buy into the need for the change, because their employees will also be impacted by it, and they will receive complaints about it. This best practice requires a long lead time to implement, as well as multiple notifications to the staff about its timing and impact on them. It is also useful to go over the granting of payroll advances with the payroll staff, so that they are prepared for the likely surge in requests for advances.

6-15 HOW CAN I REDUCE THE NUMBER OF EMPLOYEE PAYROLL–RELATED INQUIRIES?

Payroll departments spend a great deal of time answering employee questions about their pay. According to some surveys, this involves at least one-third of all department time! Though most of the questions are simple enough to answer, when they are multiplied by the number of employees in the company it is easy to see how the payroll staff can spend so much time just responding to queries.

If the payroll staff could compile a list of the most commonly asked questions by employees, it would not be an especially long list—perhaps just 10 or 20 questions for a basic payroll system, and maybe twice that amount if they also handle benefits through the payroll system. Given the high proportion of questions dealing with a limited number of issues, this is an ideal area in which to create answers to frequently asked questions (FAQs) and post them on a company intranet site. Employees can then be directed to the FAQs list, and only then asked to address the payroll staff regarding more complex questions. Sample FAQs are as follows:

- **If I am on direct deposit, at what time of day on payday will my pay be deposited in my checking account?**
  Answer: Your pay will be available in your checking account as of 8 A.M. on payday.
- **If payday falls on a weekend, when am I paid?**
  Answer: If payday falls on a weekend, you will be paid as of the first business day prior to that weekend.
- **Can I get an advance on my next paycheck?**
  Answer: No. The company policy is never to issue pay advances under any circumstances.

- **If I resign from the company, when will I be paid my final paycheck?**
  Answer: If you voluntarily leave the company, you will be paid as part of the next regularly scheduled payroll.

- **How much unused vacation time can I roll forward into next year?**
  Answer: You can roll 40 hours forward. For exceptional cases, you must apply to your department manager for a waiver.

Though these FAQs can be also listed in the employee manual, employees do not always refer to that document. By also presenting them on the intranet site (which employee tend to access more frequently, especially if it is a rich, multifunction site), there is a much greater chance that employees will access the FAQs instead of the payroll staff.

Chapter 7

Inventory Decisions

If a company has invested in inventory, the accountant faces a number of key decisions. The issue of most immediate importance is how to gain assurance regarding the accuracy of the inventory, so the inventory valuation can be included in the financial statements. Another accounting concern, though one that is not so immediate, is how to develop a system for reliably locating and dealing with obsolete inventory. This is needed to ensure that inventory is not incorrectly overvalued at year-end, when it will presumably be audited. Once identified, the obsolete inventory must be dispositioned in the most profitable manner possible. Along the same lines, the accountant must set up a lower of cost or market procedure to ensure that inventory items are not overvalued in relation to their current market value.

There are also several systems-related issues to consider. The accountant must determine what type of inventory costing system to use, the controls needed to ensure that costs are correctly recorded, and a set of measurements to monitor inventory levels. Finally, the accountant may become involved in such inventory management issues as the determination of inventory service levels, shifting inventory ownership to suppliers, and the mitigation of price protection costs. This chapter provides answers to all of these key questions. The following table itemizes the section number in which the answers to each question can be found:

Section	Decision
7-1	How do I manage inventory accuracy?
7-2	How do I identify obsolete inventory?
7-3	How do I dispose of obsolete inventory?
7-4	How do I set up a lower of cost or market system?
7-5	Which inventory costing system should I use?
7-6	Which inventory controls should I install?
7-7	What types of performance measurements should I use?
7-8	How do I maintain service levels with low inventory?
7-9	Should I shift inventory ownership to suppliers?
7-10	How do I avoid price protection costs?

7-1 HOW DO I MANAGE INVENTORY ACCURACY?

A physical inventory count can be eliminated if accurate perpetual inventory records are available. Many steps are required to implement such a system, requiring considerable effort. The controller should evaluate a company's resources prior to embarking on this process to ensure that they are sufficient to set up and maintain this system. This section contains a sequential listing of the steps that must be completed before an accurate system is achieved. This is a difficult implementation to shortcut, for missing any of the following steps will have an impact on the accuracy of the completed system. If a company skips a few steps, it will likely not achieve the requisite high levels of accuracy that it wants, and ends up having to backtrack and complete those steps at a later date. Consequently, a company should sequentially complete all of the following steps to implement a successful inventory tracking system:

1. *Select and install inventory tracking software.* The primary requirements for this software are:
   - *Track transactions.* The software should list the frequency of product usage, which allows the materials manager to determine what inventory quantities should be changed, as well as to determine which items are obsolete.
   - *Update records immediately.* The inventory data must always be up-to-date, because production planners must know what is in stock, while cycle counters require access to accurate data. Batch updating of the system is not acceptable.
   - *Report inventory records by location.* Cycle counters need inventory records that are sorted by location in order to more efficiently locate and count the inventory.
2. *Test inventory tracking software.* Create a set of typical records in the new software, and perform a series of transactions to ensure that the software functions properly. In addition, create a large number of records and perform the transactions again, to see if the response time of the system drops significantly. If the software appears to function properly, continue to the next step. Otherwise, fix the problems with the software supplier's assistance, or acquire a different software package.
3. *Revise the rack layout.* It is much easier to move racks prior to installing a perpetual inventory system, because no inventory locations must be changed in the computer system. Create aisles that are wide enough for forklift operation if this is needed for larger storage items, and cluster small parts racks together for easier parts picking. The services of a consultant are useful for arriving at the optimum warehouse configuration.
4. *Create rack locations.* A typical rack location is, for example, A-01-B-01. This means that this location code is located in Aisle A, Rack 1. Within Rack 1, it is located on Level B (numbered from the bottom to the top). Within Level B, it is located in Partition 1. Many companies skip the use of partitions, on the grounds that an aisle-rack-level numbering system will get a stock picker to within a few feet of an inventory item.

   As one progresses down an aisle, the rack numbers should progress in ascending sequence, with the odd rack numbers on the left and the even numbers on the right. Thus, the first rack on the left side of aisle D is D-01, the first rack on the right is D-02, the second rack on the left is D-03, and so on. This layout allows a stock picker to move down the center of the aisle, efficiently pulling items from stock based on sequential location codes.

5. *Lock the warehouse.* One of the main causes of record inaccuracy is removal of items from the warehouse by outside staff. To stop this removal, all entrances to the warehouse must be locked. Only warehouse personnel should be allowed access to it. All other personnel entering the warehouse should be accompanied by a member of the warehouse staff to prevent the removal of inventory.

6. *Consolidate parts.* To reduce the labor of counting the same item in multiple locations, group common parts into one place. This is not a one-shot process, for it is difficult to combine parts when there are thousands of them scattered throughout the warehouse. Expect to repeat this step at intervals, especially when entering location codes in the computer, when it tells you that the part has already been entered for a different location!

7. *Assign part numbers.* Have several experienced personnel verify all part numbers. A mislabeled part is as useless as a missing part, since the computer database will not show that it exists. Mislabeled parts also affect the inventory cost; for example, a mislabeled engine is more expensive than the item represented by its incorrect part number, which may identify it as (for example) a spark plug.

8. *Verify units of measure.* Have several experienced people verify all units of measure. Unless the software allows multiple units of measure to be used, the entire organization must adhere to one unit of measure for each item. For example, the warehouse may desire tape to be counted in rolls, but the engineering department had rather create bills of materials with tape measured in inches instead of fractions of rolls. If someone goes into the inventory database to change the unit of measure to suit his or her needs, this will also alter the extended cost of the inventory; for example, when 10 rolls of tape with an extended cost of $10 is altered so that it becomes 10 inches of tape, the cost will drop to a few pennies, even though there are still 10 rolls on the shelf. Consequently, not only must the units of measure be accurate, but the file that stores this information must be kept off limits.

9. *Pack the parts.* Pack parts into containers, seal the containers, and label them with the part number, unit of measure, and total quantity stored inside. Leave a few parts free for ready use. Open containers only when additional stock is needed. This method allows cycle counters to rapidly verify inventory balances.

10. *Count items.* Count items when there is no significant activity in the warehouse, such as during a weekend. Elaborate cross-checking of the counts, as would be done during a year-end physical inventory count, is not necessary. It is more important to have the perpetual inventory system operational before the warehouse activity increases again; any errors in the data will quickly be detected

during cycle counts and flushed out of the database. The initial counts must include a review of the part number, location, and quantity.

11. *Train the warehouse staff.* The warehouse staff should receive software training immediately before using the system, so that they do not forget how to operate the software. Enter a set of test records into the software, and have the staff simulate all common inventory transactions, such as receipts, picks, and cycle count adjustments.

12. *Enter data into the computer.* Have an experienced data entry person input the location, part number, and quantity into the computer. Once the data has been input, another person should cross-check the entered data against the original data for errors.

13. *Quick-check the data.* Scan the data for errors. If all part numbers have the same number of digits, then look for items that are too long or too short. Review location codes to see if inventory is stored in nonexistent racks. Look for units of measure that do not match the part being described. For example, is it logical to have a pint of steel in stock? Also, if item costs are available, print a list of extended costs. Excessive costs typically point to incorrect units of measure. For example, a cost of $1 per box of nails will become $500 in the inventory report if nails are incorrectly listed as individual units. All of these steps help to spot the most obvious inventory errors.

14. *Initiate cycle counts.* In brief, print out a portion of the inventory list, sorted by location. Using this report, have the warehouse staff count blocks of the inventory on a continuous basis. They should look for accurate part numbers, units of measure, locations, and quantities. The counts should concentrate on high-value or high-use items, though the entire stock should be reviewed regularly. The most important part of this step is to examine why mistakes occur. If a cycle counter finds an error, its cause must be investigated and then corrected, so that the mistake will not occur again. It is also useful to assign specific aisles to cycle counters, which tends to make them more familiar with their assigned inventory and the problems causing specific transactional errors.

The standard way to determine which inventory should be cycle counted is to count the most expensive items the most frequently. Accountants recommend this approach, because it ensures the accuracy of the most expensive items in stock, which gives them some reasonable assurance that the inventory value they record in the financial statements is approximately correct.

The problem with this approach is that the accuracy of low-cost items is considered less important—even though the absence of those items could potentially keep an order from shipping, which negatively impacts revenue.

The solution is to base cycle counts on the frequency of item usage, which means that an item that is used continually is counted the most frequently. This approach still satisfies accountants, because a high-cost item that does not move much will still be accurate with just a few counts per year, since very little can possibly happen to it if it just sits on a shelf. Conversely, an item that is constantly cycling in and out of the warehouse will be counted a great deal, which will hopefully ensure a high level of accuracy and therefore assist in avoiding stockouts that could halt shipments.

Creating a cycle count sample under a frequency-of-usage approach will require a custom report from a materials planning system. To do so, accumulate the number of putaways and picks per stock keeping unit on a rolling basis over the past few months (possibly up to a year, if inventory turnover levels are low), and then create a report that is sorted in declining order by volume of total putaways and picks. This report can be used to manually select higher-frequency items for more frequent counts.

However, this approach also requires recordkeeping to ensure that high-frequency items are indeed counted more regularly than low-frequency items. An alternative is to rearrange inventory so that higher-frequency items are stored in specific aisle areas, for which an average usage frequency is calculated; then count every item in each aisle area during a single count, and track the frequency of cycle counts for the entire block of inventory. This results in much less recordkeeping.

15. *Initiate inventory audits.* The inventory should be audited frequently, perhaps as much as once a week. This allows the accountant to track changes in the inventory accuracy level and initiate changes if the accuracy drops below acceptable levels. In addition, frequent audits are an indirect means of telling the staff that inventory accuracy is important, and must be maintained. The minimum acceptable accuracy level is 95 percent, with an error being a mistaken part number, unit of measure, quantity, or location. This accuracy level is needed to ensure accurate inventory costing, as well as to assist the materials department in planning future inventory purchases. In addition, establish a tolerance level when calculating the inventory accuracy. For example, if the computer record of a box of screws yields a quantity of 100 and the actual count results in 105 screws, then the record is accurate if the tolerance is at least 5 percent, but inaccurate if the tolerance is reduced to 1 percent. The maximum allowable tolerance should be no higher than 5 percent, with tighter tolerances being used for high-value or high-use items.

16. *Post results.* Inventory accuracy is a team project, and the warehouse staff feels more involved if the audit results are posted against the results of previous audits. Accuracy percentages should be broken out for the counting area assigned to each cycle counter, so that everyone can see who is doing the best job of reviewing and correcting inventory counts.

17. *Reward the staff.* Accurate inventories save a company thousands of dollars in many ways. This makes it cost-effective to encourage the staff to maintain and improve the accuracy level with periodic bonuses that are based on the attainment of higher levels of accuracy with tighter tolerances. Using rewards results in a significant improvement in inventory record accuracy.

The long list of requirements to fulfill before achieving an accurate perpetual inventory system makes it clear that this is not a project that yields immediate results. Unless the inventory is very small or the conversion project is heavily staffed, it is likely that a company faces many months of work before it arrives at the nirvana of an extremely accurate inventory. Consequently, one should set expectations with management that project completion is a considerable way down the road, and that only by making a major investment of time and resources will it be completed.

Despite the major effort needed to implement this system, it is still absolutely necessary as the first step in creating a closing process where there is no need to spend days determining the proper inventory valuation.

7-2 HOW DO I IDENTIFY OBSOLETE INVENTORY?

The materials review board (MRB) is responsible for evaluating all obsolete inventory, and determining the most appropriate disposition for each item. The MRB is composed of representatives from every department having any interaction with inventory issues: accounting, engineering, logistics, and production. For example, the engineering staff may need to retain some items that they are planning to incorporate into a new design, while the logistics staff may know that it is impossible to obtain a rare part, and so prefer to hold onto the few items left in stock for service parts use.

The simplest long-term way to find obsolete inventory without the assistance of a computer system is to leave the physical inventory count tags on all inventory items following completion of the annual physical count. The tags taped to any items used during the subsequent year will be thrown away at the time of use, leaving only the oldest unused items still tagged by the end of the year. One can then tour the warehouse and discuss with the MRB each of these items to see if an obsolescence reserve should be created for them. However, tags can fall off or be ripped off inventory items, especially if there is a high level of traffic in nearby bins. Though extra taping will reduce this issue, it is likely that some tag loss will occur over time.

Even a rudimentary computerized inventory tracking system is likely to record the last date on which a specific part number was removed from the warehouse for production or sale. If so, it is an easy matter to use a report writer to extract and sort this information, resulting in a report listing all inventory, starting with those products with the oldest "last used" date. By sorting the report with the oldest last usage date listed first, one can readily arrive at a sort list of items requiring further investigation for potential obsolescence. However, this approach does not yield sufficient proof that an item will never be used again, since it may be an essential component of an item that has not been scheduled for production in some time, or a service part for which demand is low.

Exhibit 7.1   Inventory Obsolescence Review Report

Description	Item No.	Location	Quantity on Hand	Last Year Usage	Planned Usage	Extended Cost
Subwoofer case	0421	A-04-C	872	520	180	$9,053
Speaker case	1098	A-06-D	148	240	120	1,020
Subwoofer	3421	D-12-A	293	14	0	24,724
Circuit board	3600	B-01-A	500	5,090	1,580	2,500
Speaker, bass	4280	C-10-C	621	2,480	578	49,200
Speaker bracket	5391	C-10-C	14	0	0	92
Wall bracket	5080	B-03-B	400	0	120	2,800
Gold connection	6233	C-04-A	3,025	8,042	5,900	9,725
Tweeter	7552	C-05-B	725	6,740	2,040	5,630

A more advanced version of the "last used" report is shown in Exhibit 7.1. It compares total inventory withdrawals against the amount on hand, which by itself may be sufficient information to conduct an obsolescence review. It also lists planned usage, which calls for information from a material requirements planning system, and which informs one of any upcoming requirements that might keep the MRB from otherwise disposing of an inventory item. An extended cost for each item is also listed, in order to give report users some idea of the write-off that might occur if an item is declared obsolete. In the exhibit, the subwoofer, speaker bracket, and wall bracket appear to be obsolete based on prior usage, but the planned use of more wall brackets would keep that item from being disposed of.

If a computer system includes a bill of materials, there is a strong likelihood that it also generates a "where used" report, listing all the bills of materials for which an inventory item is used. If there is no "where used" listed on the report for an item, it is likely that a part is no longer needed. This report is most effective if bills of materials are removed from the computer system or deactivated as soon as products are withdrawn from the market; this more clearly reveals those inventory items that are no longer needed.

An additional approach for determining whether a part is obsolete is reviewing engineering change orders. These documents show those parts being replaced by different ones, as well as when the changeover is scheduled to take place. One can then search the inventory database to see how many of the parts being replaced are still in stock, which can then be totaled, yielding another variation on the amount of obsolete inventory on hand.

A final source of information is the preceding period's obsolete inventory report. Even the best MRB will sometimes fail to dispose of acknowledged obsolete items. The accounting staff should keep track of these items and continue to notify management of those for which there is no disposition activity.

7-3 HOW DO I DISPOSE OF OBSOLETE INVENTORY?

This section outlines a number of disposition possibilities, beginning with full-price sales and moving down through options having progressively lower returns.

In some situations, one can recover nearly the entire cost of excess items by asking the service department to sell them to existing customers as replacement parts. This approach is especially useful when the excess items are for specialized parts that customers are unlikely to obtain elsewhere, since these sales can be presented to customers as valuable replacements that may not be available for much longer. Conversely, this approach is least useful for commodity items or those subject to rapid obsolescence or having a short shelf life.

It is possible that some parts should be kept on hand for a number of years, to be sold or given away as warranty replacements. This will reduce the amount of obsolescence expense, and also keeps the company from having to procure or remanufacture parts at a later date in order to meet service/repair obligations. The amount of inventory to be held in this service/repair category can be roughly calculated based on the company's experience with similar products, or with the current product if it has been sold for a sufficiently long period. Any additional inventory on hand exceeding the total amount of anticipated service/repair parts can then be disposed of. Of particular interest is the time period over which management anticipates storing parts in the service/repair category. There should be some period over which the company has historically found that there is some requirement for parts, such as 5 or 10 years. Once this predetermined period has ended, a flag in the product master file should trigger a message indicating that the remaining parts can be eliminated. Prior to doing so, management should review recent transactional experience to see if the service/repair period should be extended, or if it is now safe to eliminate the remaining stock.

Another possibility is to return the goods to the original supplier. Doing so will likely result in a restocking fee of 15 to 20 percent, which is still a bargain for otherwise useless goods. Rather than buying back parts for cash, many suppliers will only issue a credit against future purchases. This option becomes less likely if the company has owned the goods for a very long time, since the supplier may no longer have a need for them or no longer stocks them at all. Of course, this approach fails if the supplier will only issue a credit and the company has no need for other parts sold by the supplier.

Some types of inventory are categorized by suppliers as non-cancelable and non-returnable (NCNR), usually because the inventory is so customized that they cannot expect to resell it elsewhere. If so, the goods will be difficult to disposition, so it is best to install a variety of up-front procedures to ensure that less NCNR inventory is ordered or left unused by the company, thereby reducing the amount of future write-offs. Here are some options to consider:

- Designate a field in the inventory item master file as the NCNR flag, and use it to designate which inventory items are categorized as NCNR by suppliers.

- Using the NCNR flag, modify the corporate material requirements planning system to forward all automatically generated purchase orders for these items to the materials planning staff, who verifies that they are really needed.

- Use the NCNR flag to create reports showing any NCNR inventory that will no longer be usable when an engineering change order is activated, when a bill of materials is modified for some other reason, or when a customer cancels a sales order.

- Use the NCNR flag to report on any scheduled production requiring NCNR items that is based on a forecast, rather than actual demand. When management realize the extra risk associated with this type of inventory, they tend to reduce the size of their forecasts.

- Finally, the NCNR status of inventory will be altered by suppliers from time to time, so be sure to update the NCNR flags in the item master file at least once a year.

It may be possible to sell goods online through an auction service. Though the best-known is eBay, there are other sites designed exclusively for the disposition of excess goods, such as www.salvagesale.com. These sites are more proactive in maintaining contact with potential buyers within specific commodity categories, and so can sometimes generate higher resale prices.

A poor way to sell off excess inventory to salvage contractors is to allow them to pick over the items for sale, only selecting those items they are certain to make a profit on. By doing so, the bulk of the excess inventory will still be parked in the warehouse when the contractors are gone. Instead, divide the inventory into batches, each one containing some items of value, which a salvage contractor must purchase in total in order to obtain that subset of items he really wants. Then have the contractors bid on each batch. Though the total amount of funds realized may not be much higher than would have been the case if the contractors had cherry-picked the inventory, they will take on the burden of removing the inventory from the warehouse, thereby allowing the company to avoid disposal expenses.

There are some instances where a company can donate excess inventory to a charity. By doing so, it can claim a tax deduction for the book value of the donated items. This will not generate any cash flow if the company has no reportable income, though the deduction can contribute to a net operating loss carryforward that can be carried into a different tax reporting year. If this approach looks viable, request a copy of nonprofit status from the receiving entity, proving that it has been granted nonprofit status under section 501(c)(3) of the Internal Revenue Service tax code.

One of the major channels for inventory donations is the National Association for the Exchange of Industrial Resources (www.naeir.org), which accepts new items from donors and distributes them to nonprofits and schools. Here is how the process works:

1. Create a list of items to donate, with a description, quantity, and retail value.
2. Fax the list to NAEIR at 309–343–0862.
3. NAEIR will send back an acceptance letter if they can use the inventory. If they cannot use it, do not ship it.

4. Ship the accepted items to NAEIR (the sender pays the freight).
5. NAEIR issues documentation needed for a tax claim. For tax purposes, a donating company can deduct its cost, plus half the difference between its cost and the fair market value, with a maximum deduction of twice its cost.

On the other end of the transaction, nonprofits and schools pay a $595 annual fee to NAEIR. In exchange, they receive a catalog of what NAEIR has in stock five times a year. NAEIR allocates inventory from each catalog on a weekly basis, over a 10-week period (after which they issue a new catalog). They do this so that their stocks of high-demand items are not taken as soon as each new catalog is issued. Each member can request items from the catalog, but there is no assurance that there will be enough inventory to go around.

Because NAEIR accepts only certain types of inventory that its members need, this is not a catchall avenue for the disposition of inventory, and so should be considered only one of a variety of inventory disposition options.

Finally, even if there is no hope of obtaining any form of compensation for obsolete goods, strongly consider throwing them in the dumpster. By doing so, there will be more storage space in the warehouse, allowing one to allocate the space to other uses. Further, the amount of inventory insurance coverage will be less, resulting in a smaller annual insurance premium. Depending on the local tax jurisdiction, one can also avoid paying a property tax on the inventory that has been disposed of. Further, one can also reduce the number of inventory items to track in the warehouse database, which can lead to a reduction in the number of cycle-counting hours required per day to review the entire inventory on a recurring basis.

7-4 HOW DO I SET UP A LOWER OF COST OR MARKET SYSTEM?

The lower of cost or market (LCM) rule states that the cost of inventory cannot be recorded higher than its replacement cost on the open market; the replacement cost is bounded at the high end by its eventual selling price, less costs of disposal, nor can it be recorded lower than that price, less a normal profit percentage. The concept is best demonstrated with the four scenarios listed in the following example:

Item	Selling Price	Completion/ Selling – Cost	Upper Price = Boundary	Normal – Profit	Lower Price = Boundary	Existing Inventory Cost	Replacement Cost (1)	Market Value (2)	LCM
A	$ 15.00	$ 4.00	$ 11.00	$ 2.20	$ 8.80	$ 8.00	$ 12.50	$ 11.00	$ 8.00
B	40.15	6.00	34.15	5.75	28.40	35.00	34.50	34.15	34.15
C	20.00	6.50	13.50	3.00	10.50	17.00	12.00	12.00	12.00
D	10.50	2.35	8.15	2.25	5.90	8.00	5.25	5.90	5.90

(1) The cost at which an inventory item could be purchased on the open market.
(2) Replacement cost, bracketed by the upper and lower price boundaries.

In the example, the numbers in the first six columns are used to derive the upper and lower boundaries of the market values that will be used for the lower of cost or market calculation. By subtracting the completion and selling costs from each product's selling price, we establish the upper price boundary (in bold) of the market cost calculation. By then subtracting the normal profit from the upper cost boundary of each product, we establish the lower price boundary. Using this information, the LCM calculation for each of the listed products is as follows:

- *Product A, replacement cost higher than existing inventory cost.* The market price cannot be higher than the upper boundary of $11.00, which is still higher than the existing inventory cost of $8.00. Thus, the LCM is the same as the existing inventory cost.

- *Product B, replacement cost lower than existing inventory cost, but higher than upper price boundary.* The replacement cost of $34.50 exceeds the upper price boundary of $34.15, so the market value is designated at $34.15. This is lower than the existing inventory cost, so the LCM becomes $34.15.

- *Product C, replacement cost lower than existing inventory cost, and within price boundaries.* The replacement cost of $12.00 is within the upper and lower price boundaries, and so is used as the market value. This is lower than the existing inventory cost of $17.00, so the LCM becomes $12.00.

- *Product D, replacement cost lower than existing inventory cost, but lower than lower price boundary.* The replacement cost of $5.25 is below the lower price boundary of $5.90, so the market value is designated as $5.90. This is lower than the existing inventory cost of $8.00, so the LCM becomes $5.90.

The lower of cost or market calculation is likely to be conducted at such infrequent intervals that the inventory accountant forgets how the calculation was made in the past. Thus, there is a considerable risk that the calculations will be conducted differently each time, yielding inconsistent results. To avoid this problem, consider including in the accounting procedures manual a clear definition of the calculation to be followed. A sample procedure is shown in Exhibit 7.2.

7-5 WHICH INVENTORY COSTING SYSTEM SHOULD I USE?

There is no single inventory costing system that will work perfectly for every company, so this section presents the essentials of a number of costing systems, from which the reader can choose the most appropriate system. When making a selection, a guiding principle is that the costing system used should be as simple to calculate and easy to maintain as possible. The costing systems are as follows:

Exhibit 7.2   Lower of Cost or Market Procedure:

Use this procedure to periodically adjust the inventory valuation for those items whose market value has dropped below their recorded cost.

1. Export the extended inventory valuation report to an electronic spreadsheet. Sort it by declining extended dollar cost, and delete the 80% of inventory items that do not comprise the top 20% of inventory valuation. Sort the remaining 20% of inventory items by either part number or item description. Print the report.
2. Send a copy of the report to the materials manager, with instructions to compare unit costs for each item on the list to market prices, and be sure to mutually agree upon a due date for completion of the review.
3. When the materials management staff has completed its review, meet with the materials manager to go over its results and discuss any major adjustments. Have the materials management staff write down the valuation of selected items in the inventory database whose cost exceeds their market value.
4. Have the accounting staff expense the value of the write-down in the accounting records.
5. Write a memo detailing the results of the lower of cost or market calculation. Attach one copy to the journal entry used to write down the valuation, and issue another copy to the materials manager.

THE FIRST-IN, FIRST-OUT (FIFO) METHOD

A computer manufacturer knows that the component parts it purchases are subject to extremely rapid rates of obsolescence, sometimes rendering a part worthless in a month or two. Accordingly, it will be sure to use up the oldest items in stock first, rather than running the risk of scrapping them a short way into the future. For this type of environment, the first-in first-out (FIFO) method is the ideal way to deal with the flow of costs. This method assumes that the oldest parts in stock are always used first, which means that their associated old costs are used first, as well.

The concept is best illustrated with an example, which we show in Exhibit 7.3. In the first row, we create a single layer of inventory that results in 50 units of inventory, at a per-unit cost of $10.00. So far, the extended cost of the inventory is the same as we saw under the LIFO, but that will change as we proceed to the second row of data. In this row, we have monthly inventory usage of 350 units, which FIFO assumes will use the entire stock of 50 inventory units that were left over at the end of the preceding month, as well as 300 units that were purchased in the current month. This wipes out the first layer of inventory, leaving us with a single new layer that is composed of 700 units at a cost of $9.58 per unit. In the third row, there is 400 units of usage, which again comes from the first inventory layer, shrinking it down to just 300 units. However, since extra stock was purchased in the same period, we now have an extra inventory layer that is comprised of 250 units, at a cost of $10.65 per unit. The rest of the exhibit proceeds using the same FIFO layering assumptions.

There are several factors to consider before implementing a FIFO costing system. They are as follows:

- *Fewer inventory layers.* The FIFO system generally results in fewer layers of inventory costs in the inventory database than would a last-in, first-out (LIFO) system, because a LIFO system will leave some layers of costs completely untouched for long time periods if inventory levels do not drop, whereas a FIFO system will continually clear out old layers of costs, so that multiple costing layers do not have a chance to accumulate.

- *Reduces taxes payable in periods of declining costs.* Though it is very unusual to see declining inventory costs, it sometimes occurs in industries where there is either ferocious price competition among suppliers, or else extremely high rates of innovation that in turn lead to cost reductions. In such cases, using the earliest costs first will result in the immediate recognition of the highest possible expense, which reduces the reported profit level and therefore reduces taxes payable.

- *Shows higher profits in periods of rising costs.* Since it charges off the earliest costs first, any very recent increase in costs will be stored in inventory, rather than being immediately recognized. This will result in higher levels of reported profits, though the attendant income tax liability will also be higher.

- *Less risk of outdated costs in inventory.* Because old costs are used first in a FIFO system, there is no way for old and outdated costs to accumulate in inventory. This prevents the management group from having to worry about the adverse impact of inventory reductions on reported levels of profit, either with excessively high or low charges to the cost of goods sold. This avoids the dilemma noted earlier for LIFO, where just-in-time systems may not be implemented if the result will be a dramatically different cost of goods sold.

In short, the FIFO cost layering system tends to result in the storage of the most recently incurred costs in inventory and higher levels of reported profits. It is most useful for those companies whose main concern is reporting high profits rather reducing income taxes.

THE LAST-IN, FIRST-OUT (LIFO) METHOD

In a supermarket, the shelves are stocked several rows deep with products. A shopper will walk by and pick products from the front row. If the stocking person is lazy, he will then add products to the front row locations from which products were just taken, rather than shifting the oldest products to the front row and putting new ones in the back. This concept of always taking the newest products first is called last-in first-out (LIFO). The following factors must be considered before implementing a LIFO system:

Exhibit 7.3 FIFO Costing Part Number BK0043

Column 1	Column 2	Column 3	Column 4	Column 5	Column 6	Column 7	Column 8	Column 9
Date Purchased	Quantity Purchased	Cost Per Unit	Monthly Usage	Net Inventory Remaining	Cost of 1st Inventory Layer	Cost of 2nd Inventory Layer	Cost of 3rd Inventory Layer	Extended Inventory Cost
05/03/07	500	$10.00	450	50	$(50 \times \$10.00)$	—	—	$500
06/04/07	1,000	$9.58	350	700	$(700 \times \$9.58)$	—	—	$6,706
07/11/07	250	$10.65	400	550	$(300 \times \$9.58)$	$(250 \times \$10.65)$	—	$5,537
08/01/07	475	$10.25	350	675	$(200 \times \$10.65)$	$(475 \times \$10.25)$	—	$6,999
08/30/07	375	$10.40	400	650	$(275 \times \$10.40)$	$(375 \times \$10.40)$	—	$6,760
09/09/07	850	$9.50	700	800	$(800 \times \$9.50)$	—	—	$7,600
12/12/07	700	$9.75	900	600	$(600 \times \$9.75)$	—	—	$5,850
02/08/08	650	$9.85	800	450	$(450 \times \$9.85)$	—	—	$4,433
05/07/08	200	$10.80	0	650	$(450 \times \$9.85)$	$(200 \times \$10.80)$	—	$6,593
09/23/08	600	$9.85	750	500	$(500 \times \$9.85)$	—	—	$4,925

173

- *Many layers.* The LIFO cost flow approach can result in a large number of inventory layers. Though this is not important when a computerized accounting system is used that will automatically track a large number of such layers, it can be burdensome if the cost layers are manually tracked.

- *Alters the inventory valuation.* If there are significant changes in product costs over time, the earliest inventory layers may contain costs that are wildly different from market conditions in the current period, which could result in the recognition of unusually high or low costs if these cost layers are ever accessed. Also, LIFO costs can never be reduced to the lower of cost or market, thereby perpetuating any unusually high inventory values in the various inventory layers.

- *Interferes with the implementation of just-in-time systems.* As noted in the previous bullet point, clearing out the final cost layers of a LIFO system can result in unusual cost of goods sold figures. If these results will cause a significant skewing of reported profitability, company management may be put in the unusual position of opposing the implementation of advanced manufacturing concepts, such as just-in-time, that reduce or eliminate inventory levels.

- *Reduces taxes payable in periods of rising costs.* In an inflationary environment, costs that are charged off to the cost of goods sold as soon as they are incurred will result in a higher cost of goods sold and a lower level of profitability, which in turn results in a lower tax liability. This is the principle reason why LIFO is used by most companies.

- *Requires consistent usage for all reporting.* Under IRS rules, if a company uses LIFO to value its inventory for tax reporting purposes, then it must do the same for its external financial reports. The result of this rule is that a company cannot report lower earnings for tax purposes and higher earnings for all other purposes by using an alternative inventory valuation method. However, it is still possible to mention what profits would have been if some other method had been used, but only in the form of a footnote appended to the financial statements. If financial reports are generated only for internal management consumption, then any valuation method may be used.

In short, LIFO is used primarily for reducing a company's income tax liability. This single focus can cause problems, such as too many cost layers, an excessively low inventory valuation, and a fear of inventory reductions due to the recognition of inventory cost layers that may contain very low per-unit costs, which will result in high levels of recognized profit and therefore a higher tax liability. Given these issues, one should carefully consider the utility of tax avoidance before implementing a LIFO cost layering system.

As an example, The Magic Pen Company has made 10 purchases, which are itemized in Exhibit 7.4. In the exhibit, the company has purchased 500 units of a product with part number BK0043 on May 3, 2007 (as noted in the first row of data), and uses 450 units during that month, leaving the company with 50 units. These 50 units were all purchased at a cost of $10.00 each, so they are itemized in Column 6 as the first layer of inventory costs for this product. In the next row of

Exhibit 7.4 LIFO Costing Part Number BK0043

Column 1	Column 2	Column 3	Column 4	Column 5	Column 6	Column 7	Column 8	Column 9	Column 10
Date Purchased	Quantity Purchased	Cost Per Unit	Monthly Usage	Net Inventory Remaining	Cost of 1st Inventory Layer	Cost of 2nd Inventory Layer	Cost of 3rd Inventory Layer	Cost of 4th Inventory Layer	Extended Inventory Cost
05/03/07	500	$10.00	450	50	(50×$10.00)	—	—	—	$500
06/04/07	1,000	$9.58	350	700	(50×$10.00)	(650×$9.58)	—	—	$6,727
07/11/07	250	$10.65	400	550	(50×$10.00)	(500×$9.58)	—	—	$5,290
08/01/07	475	$10.25	350	675	(50×$10.00)	(500×$9.58)	(125×$10.25)	—	$6,571
08/30/07	375	$10.40	400	650	(50×$10.00)	(500×$9.58)	(100×$10.25)	—	$6,315
09/09/07	850	$9.50	700	800	(50×$10.00)	(500×$9.58)	(100×$10.25)	(150×$9.50)	$7,740
12/12/07	700	$9.75	900	600	(50×$10.00)	(500×$9.58)	(50×$9.58)	—	$5,769
02/08/08	650	$9.85	800	450	(50×$10.00)	(400×$9.58)	—	—	$4,332
05/07/08	200	$10.80	0	650	(50×$10.00)	(400×$9.58)	(200×$10.80)	—	$6,492
09/23/08	600	$9.85	750	500	(50×$10.00)	(400×$9.58)	(50×$9.85)	—	$4,825

data, an additional 1,000 units were bought on June 4, 2007, of which only 350 units were used. This leaves an additional 650 units at a purchase price of $9.58, which are placed in the second inventory layer, as noted on Column 7. In the third row, there is a net decrease in the amount of inventory, so this reduction comes out of the second (or last) inventory layer in Column 7; the earliest layer, as described in Column 6, remains untouched, since it was the first layer of costs added, and will not be used until all other inventory has been eliminated. The exhibit continues through seven more transactions, at one point increasing to four layers of inventory costs.

THE DOLLAR VALUE LIFO METHOD

This method computes a conversion price index for the year-end inventory in comparison to the base year cost. This index is computed separately for each company business unit. The conversion price index can be computed with the *double-extension method*. Under this approach, the total extended cost of the inventory at both base year prices and the most recent prices are calculated. Then the total inventory cost at the most recent prices is divided by the total inventory cost at base year prices, resulting in a conversion price percentage, or index. The index represents the change in overall prices between the current year and the base year. This index must be computed and retained for each year in which the LIFO method is used.

There are two problems with the double-extension method. First, it requires a massive volume of calculations if there are many items in inventory. Second, tax regulations require that any new item added to inventory, no matter how many years after the establishment of the base year, have a base year cost included in the LIFO database for purposes of calculating the index. This base year cost is supposed to be the one in existence at the time of the base year, which may require considerable research to determine or estimate. Only if it is impossible to determine a base year cost can the current cost of a new inventory item be used as the base year cost. For these reasons, the double-extension inventory valuation method is not recommended in most cases.

As an example, a company carries a single item of inventory in stock. It has retained the following year-end information about the item for the past four years:

Year	Ending Unit Quantity	Ending Current Price	Extended at Current Year-end Price
1	3,500	$32.00	$112,000
2	7,000	34.50	241,500
3	5,500	36.00	198,000
4	7,250	37.50	271,875

The first year is the base year upon which the double-extension index will be based in later years. In the second year, we extend the total year-end inventory by both the base year price and the current year price, as follows:

Year-end Quantity	Base Year Cost	Extended at Base Year Cost	Ending Current Price	Extended at Ending Current Price
7,000	$32.00	$224,000	$34.50	$241,500

To arrive at the index between year 2 and the base year, we divide the extended ending current price of $241,500 by the extended base year cost of $224,000, yielding an index of *107.8 percent*.

The next step is to calculate the incremental amount of inventory added in year 2, determine its cost using base year prices, and then multiply this extended amount by our index of 107.8 percent to arrive at the cost of the incremental year two LIFO layer. The incremental amount of inventory added is the year-end quantity of 7,000 units, less the beginning balance of 3,500 units, which is 3,500 units. When multiplied by the base year cost of $32.00, we arrive at an incremental increase in inventory of $112,000. Finally, we multiply the $112,000 by the price index of 107.8 percent to determine that the cost of the year 2 LIFO layer is $120,736.

Thus, at the end of year 2, the total double-extension LIFO inventory valuation is the base year valuation of $112,000 plus the year-2 layer's valuation of $120,736, totaling $232,736.

In year 3, the amount of ending inventory has declined from the previous year, so no new layering calculation is required. Instead, we assume that the entire reduction of 1,500 units during that year were taken from the year-2 inventory layer. To calculate the amount of this reduction, we multiply the remaining amount of the year-2 layer (5,500 units less the base year amount of 3,500 units, or 2,000 units) times the ending base year price of $32.00 and the year-2 index of 107.8 percent. This calculation results in a new year-2 layer of $68,992.

Thus, at the end of year 3, the total double-extension LIFO inventory valuation is the base layer of $112,000 plus the reduced year-2 layer of $68,992, totaling $180,992.

In year 4, there is an increase in inventory, so we can calculate the presence of a new layer using the following table:

Year-end Quantity	Base Year Cost	Extended at Base Year Cost	Ending Current Price	Extended at Ending Current Price
7,250	$32.00	$232,000	$37.50	$271,875

Again, we divide the extended ending current price of $271,875 by the extended base year cost of $232,000, yielding an index of *117.2 percent*. To complete the calculation, we then multiply the incremental increase in inventory over year 3 of 1,750 units, multiply it by the base year cost of $32.00/unit, and then multiply the result by our new index of 117.2 percent to arrive at a year-4 LIFO layer of $65,632.

Thus, after four years of inventory layering calculations, the double-extension LIFO valuation consists of the following three layers:

Layer Type	Layer Valuation	Layer Index
Base layer	$112,000	0.0%
Year 2 layer	68,992	107.8%
Year 4 layer	65,632	117.2%
Total	$246,624	—

THE LINK CHAIN METHOD

Another way to calculate the dollar-value LIFO inventory is to use the link-chain method. This approach is designed to avoid the problem encountered during double-extension calculations, where one must determine the base year cost of each new item added to inventory. However, tax regulations require that the link-chain method be used for tax reporting purposes only if it can be clearly demonstrated that all other dollar-value LIFO calculation methods are not applicable due to high rates of churn in the types of items included in inventory.

The link-chain method creates inventory layers by comparing year-end prices to prices at the beginning of each year, thereby avoiding the problems associated with comparisons to a base year that may be many years in the past. This results in a rolling cumulative index that is linked (hence the name) to the index derived in the preceding year. Tax regulations allow one to create the index using a representative sample of the total inventory valuation that must comprise at least one-half of the total inventory valuation. In brief, a link-chain calculation is derived by extending the cost of inventory at both beginning-of-year and end-of-year prices to arrive at a pricing index within the current year; this index is then multiplied by the ongoing cumulative index from the previous year to arrive at a new cumulative index that is used to price out the new inventory layer for the most recent year.

The following example of the link-chain method assumes the same inventory information just used for the double-extension example. However, we have also noted the beginning inventory cost for each year and included the extended beginning inventory cost for each year, which facilitates calculations under the link-chain method:

Year	Ending Unit Quantity	Beginning of Year Cost/Each	End of Year Cost/Each	Extended at Beginning of Year Price	Extended at End of Year Price
1	3,500	$—	$32.00	$—	$112,000
2	7,000	32.00	34.50	224,000	241,500
3	5,500	34.50	36.00	189,750	198,000
4	7,250	36.00	37.50	261,000	271,875

As was the case for the double-extension method, there is no index for year 1, which is the base year. In year 2, the index will be the extended year-end price of $241,500 divided by the extended beginning-of-year price of $224,000, or 107.8 percent. This is the same percentage calculated for year 2 under the double-extension method, because the beginning-of-year price is the same as the base price used under the double-extension method.

We then determine the value of the year-2 inventory layer by first dividing the extended year-end price of $241,500 by the cumulative index of 107.8 percent to arrive at an inventory valuation restated to the base year cost of $224,026. We then subtract the year-1 base layer of $112,000 from the $224,026 to arrive at a new layer at the base year cost of $112,026, which we then multiply by the cumulative index of 107.8 percent to bring it back to current year prices. This results in a year-2 inventory layer of $120,764. At this point, the inventory layers are as follows:

Layer Type	Base Year Valuation	LIFO Layer Valuation	Cumulative Index
Base layer	$112,000	$112,000	0.0%
Year 2 layer	112,026	120,764	107.8%
Total	$224,026	$232,764	—

In year 3, the index will be the extended year-end price of $198,000 divided by the extended beginning-of-year price of $189,750, or 104.3 percent. Since this is the first year in which the base year was not used to compile beginning-of-year costs, we must first derive the cumulative index, which is calculated by multiplying the preceding year's cumulative index of 107.8 percent by the new year-3 index of 104.3 percent, resulting in a new cumulative index of 112.4 percent. By dividing year 3's extended year-end inventory of $198,000 by this cumulative index, we arrive at inventory priced at base year costs of $176,157.

This is less than the amount recorded in year 2, so there will be no inventory layer. Instead, we must reduce the inventory layer recorded for year 2. To do so, we subtract the base year layer of $112,000 from the $176,157 to arrive at a reduced year-2 layer of $64,157 at base year costs. We then multiply the $64,157 by the cumulative index in year 2 of 107.8 percent to arrive at a inventory valuation for the year-2 layer of $69,161. At this point, the inventory layers and associated cumulative indexes are as follows:

Layer Type	Base Year Valuation	LIFO Layer Valuation	Cumulative Index
Base layer	$112,000	$112,000	0.0%
Year 2 layer	64,157	69,161	107.8%
Year 3 layer	—	—	112.4%
Total	$176,157	$181,161	—

In year 4, the index will be the extended year-end price of $271,875 divided by the extended beginning-of-year price of $261,000, or 104.2 percent. We then derive the new cumulative index by multiplying the preceding year's cumulative index of 112.4 percent by the year-4 index of 104.2 percent, resulting in a new cumulative index of 117.1 percent. By dividing year 4's extended year-end inventory of $271,875 by this cumulative index, we arrive at inventory priced at base year costs of $232,173. We then subtract the preexisting base year inventory valuation for all previous layers of $176,157 from this amount to arrive at the base year valuation of the year-4 inventory layer, which is $56,016. Finally, we multiply the $56,016 by the cumulative index in year 4 of 117.1 percent to arrive at an inventory valuation for the year-4 layer of $62,575. At this point, the inventory layers and associated cumulative indexes are as follows:

Layer Type	Base Year Valuation	LIFO Layer Valuation	Cumulative Index
Base layer	$112,000	$112,000	0.0%
Year 2 layer	64,157	69,161	107.8%
Year 3 layer	—	—	112.4%
Year 4 layer	56,016	62,575	117.1%
Total	$232,173	$243,736	—

Compare the results of this calculation with those from the double-extension method. The indexes are nearly identical, as are the final LIFO layer valuations. The primary differences between the two methods is the avoidance of a base year cost determination for any new items subsequently added to inventory, for which a current cost is used instead.

THE WEIGHTED-AVERAGE METHOD

The weighted-average costing method is calculated exactly in accordance with its name—it is a weighted average of the costs in inventory. It has the singular advantage of not requiring a database that itemizes the many potential layers of inventory at the different costs at which they were acquired. Instead, the weighted average of all units in stock is determined, at which point *all* of the units in stock are accorded that weighted-average value. When parts are used from stock, they are all issued at the same weighted-average cost. If new units are added to stock, then the costs of the additions are added to the weighted average of all existing items in stock, which will result in a new, slightly modified weighted average for *all* of the parts in inventory (both the old and new ones).

This system has no particular advantage in relation to income taxes, since it does not skew the recognition of income based on trends in either increasing or declining costs. This makes it a good choice for those organizations that do not want to deal with tax planning. It is also useful for very small inventory valuations, where there would not be any significant change in the reported level of income even if the LIFO or FIFO methods were to be used.

Exhibit 7.5 illustrates the weighted-average calculation for inventory valuations, using a series of 10 purchases of inventory. There is a maximum of one purchase per month, with usage (reductions from stock) also occurring in most months. Each of the columns in the exhibit show how the average cost is calculated after each purchase and usage transaction.

We begin the illustration with the first row of calculations, which shows that we have purchased 500 units of item BK0043 on May 3, 2007. These units cost $10.00 per unit. During the month in which the units were purchased, 450 units were sent to production, leaving 50 units in stock. Since there has been only one purchase thus far, we can easily calculate, as shown in column 7, that the total inventory valuation is $500, by multiplying the unit cost of $10.00 (in column 3) by the number of units left in stock (in column 5). So far, we have a per-unit valuation of $10.00.

Next we proceed to the second row of the exhibit, where we have purchased another 1,000 units of BK0043 on June 4, 2007. This purchase was less expensive, since the purchasing volume was larger, so the per-unit cost for this purchase is only $9.58. Only 350 units are sent to production during the month, so we now have 700 units in stock, of which 650 are added from the most recent purchase. To determine the new weighted-average cost of the total inventory, we first determine the extended cost of this newest addition to the inventory. As noted in column 7, we arrive at $6,227 by multiplying the value in column 3 by the value in column 6. We then add this amount to the existing total inventory valuation ($6,227 plus $500) to arrive at the new extended inventory cost of $6,727, as noted in column 8. Finally, we divide this new extended cost in column 8 by the total number of units now in stock, as shown in column 5, to arrive at our new per-unit cost of $9.61.

The third row reveals an additional inventory purchase of 250 units on July 11, 2007, but more units are sent to production during that month than were bought, so the total number of units in inventory drops to 550 (column 5). This inventory reduction requires no review of inventory layers, as was the case for the LIFO and FIFO calculations. Instead, we simply charge off the 150-unit reduction at the average per-unit cost of $9.61. As a result, the ending inventory valuation drops to $5,286, with the same per-unit cost of $9.61. Thus, reductions in inventory quantities under the average costing method require little calculation—just charge off the requisite number of units at the current average cost.

The remaining rows of the exhibit repeat the concepts just noted, alternatively adding units to and deleting them from stock. Though there are a number of columns noted in this exhibit that one must examine, it is really a simple concept to understand and work with. The typical computerized accounting system will perform all of these calculations automatically.

THE SPECIFIC IDENTIFICATION METHOD

When each individual item of inventory can be clearly identified, it is possible to create inventory costing records for each one, rather than summarizing costs by general inventory type. This approach is rarely used, since the amount of paperwork and effort

Exhibit 7.5 Average Costing Part Number BK0043

Column 1	Column 2	Column 3	Column 4	Column 5	Column 6	Column 7	Column 8	Column 9
Date Purchased	Quantity Purchased	Cost per Unit	Monthly Usage	Net Inventory Remaining	Net Change in Inventory During Period	Extended Cost of New Inventory Layer	Extended Inventory Cost	Average Inventory Cost/Unit
05/03/07	500	$10.00	450	50	50	$500	$500	$10.00
06/04/07	1,000	$9.58	350	700	650	$6,227	$6,727	$9.61
07/11/07	250	$10.65	400	550	−150	$0	$5,286	$9.61
08/01/07	475	$10.25	350	675	125	$1,281	$6,567	$9.73
08/30/07	375	$10.40	400	650	−25	$0	$6,324	$9.73
09/09/07	850	$9.50	700	800	150	$1,425	$7,749	$9.69
12/12/07	700	$9.75	900	600	−200	$0	$5,811	$9.69
02/08/08	650	$9.85	800	450	−150	$0	$4,359	$9.69
05/07/08	200	$10.80	0	650	200	$2,160	$6,519	$10.03
09/23/08	600	$9.85	750	500	−150	$0	$5,014	$10.03

associated with developing unit costs is far greater than under all other valuation techniques. It is most applicable in businesses such as home construction, where there are very few units of inventory to track, and where each item is truly unique.

7-6 WHICH INVENTORY CONTROLS SHOULD I INSTALL?

The accountant can certainly become involved in a plethora of controls that operate throughout the receiving, storage, picking, and shipping functions. However, the inventory controls of most importance to the accounting function are those relating to inventory valuation, since the accountant is directly responsible for this area. The following seven controls should be considered primary controls over the inventory valuation process:

1. *Review the bill of materials and labor routing change log.* Alterations to the bill of materials or labor routing files can have a significant impact on the inventory valuation. To guard against unauthorized changes to these records, enable the transaction change log of the software (if such a feature exists) and incorporate a review of the change log into the month-end valuation calculation procedure.
2. *Compare unextended product costs to those for prior periods.* Product costs of all types can change for a variety of reasons. An easy way to spot these changes is to create and regularly review a report that compares the unextended cost of each product with its cost in a prior period. Any significant changes can then be traced back to the underlying costing information to see exactly what caused each change. The main problem with this control is that many less expensive accounting systems do not retain historical inventory records. If so, the information should be exported to an electronic spreadsheet or separate database once a month, where historical records can then be kept. An example of a cost changes report is shown in Exhibit 7.6.
3. *Review sorted list of extended product costs in declining dollar order.* This report is more commonly available than the historical tracking report noted in control

Exhibit 7.6 Cost Changes Report

Part Description	Beginning Unit Cost	Cost Changes	Ending Unit Costs	Remarks
Power unit	820.00	+30.00	850.00	Price increase
Fabric	142.60		142.60	
Paint	127.54	−22.54	105.00	Modified paint type
Instruments	93.14	−1.14	92.00	New altimeter
Exhaust stock	34.17		34.17	
Rubber grommet	19.06	−.06	19.00	New material
Aluminum forging	32.14	−2.00	30.14	Substitute forging
Cushion	14.70		14.70	
Total	**1,283.35**	**4.26**	**1,287.61**	

number 2, but contains less information. The report lists the extended costs of all inventory on hand for each inventory item, sorted in declining order of cost. By scanning the report, one can readily spot items that have unusually large or small valuations. However, finding these items requires some knowledge of what costs were in previous periods. Also, a lengthy inventory list makes it difficult to efficiently locate costing problems. Thus, this report is inferior to the unextended historical cost comparison report from a control perspective.

4. *Review variances from standard cost.* When the materials management department creates a standard cost for an item, it is usually intended to be a very close approximation of the current market price for that item. Consequently, an excellent control is to run a monthly report comparing the standard cost and most recent price paid for all items, with only those items appearing on the report for which a significant dollar variance has occurred. This can indicate the presence of such purchasing problems as supplier kickbacks or special-order purchases that result in higher prices.

5. *Investigate entries made to the inventory or cost of goods sold accounts.* Because the inventory and cost-of-goods-sold accounts are so large, it is more common for employees attempting to hide fraudulent transactions to dump them into these accounts. Accordingly, part of the standard month-end closing procedure should include the printing and analysis of a report listing only the manual journal entries made to these two accounts. This is also a good audit procedure for the internal auditing department to complete from time to time.

6. *Review inventory layering calculations.* Most inventory layering systems are automatically maintained through a computer system, and cannot be altered. In these cases, there is no need to verify the layering calculations. However, if the layering information is manually maintained, one should schedule periodic reviews of the underlying calculations to ensure proper cost layering. This usually involves tracing costs back to specific supplier invoices. However, one should also trace supplier invoices forward to the layering calculations, since it is quite possible that invoices have been excluded from the calculations. Also, verify consistency in the allocation of freight and sales tax costs to inventory items in the layering calculations.

7. *Verify the calculation and allocation of overhead cost pools.* Overhead costs are usually assigned to inventory as the result of a manually derived summarization and allocation of overhead costs. This can be a lengthy calculation, subject to error. The best control over this process is a standard procedure that clearly defines which costs to include in the pools and precisely how these costs are to be allocated. In addition, regularly review the types of costs included in the calculations, verify that the correct proportions of these costs are included, and ensure that the costs are being correctly allocated to inventory. A further control is to track the total amount of overhead accumulated in each reporting period—any sudden change in the amount may indicate an error in the overhead cost summarization.

The first three of the following controls are supplemental to the primary ones already noted, mostly because they fall outside the normal month-end inventory valuation procedure. Instead, they can be completed at any time, with a frequency level dictated by the level of planned risk mitigation. The fourth control is an access control to prevent employees from modifying key computer records. The controls are as follows:

1. *Audit inventory material costs.* Inventory costs are usually assigned either through a standard costing procedure or as part of some inventory layering concept such as LIFO or FIFO. In the case of standard costs, one should regularly compare them to the actual costs of materials purchased to see if any standard costs should be updated to bring them more in line with actual costs incurred. If it is company policy to update standard costs only at lengthy intervals, then verify that the variance between actual and standard costs is being written off to the cost of goods sold.

   If inventory layering is used to store inventory costs, then periodically audit the costs in the most recently used layers, tracing inventory costs back to specific supplier invoices.

2. *Audit production setup cost calculations.* If production setup costs are included in inventory unit costs, there is a possibility of substantial costing errors if the assumed number of units produced in a production run is incorrect. For example, if the cost of a production setup is $1,000 and the production run is 1,000 units, then the setup cost should be $1 per unit. However, if someone wanted to artificially increase the inventory valuation in order to increase profits, the assumed production run size could be reduced. In the example, if the production run assumption were dropped to 100 units, the cost per unit would increase tenfold to $10. A reasonable control over this problem is to regularly review setup cost calculations. An early warning indicator of this problem is to run a report comparing setup costs over time for each product to see if there are any sudden changes in costs. Also, access to the computer file storing this information should be strictly limited.

3. *Review inventory for obsolete items.* The single largest cause of inventory valuation errors is the presence of large amounts of obsolete inventory. To avoid this problem, periodically print a report that lists which inventory items have *not* been used recently, including the extended cost of these items. A more accurate variation is to print a report itemizing all inventory items for which there are no current production requirements (only possible if a material requirements planning system is in place). Alternatively, create a report that compares the amount of inventory on hand to annual historical usage of each item. With this information in hand, one should then schedule regular meetings with the materials manager to determine what inventory items should be scrapped, sold off, or returned to suppliers. This concept is addressed more extensively in Section 7-2.

4. *Control updates to bill of materials and labor routing costs.* The key sources of costing information are the bill of materials and labor routing records for each product. One can easily make a few modifications to these records in order to

substantially alter inventory costs. To prevent such changes from occurring, always impose strict security access over these records. If the accounting software has a change-tracking feature that stores data about who made changes and what changes were made, then be sure to use this feature. If used, periodically print a report (if available) detailing all changes made to the records, and review it for evidence of unauthorized access.

Because there are so many elements involved in inventory that can lead to an incorrect inventory valuation, it is best to use all of the preceding controls as part of a comprehensive system of valuation controls. Given the level of risk mitigation involved, there is a greater payoff in using all of the controls than in eliminating a few.

An additional inventory valuation activity is to conduct a periodic lower of cost or market (LCM) valuation, which is outlined in Section 7-4. The following two controls are sufficient for ensuring that an LCM analysis is completed on a regular basis:

1. *Follow a schedule of lower or cost or market reviews.* The primary difficulty with LCM reviews is that they are not done at all. Adding them to the financial closing procedure, at least on a quarterly basis, will ensure that they are regularly completed.
2. *Follow a standard procedure for lower of cost or market reviews.* It is not uncommon for an LCM review to be very informal—perhaps a brief discussion with the purchasing staff once a year regarding pricing levels for a few major items. This approach does not ensure that all valuation problems will be uncovered. A better approach is to formulate a standard LCM procedure.

7-7 WHAT TYPES OF PERFORMANCE MEASUREMENTS SHOULD I USE?

The classic performance measurement used by accountants is inventory turnover. Unfortunately, this measurement reveals only at an aggregated level the amount of inventory on hand in relation to sales. There are other measurements available that reveal a great many more issues that contribute to a company's gross inventory investment. This section itemizes the most useful ones.

PERCENTAGE OF NEW PARTS USED IN NEW PRODUCTS

A continuing problem for a company's logistics staff is the volume of new parts that the engineering department specifies for each new product. This can result in an extraordinary number of parts to keep track of, which entails additional purchasing and materials handling costs. From the perspective of saving costs for the entire company, it makes a great deal of sense to encourage engineers to design products that share components with existing products. This approach leverages new products from the existing workload of the purchasing and materials handling staffs, and has the added benefit of avoiding an investment in new parts inventory. For these reasons, the percentage of new parts used in new products is an excellent choice of performance measurement.

To measure it, divide the number of *new* parts in a bill of materials by the *total* number of parts in a bill of materials. Many companies may not include fittings and fasteners in the bill of materials, since they keep large quantities of these items on hand at all times and charge them off to current expenses. If so, the number of parts to include in the calculation will usually decline greatly, making the measurement much easier to complete. The formula is as follows:

$$\frac{\text{Number of new parts in bill of materials}}{\text{Total number of parts in bill of materials}}$$

Engineers may argue against the use of this measurement on the grounds that it provides a disincentive for them to locate more reliable and/or less expensive parts with which to replace existing components. Though this measure can act as a block to such beneficial activities, a measurement system can avoid this problem by also focusing on long-term declines in the cost of products or increases in the level of quality.

BILL OF MATERIALS ACCURACY

The engineering department is responsible for the release of a bill of materials for each product that it designs. The bill of materials should specify exactly what components are needed to build a product, plus the quantities required for each part. The logistics staff uses this information to ensure that the correct parts are available when the manufacturing process begins. At least a 98 percent accuracy rating is needed for this measurement in order to manufacture products with a minimum of stoppages due to missing parts.

To calculate the measurement, divide the number of accurate parts (defined as the correct part number, unit of measure, and quantity) listed in a bill of materials by the total number of parts listed in the bill. The formula is as follows:

$$\frac{\text{Number of accurate parts listed in bill of materials}}{\text{Total number of parts listed in bill of materials}}$$

Though the minimum acceptable level of accuracy is 98 percent, this is an area where nothing less than a 100 percent accuracy level is required in order to ensure that the production process runs smoothly. Consequently, a great deal of attention should be focused squarely on this measurement.

The timing of the release of the bill of materials is another problem. If an engineering staff is late in issuing a proper bill of materials, then the logistics group must scramble to bring in the correct parts in time for the start of the production process. Measuring the timing of the bill's release as well as its accuracy can avoid this problem by focusing the engineering staff's attention on it.

INVENTORY AVAILABILITY

One of the primary reasons for having inventory is to satisfy customer demand in a timely manner. Maintaining a high level of inventory availability is usually cited as the primary reason why companies keep such high levels of finished goods and service parts on hand. Given this logic, one should measure a company's success in filling orders to see whether high inventory retention is working as a policy.

To measure inventory availability, divide the total number of completed orders received by customers no later than their required date during the measurement period by the total number of completed orders that customers should have received during the measurement period. The calculation follows:

$$\frac{\text{Total number of completed orders received by customer by required date}}{\text{Total number of orders that should have been completed}}$$

The measurement emphasizes a successful order fulfillment as one *received* by the customer on time, since the customer is not being served properly if the order was merely shipped as of the required due date. Most company systems have no provision for tracking customer receipt dates. To avoid this problem, a company can train the order entry staff to subtract shipping time from a customer's required date upon receipt of the order, and enter the shortened date in the order entry system.

A company can falsely assume that it has a high availability rate if it counts any sort of partial shipment as a completed order in the numerator, possibly on the grounds that it has successfully shipped nearly all of an order. This measurement approach certainly does not represent the view of the customer, which may very well stop using the company on the basis of a "completed" order, which it sees as a failure.

AVERAGE BACK-ORDER LENGTH

When a company focuses solely on the inventory availability measurement just described, the status of any items placed on back order tends to fall off the map. If a customer cannot receive a shipment on time, it at least wants to receive it as soon thereafter as possible, so a company should also track the average length of its back-ordered items to ensure that customers are not excessively dissatisfied.

To measure the average back-order length, compile a list of all customer orders that were not shipped on time and summarize from this list the total number of days that each order has gone past the customer receipt date without being shipped. Then divide this total number of days by the total number of back-ordered customer orders. The calculation follows:

$$\frac{\text{Sum of the [Number of days past the required customer receipt date for each order]}}{\text{Total number of back-ordered customer orders}}$$

Though the measurement is useful enough by itself, management will probably want to see an accompanying list of the oldest back-ordered items so it can resolve them as soon as possible.

INVENTORY ACCURACY

If a company's inventory records are inaccurate, timely production of its products becomes a near-impossibility. For example, if a key part is not located at the spot in the warehouse where its record indicates it should be, or its indicated quantity is incorrect, then the materials handling staff must frantically search for it and probably issue a rush order to a supplier for more of it, while the production line remains idle, waiting for the key raw materials. To avoid this problem, a company must ensure not only that the quantity and location of a raw material are correct, but also that its units of measure and part number are accurate. If any of these four items are wrong, there is a strong chance that the production process will be negatively impacted. Thus, inventory accuracy is one of the most important materials handling measurements.

The measurement is to divide the number of accurate test items sampled by the total number of items sampled. The definition of an accurate test item is one whose actual quantity, unit of measure, description, and location match those indicated in the warehouse records. If any one of these items is incorrect, then the test item should be considered inaccurate. The formula is as follows:

$$\frac{\text{Number of accurate test items}}{\text{Total number of items sampled}}$$

It is extremely important to conduct this measurement using all four of the criteria noted in the formula derivation. The quantity, unit of measure, description, and location must match the inventory record. If this is not the case, then the reason for using it—ensuring that the correct amount of inventory is on hand for production needs—will be invalidated. For example, even if the inventory is available in the correct quantity, if its location code is wrong, then no one can find it in order to use it in the production process. Similarly, the quantity recorded may exactly match the amount located in the warehouse, but this will still lead to an incorrect quantity if the unit of measure in the inventory record is something different, such as dozens instead of *inches*.

INVENTORY TURNOVER

Inventory is frequently the largest component of a company's working capital; in such situations, if inventory is not being used up by operations at a reasonable pace, then a company has invested a large part of its cash in an asset that may be difficult to liquidate in short order. Accordingly, keeping close track of the rate of inventory turnover is a significant function of management. Turnover should be tracked on a trend line in order to see if there are gradual reductions in the rate of turnover, which can indicate that corrective action is required to eliminate excess inventory stocks.

The most simple turnover calculation is to divide the period-end inventory into the annualized cost of sales. One can also use an *average* inventory figure in the denominator, which avoids sudden changes in the inventory level that are likely to occur on any specific period-end date. The formula is as follows:

$$\frac{\text{Cost of goods sold}}{\text{Inventory}}$$

A variation on the preceding formula is to divide it into 365 days, which yields the number of days of inventory on hand. This may be more understandable to the layman; for example, 43 days of inventory is clearer than 8.5 inventory turns, even though they represent the same situation. The formula is as follows:

$$365\% \left(\frac{\text{Cost of Goods Sold}}{\text{Inventory}} \right)$$

The turnover ratio can be skewed by changes in the underlying costing methods used to allocate direct labor and especially overhead cost pools to the inventory. For example, if additional categories of costs are added to the overhead cost pool, then the allocation to inventory will increase, which will reduce the reported level of inventory turnover—even though the turnover level under the original calculation method has not changed at all. The problem can also arise if the method of allocating costs is changed; for example, it may be shifted from an allocation based on labor hours worked to one based on machine hours worked, which can alter the total amount of overhead costs assigned to inventory. The problem can also arise if the inventory valuation is based on standard costs, and the underlying standards are altered. In all three cases, the amount of inventory on hand has not changed, but the costing systems used have altered the reported level of inventory costs, which impacts the reported level of turnover.

A separate issue is that the basic inventory turnover figure may not be sufficient evidence of exactly where an inventory overage problem may lie. Accordingly, one can subdivide the measurement so that there are separate calculations for raw materials, work-in-process, and finished goods (which perhaps can be subdivided further by location). This approach allows for more precise management of inventory-related problems.

OBSOLETE INVENTORY PERCENTAGE

A company needs to know the proportion of its inventory that is obsolete, for several reasons. First, external auditors will require that an obsolescence reserve be set up against these items, which drastically lowers the inventory value and creates a charge against current earnings. Second, constantly monitoring the level of obsolescence allows a company to work on eliminating the inventory through such means as returns to suppliers, taxable donations, and reduced-price sales to customers. Finally, obsolete inventory takes up valuable warehouse space that could otherwise be put to other uses; monitoring it with the obsolete inventory percentage allows management to eliminate these items in order to reduce space requirements.

The measurement is to summarize the cost of all inventory items having no recent usage, and divide by the total inventory valuation. The amount used in the numerator is subject to some interpretation, since there may be occasional usage that will eventually use up the amount left in stock, despite the fact that it has not been used for some time. An alternative summarization method for the numerator that avoids this problem is to include only those inventory items that do not appear on any bill of materials for a currently produced item. The formula is as follows:

$$\frac{\text{Cost of inventory items with no recent usage}}{\text{Total inventory cost}}$$

PERCENTAGE OF RETURNABLE INVENTORY

Over time, a company will tend to accumulate either more inventory than it can use, or inventory that is no longer used at all. These overaccumulations may be caused by an excessively large purchase, or the scaling back of production needs below original expectations, or perhaps a change in a product design that leaves some components completely unnecessary. Whatever the reason may be, it is useful to review the inventory occasionally in order to determine what proportion of it can be returned to suppliers for cash or credit.

The measurement is to summarize all inventory items for which suppliers have indicated that they will accept a return in exchange for cash or credit. For these items, one may use in the numerator either the listed book value of returnable items or the net amount of cash that can be realized by returning them (which will usually include a restocking fee charged by suppliers). The first variation is used when a company is more interested in the amount of total inventory that it can eliminate from its accounting records, while the second approach is used when it is more interested in the amount of cash that can be realized through the transaction. The denominator is the book value of the entire inventory. The formula is as follows:

$$\frac{\text{Dollars of returnable inventory}}{\text{Total dollars of inventory}}$$

Even though a large proportion of the inventory may initially appear to be returnable, one must also consider that near-term production needs may entail the repurchase of some of those items, resulting in additional freight charges to bring them back into the warehouse. Consequently, the underlying details of the measurement should be reviewed in order to ascertain not only which items can be returned, but also more specifically which ones can be returned that will not be needed in the near term. This will involve the judgment of the logistics staff, perhaps aided by a reorder quantity calculation, to see if it is cost justifiable to return goods to a supplier that eventually will be needed again. A reduced version of the measurement that avoids this problem is to include in the numerator only those inventory items for which there is no production need whatsoever, irrespective of the timeline involved.

7-8 HOW DO I MAINTAIN SERVICE LEVELS WITH LOW INVENTORY?

A major ongoing debate within many departments of a company is the appropriate level of inventory to maintain. If the market and sales managers want to achieve high service levels, then stocking a high level of inventory seems necessary. However, this increases working capital requirements and greatly increases the risk of incurring obsolete inventory expenses. The accountant may find it helpful to use a set of analysis tools to assist management with the calculation of the best possible investment level for service parts. Here are some tools to consider:

- *Throughput per customer.* Know which customers generate the company's cash flow. This requires a knowledge of exactly which products each customer purchases on an annualized basis, as well as the throughput (revenue minus totally variable costs) of those products. It is entirely possible that a high-volume customer may generate such an insignificant amount of cash that it is not worth an excessive level of servicing, so there is no need to maintain a large inventory of specialized service parts for it.

- *Customer quality standards.* Ever notice how some customers are pickier than others? Some customers will require replacement of parts that would be considered well within the quality specifications of other customers. If these customers are the same ones with low throughput levels (see last item), then the company needs to question not only its stocking levels, but also why it permits them to be customers. Consequently, be sure to review the proportion of inventory returns by customer.

- *Customer complaints.* Which inventory items do customers actually want the company to have on hand for immediate delivery? Management may be surprised to find that only a few items are "hot buttons," and those hot buttons may not even be overly expensive to keep on hand. It makes sense to spend a few hours combing through the customer complaints log to see which stockouts actually caused a problem. If the company does not have this information, then set up an inexpensive online survey through an online surveying service such as Survey Monkey ($20/month for a 1,000-response survey) and ask the customers.

- *Call the user.* Notice that the header for this point is "call the user," not "call the customer." There is a specific person within the customer's organization who is waiting for the company's service parts to arrive. Find out who it is, and ask her how soon she needs parts from the company. Not only is this a great way to maintain customer contact and build repeat business, but the company can also obtain an excellent view of precisely how its product is used, and therefore how rapidly its system needs to fulfill any orders for the product. For example, if a service part is needed by the customer on a key piece of manufacturing equipment that will bring down the customer's entire assembly line, then pre-positioning the part in a nearby warehouse or on-site may be the level of servicing inventory required. Alternatively, if the part is used only on backup equipment that is rarely used, then a week-long delay may be entirely acceptable.

A key point is that not one of the items listed in this toolkit includes the more common metrics, such as fulfillment rates, service levels, demand accuracy, or the percentage of obsolete inventory. The appropriate level of inventory is extremely difficult to determine when using such aggregate measures, because service levels can vary so dramatically by individual product.

The typical warehouse may contain several thousand different products, so conducting an analysis with the preceding toolkit for each individual item would be prohibitively expensive. Instead, aggregate products by customer to see which ones are used only by low-throughput customers, and then assign them a low level of stocking priority. Next, aggregate products by type, and determine the level of customer need for each inventory type by using the direct contact or customer complaint tools. This quick aggregation approach greatly reduces the effort required to determine the correct stocking levels needed for different types of inventory.

The preceding discussion addressed ways to determine inventory levels for individual inventory items. In addition, some general techniques are available for reducing *all* types of inventory without reducing service levels. They are as follows:

- *Consolidate smaller, local warehouses into a single regional warehouse.* By doing so, the company needs to maintain safety stock only at one location, rather than once at each warehouse.
- *Centralize slow-moving inventory.* If an item turns over very slowly, then it may be cost-effective to store it in just one place (not even in a few regional warehouses). The trade-off here is an absolute minimum amount of safety stock versus possibly higher shipping costs.
- *Buy in smaller quantities.* This may result in more frequent deliveries, so there may be a cost trade-off. At a minimum, avoid any purchasing "deals" where the company buys vast quantities of goods in exchange for a price break.
- *Shrink production runs.* A major cause of excessive inventory is production runs that greatly exceed the amount of customer orders. If there are no orders, don't

load up the warehouse with extra units. And above all, don't operate the production equipment just to keep the staff busy. If there is no demand, then do not produce it.

- *Shrink the number of product options.* Does the company really need to sell a product in blue, green, red, and pink, as well as with an optional confabulator? Though marketing will be annoyed, try to stock only one or two product variations. At a minimum, store only a moderate number of subunits that can be quickly altered at the last minute into a variety of configurations, rather than storing lots of the final configurations.

Another concept that can reduce inventory levels without impacting service levels is risk pooling. This is the concept that safety stock levels can be reduced for parts that are used in a large number of products, because fluctuations in the demand levels of parent products will offset each other, resulting in a lower safety stock level.

For example, engineers are usually instructed to use common parts in more than one product, so that fewer total parts can be stocked (another inventory reduction technique). A useful side benefit of this approach is that the fluctuations in the demand levels of a single part by multiple parent products will offset each other. This results in a smaller standard deviation in usage levels for a part having multiple sources of demand, as opposed to the usage deviation for parts with fewer sources of demand.

In order to reduce safety stock levels for parts having multiple sources of demand, use a simple trial-and-error approach of determining the actual stockout level of these items over a rolling three-month period, and gradually reducing the in-stock balance until the mandated service level is reached. For these items, the safety stock level will likely be substantially below the average corporate safety stock level.

This section has addressed multiple ways to reduce inventory levels without impacting service levels: by the profit level generated, actual customer need, storage centralization, product configuration, purchasing and producing in smaller quantities, and risk pooling. Only by attacking the problem with most of these tools will a company experience a significant decline in its inventory levels while continuing to provide a high level of customer support.

7-9 SHOULD I SHIFT INVENTORY OWNERSHIP TO SUPPLIERS?

If a company is attempting to reduce its inventory investment, the materials management staff may suggest that raw materials be shifted back to suppliers as consignment inventory that is stored on the company's premises.

The most common approach to consignment inventory management is for the supplier to maintain a sufficient quantity of inventory at the company to ensure a sufficient on-hand supply until its next replenishment visit. During each visit, the supplier counts the amount of inventory used since its last visit, replenishes stock, and invoices the company for the amount used. Though this approach initially appears to be a good one from the perspective of the company, it has some problems.

From a cost perspective, the company will still incur the cost of the storage space taken up by the consigned inventory. This storage space may be significant, since the supplier will prefer to retain sufficient on-site inventory to keep it from returning to review the inventory too frequently. Also, the company may be held liable for any consignment inventory that becomes obsolete, especially if the supplier has custom-designed the goods for the company. Further, there is a significant cost associated with the initial consignment contract creation, as well as ongoing contract maintenance. And finally, suppliers may find ways to shift the financing cost of that inventory back onto the company, either through higher prices or lower product quality.

An additional problem is that many materials management systems are not designed to track consignment inventory, requiring painstaking manual procedures to coordinate activities with suppliers.

The impact of these issues is that working capital will decline somewhat, while materials and administrative costs will increase. A better approach is to work with suppliers to mutually reduce the total amount of inventory in the supply chain. Since inventory is mostly a buffer to compensate for variations in the output of the supplier and the demand of the company, it is better to coordinate forecasts, thereby reducing the need for the buffer.

Consequently, the accountant should spend considerable time analyzing the total cost of a proposed inventory consignment arrangement, not just the proposed initial improvement in cash flow.

7-10 HOW DO I AVOID PRICE PROTECTION COSTS?

A company with a distribution network sometimes finds it necessary to engage in price protection, where it reimburses its distributors for any price reductions on products they still have in stock. By doing so, the distributor does not have to sell at a loss. This is a particular concern in the consumer electronics market, where product prices decline continually as a result of price wars.

There are several ways to minimize these price protection costs. First, deliberately ship in smaller quantities, with more frequent replenishment cycles, thereby preventing distributors from building up large inventory stockpiles on which price protection payments must be made. If distributors resist this approach, then offer them incentives to do so that cost less than the projected savings from the price protection costs.

Second, join with the distributors in using collaborative forecasting and replenishment. Ideally, this means that the company has direct access to each distributor's inventory database, and can see sales trends and stocking levels in real-time. This allows the company to precisely tailor the size and timing of shipments to avoid price protection costs.

Third, do not allow distributors to order in excessively large volumes. This can be most easily done by not offering volume discounts. However, overordering can be a significant problem simply because price protection and inventory return policies are excessively liberal, since distributors know they can return whatever they do not sell. Thus, some degree of restriction in these policies will almost certainly lead to less overordering.

Chapter 8

Cost Allocation Decisions

At a basic level, the allocation of overhead costs is simply a response to meet the requirements of various accounting standards. However, overhead allocation can also be used (and misused) to arrive at a number of decisions, such as the profitability of products, customers, and operating divisions. This chapter shows how to properly use cost allocation through the use of activity-based costing, while also revealing several flaws in the use of any allocation technique that can result in incorrect management decisions. The following table itemizes the section number in which the answers to each question posed in this chapter can be found:

Section	Decision
8-1	What is the basic method for calculating overhead?
8-2	How does activity-based costing work?
8-3	How should I use activity-based costing?
8-4	Are there any problems with activity-based costing?
8-5	How do just-in-time systems impact cost allocation?
8-6	How does overhead allocation impact automated production systems?
8-7	How does overhead allocation impact low-volume products?
8-8	How does overhead allocation impact low-profit products?
8-9	How do I allocate joint and byproduct costs?

8-1 WHAT IS THE BASIC METHOD FOR CALCULATING OVERHEAD?

There are two factors that go into the production of the overhead number. One is the compilation of the overhead pool, which yields the grand total of all overhead costs that will subsequently be allocated to each product. The second factor is the allocation method that is used to determine how much of the fixed cost is allocated to each unit.

The overhead cost pool can contain a wide array of costs that are related to the production of a specific product in varying degrees. For example, there may be machine-specific costs, such as setup, depreciation, maintenance, and repairs, that have some reasonably traceable connection to a specific product at the batch level. Other overhead costs, such as building maintenance or insurance, are related more closely to the building in which the production operation is housed, and have a much looser connection to a specific product. The overhead cost pool may also contain costs for the management or production scheduling of an entire production line, as well as the costs of distributing product to customers. Given the wide-ranging nature of these costs, it is evident that a hodgepodge of costs is being accumulated into a single cost pool, which almost certainly will result in very inaccurate allocations to individual products.

The allocation method is the other factor that impacts the cost of overhead. The most common method of allocation is based on the amount of direct labor dollars used to create a product. This method can cause considerable cost misallocations, because the amount of labor in a product may be so much smaller than the quantity of overhead cost to be allocated that anywhere from $1 to $4 may be allocated to a product for every $1 of direct labor cost in it. Given the high ratio of overhead to direct labor, it is very easy for the amount of overhead charged to a product to swing drastically in response to a relatively minor shift in direct labor costs. A classic example of this problem is what happens when a company decides to automate a product line. When it does so, it incurs extra costs associated with new machinery, which adds to the overhead cost pool. Meanwhile, the amount of direct labor in the product plummets, due to the increased level of automation. Consequently, the increased amount of overhead, which is directly associated with the newly automated production line, is allocated to other products whose production has not yet been automated. This means that the overhead cost of a product that is created by an automated production line does not have enough overhead cost allocated to it, while the overhead cost assigned to more labor-intensive products is too high.

There are solutions to the problems of excessively congregated cost pools, as well as allocations based on direct labor. One is to split the single overhead allocation pool into a small number of overhead cost pools. Each of these pools should contain costs that are closely related to each other. For example, there may be an assembly overhead cost pool (as noted in Exhibit 8.1) that contains only those overhead costs associated with the assembly operation, such as janitorial costs, the depreciation and maintenance on assembly equipment, and the supervision costs of that area. Similarly, there can be another cost pool (as also noted in Exhibit 8.1) that summarizes all fabrication costs. This pool may contain all costs associated with the manufacture and procurement of all component parts, which includes the costs of machinery setup, depreciation, and maintenance, as well as purchasing salaries. Finally, there can be an overall plant overhead cost pool that includes the costs of building maintenance, supervision, taxes, and insurance. It may not be useful to exceed this relatively limited number of cost pools, for the complexity of cost tracking can become excessive. The result of this process is a much better summarization of costs.

Each of the newly created cost pools can then be assigned a separate cost allocation method that has a direct relationship between the cost pool and the product being created. For example, the principal activity in the assembly operation is direct labor, so this time-honored allocation method can be retained when allocating the costs of the assembly overhead cost pool to products. However, the principal activity in the fabrication area is machine hours, so this becomes the basis of allocation for fabrication overhead costs. Finally, all building-related costs are best apportioned through the total square footage of all machinery, inventory, and related operations

Exhibit 8.1   Bill of Materials with Multiple Overhead Costs

Component Description	Unit of Measure	Batch Range	Scrap %	Quantity	Cost/ Each	Total Cost
Base	Ea	500–1,000	—	1	$17.00	$17.00
Switch	Ea	1,000–2,000	—	1	.75	.75
Spring	Ea	5,000–8,000	—	4	.25	1.00
Extension Arm, Lower	Ea	250–500	8%	1	3.75	4.05
Extension Arm, Upper	Ea	250–500	8%	1	4.25	4.59
Adjustment Knob	Ea	400–800	5%	2	.75	1.58
Bulb Holder	Ea	1,000–5,000	—	1	.30	.30
Bulb	Ea	2,000–2,500	1%	1	2.15	2.17
Bulb Lens	Ea	500–1,000	2%	1	1.50	1.53
Fabrication Labor	Hr	250–500 Units	—	2.5	18.00	45.00
Assembly Labor	Hr	250–500 Units	—	2.0	12.50	25.00
Assembly Overhead	Assembly Labor Hr	500–1,000 Hours	—	2.0	3.25	6.50
Fabrication Overhead	Fabrication Machine Hour	625–1,250 Hours	—	2.5	1.20	3.00
Plant Overhead	Square Footage	5,000 Square Feet	—	1	1.75	1.75
Total Cost				—	—	$114.22

used by each product, so square footage becomes the basis of allocation for this cost pool.

The result of these changes, as noted in Exhibit 8.1, is an altered bill of materials that replaces a single overhead cost line item with three different overhead costs, each one being allocated based on the most logical allocation measure.

8-2 HOW DOES ACTIVITY-BASED COSTING WORK?

Activity-based costing (ABC) was invented in order to bring some relevance to the allocation of overhead, which results in better information and related management decisions.

An ABC system begins with a determination of the scope of the project. This is a critical item, for creating an ABC system that encompasses every aspect of every department of all corporate subsidiaries will take an inordinate amount of time and resources, and may never show valuable results for several years, if ever. To control this problem, we first determine the range of activities that the ABC system is to encompass, and the results desired from the system. It is not usually necessary to create an ABC system for simple processes for which the costs can be readily separated and reported on. Instead, activities that are deserving of inclusion in an ABC system are those that include many machines, involve complex processes, use automation, require many machine setups, or support a diverse product line. These are areas in which costs are difficult to clearly and indisputably assign to products or other cost objects.

Another scope issue is the extent to which the ABC system is to be integrated into the existing accounting system. If the project is to be handled on a periodic recalculation basis, rather than one that is automatically updated whenever new information is introduced into the accounting system, then all linkages can be no more than manual retyping of existing information into a separate ABC. However, a fully integrated ABC system will require the extensive coding of software interfaces between the two systems, which is both time-consuming and expensive. These changes may include some alteration of the corporate chart of accounts, the cost center structure, and the cost and revenue distributions used by the accounts payable and billing functions. These are major changes, so the level of system integration should be a large proportion of the scope discussions.

A final scope issue is a determination of how many costs from nonproduction areas should be included in the system. For those companies that have proportionately large production departments, this may not be an issue; but for service companies or those with large development departments, these other costs can be a sizeable proportion of total costs, and so should be included in the ABC system. These costs can come from areas as diverse as the R&D, product design, marketing, distribution, computer services, janitorial, and administration functions. Adding each new functional area will increase the administrative cost of the ABC system, so a key issue in scope determination is whether the cost of each functional area is large enough to have an impact on the activity costs calculated by the ABC system. Costs with negligible impact should be excluded.

Once we have determined the scope, next we must separate all direct materials and labor costs and set them to one side. These costs are quite adequately identified by most existing accounting systems already, so it is usually a simple matter to identify and segregate the general ledger accounts in which these costs are stored. The remaining costs in the general ledger should be ones that can be allocated.

Next, using our statement of the scope of the project, we can identify those costs in the general ledger that are to be allocated through the ABC system. For example, if the primary concern of the new system is to determine the cost of the sales effort on each product sale, then finding the sales and marketing costs will be the primary concern. Alternatively, if the purpose of the ABC system is to find the distribution cost per unit, then only those costs associated with warehousing, shipping, and freight must be located.

With the designated overhead costs in hand, we then proceed to store costs into secondary, or resource, cost pools. A secondary cost pool is one that provides services to other company functions, without directly providing services to any activities that create products or services. Examples of resource costs are administrative salaries, building maintenance, and computer services. The costs stored in these cost pools will later be charged to other cost pools with various activity measures, so the costs should be stored in separate pools that can be allocated with similar allocation measures. For example, computer services costs may be allocated to other cost pools based on the number of personal computers used, so any costs that can be reasonably and logically allocated based on the number of personal computers used should be stored in the same resource cost pool.

In a similar manner, we then store all remaining overhead costs in a set of primary cost pools. There can be a very large number of cost pools for the storage of similar costs, but one should consider that the cost of administering the ABC system (unless it is a rare case of full automation) will increase with each cost pool added. Accordingly, it is best to keep the number of cost pools under 10. There are a few standard cost pool descriptions that are used in most companies. They are as follows:

- *Batch-related cost pools.* Many costs, such as purchasing, receiving, production control, shop floor control, tooling, setup labor, supervision, training, materials handling, and quality control are related to the length of production batches.

- *Product line–related cost pools.* A group of products may have incurred the same research and development, advertising, purchasing, and distribution costs. It may be necessary to split this category into separate cost pools if there are a number of different distribution channels, if the costs of the channels differ dramatically from each other.

- *Facility-related cost pools.* Some costs cannot be directly allocated to specific products, because they relate more closely to the entire facility. These costs include building insurance, building maintenance, and facility depreciation.

Other cost pools can be added to these three basic cost pools, if the results will yield a significantly improved level of accuracy, or if the extra cost pools will lead to the attainment of the goals and scope that were set at the beginning of the project. In particular, the batch-related cost pool can be subdivided into a number of smaller cost pools depending on the number of different operations within a facility. For example, a candy-making plant will have a line of cookers, the cost of which can be included in one cost pool, while the cost of its candy extruder machines can be segregated into a separate cost pool and its cellophane wrapper machines into yet another cost pool. Costs may be allocated quite differently, depending on the type of machine used, so separating this category into a number of smaller cost pools may make sense.

Costs cannot always be directly mapped from general ledger accounts into cost pools. Instead, there may be valid reasons for splitting general ledger costs into different cost pools. If so, an allocation method must be found that logically splits these costs. This method is termed a resource driver. Examples of resource drivers are the number of products produced, direct labor hours, and the number of production orders used. Whatever the type of resource driver selected, it should provide a logical and defendable means for redirecting costs from a general ledger account into a cost pool. There should be a minimal number of resource drivers, because time and effort is required to accumulate each one. In reality, most companies will use management judgment to arrive at a set percentage of each account that is allocated to cost pools, rather than using any formal resource driver at all. For example, the cost of computer depreciation may be allocated 50 percent to a secondary cost pool, 40 percent to a batch-related primary cost pool, and 10 percent to a facility-related primary cost pool, because these percentages roughly reflect the number of personal computers located at various parts of the facility, which in turn is considered a reasonable means for spreading these costs among different cost pools.

There are varying levels of detailed analysis that one can use to assign costs to cost pools. The level of analysis will be largely driven by the need for increasingly detailed levels of information; if there is less need for accuracy, then a less expensive method can be used. For example, if there are three cost pools into which the salaries of the purchasing department can be stored, depending on the actual activities conducted, then the easiest and least accurate approach is to make a management decision to send a certain percentage of the total cost into each one. A higher level of accuracy would require that the employees be split up into job categories, with varying percentages being allocated from each category. Finally, the highest level of accuracy would require time tracking by employee, with a fresh recalculation after every set of time-sheets is collected. The level of accuracy needed, the size of the costs being allocated, and the cost of the related data collection, will drive the decision to collect information at progressively higher levels of accuracy.

The next step is to allocate all of the costs stored in the secondary cost pools into the primary cost pools. This is done with activity drivers, which we will explain shortly. By allocating these cost pools to primary cost pools, we cause a redistribution of costs to occur that then can be further allocated from the primary cost pools, with considerable accuracy, to cost objects. This subsidiary step of allocating costs from resource cost centers to primary cost centers can be avoided by sending all costs straight from the general ledger to the primary cost pools, but several studies have shown that this more direct approach does not do as good a job of accurately allocating costs. The use of resource cost centers more precisely reflects how costs flow through an organization—from resource activities such as the computer services department to other departments, which in turn are focused on activities that are used to create cost objects.

Now that all costs have been allocated into primary cost pools, we must find a way to accurately charge these costs to cost objects, which are the users of the costs. Examples of cost objects are products and customers. We perform this allocation with an activity driver. This is a variable that explains the consumption of costs from a cost pool. There should be a clearly defined cause-and-effect relationship between the cost pool and the activity, so that there is a solid and defensible reason for using a specific activity driver. This is a very key area, for the use of specific activity drivers will change the amount of costs charged to cost objects, which can raise the ire of the managers who are responsible for those cost objects. Exhibit 8.2 itemizes a number of activity drivers that relate to specific types of costs.

The list of activities presented in Exhibit 8.2 is by no means comprehensive. Each company has unique processes and costs that may result in the selection of different activity drivers from the ones noted here. There are several key issues to consider when selecting an activity driver. They are as follows:

Exhibit 8.2   Activity Drivers for Specific Types of Costs

Cost Type	Related Activity Driver
Accounting costs	Number of billings
Accounting costs	Number of cash receipts
Accounting costs	Number of check payments
Accounting costs	Number of general ledger entries
Accounting costs	Number of reports issued
Administration costs	Hours charged to lawsuits
Administration costs	Number of stockholder contacts
Engineering costs	Hours charged to design work
Engineering costs	Hours charged to process planning
Engineering costs	Hours charged to tool design
Engineering costs	Number of engineering change orders
Facility costs	Amount of space utilization
Human resources costs	Employee headcount
Human resources costs	Number of benefits changes
Human resources costs	Number of insurance claims
Human resources costs	Number of pension changes
Human resources costs	Number of recruiting contacts
Human resources costs	Number of training hours
Manufacturing costs	Number of direct labor hours
Manufacturing costs	Number of field support visits
Manufacturing costs	Number of jobs scheduled
Manufacturing costs	Number of machine hours
Manufacturing costs	Number of machine setups
Manufacturing costs	Number of maintenance work orders
Manufacturing costs	Number of parts in product
Manufacturing costs	Number of parts in stock
Manufacturing costs	Number of price negotiations
Manufacturing costs	Number of purchase orders
Manufacturing costs	Number of scheduling changes
Manufacturing costs	Number of shipments
Marketing and sales costs	Number of customer service contacts
Marketing and sales costs	Number of orders processed
Marketing and sales costs	Number of sales contacts made
Quality control costs	Number of inspections
Quality control costs	Number of supplier reviews
Storage time (e.g., depreciation, taxes)	Inventory turnover
Storage transactions (e.g., receiving)	Number of times handled

- *Minimize data collection.* Very few activity drivers are already tracked through the existing accounting system, since few of them involve costs. Instead, they are more related to actions, such as the number of supplier reviews, or the number of customer orders processed. These are numbers that may not be tracked anywhere in the existing system, and so will require extra effort to compile. Consequently, if there are few differences between several potential activity drivers, pick the one that is already being measured, thereby saving the maintenance work for the ABC system.

- *Pick low-cost measurements.* If it is apparent that the only reasonable activity measures are ones that must be collected "from scratch," then (all other items being equal) pick the one with the lowest data collection cost. This is a particularly important consideration if the ABC project is operating on a tight budget, or if there is concern by employees that the new system is taking up too many resources.
- *Verify a cause-and-effect relationship.* The activity driver must have a direct bearing on the incurrence of the costs in the cost pool. To test this, perform a regression analysis; if the regression reveals that changes in the activity driver have a direct and considerable impact on the size of the cost pool, then it is a good driver to use. It is also useful if the potential activity driver is one that can be used as an element of improvement change. For example, if management can focus the attention of the organization on reducing the quantity of the activity driver, then this will result in a smaller cost pool.

Once an activity driver has been selected for each cost pool, we then divide the total volume of each activity for the accounting period into the total amount of costs accumulated into each cost pool to derive a cost per unit of activity. For example, if the activity measure is the number of insurance claims processed, and there are 350 in the period, then if they were to be divided into a human resources benefits cost pool of $192,000, the resulting cost per claim processed would be $549.

Our next step is to determine the quantity of each activity that is used by the cost object. To do so, we need a measurement system that accumulates the quantity of activity drivers used for each cost object. This measurement system may very well not be in existence yet, and so must be specially constructed for the ABC system. If the cost of this added data collection is substantial, then there will be considerable pressure to reduce the number of activity drivers, which represents a trade-off between accuracy and system cost.

Finally, we have reached our goal, which is to accurately assign overhead costs to cost objects. To do so, we multiply the cost per unit of activity by the number of units of each activity used by the cost objects. This should flush out all of the costs located in the cost pools and assign them to cost objects in their entirety. By doing so, we have found not only a defensible way to assign overhead costs in a manner that is understandable, but more importantly, a way that managers can use to reduce those costs. For example, if the activity measure for the overhead costs associated with the purchasing function's cost is the number of different parts ordered for each product, then managers can focus on reducing the activity measure, which entails a reduction in the number of different parts included in each product. By doing so, the amount of purchasing overhead will indeed be reduced, for it is directly associated with and influenced by this activity driver. Thus, the ABC system is an excellent way to focus attention on costs that can be eliminated.

The explanation of ABC has been a lengthy one, so let us briefly recap it. After setting the scope of the ABC system, we allocate costs from the general ledger to secondary and primary cost pools, using resource drivers. We then allocate the costs of the secondary cost pools to the primary ones. Next, we create activity drivers that are closely associated with the costs in each of the cost pools, and derive a cost per unit of activity. We then accumulate the number of units of each activity that are used by each cost object (such as a product or customer), and multiply the number of these units by the cost per activity driver. This procedure completely allocates all overhead costs to the cost objects in a reasonable and logical manner. An overview of the process is shown in Exhibit 8.3.

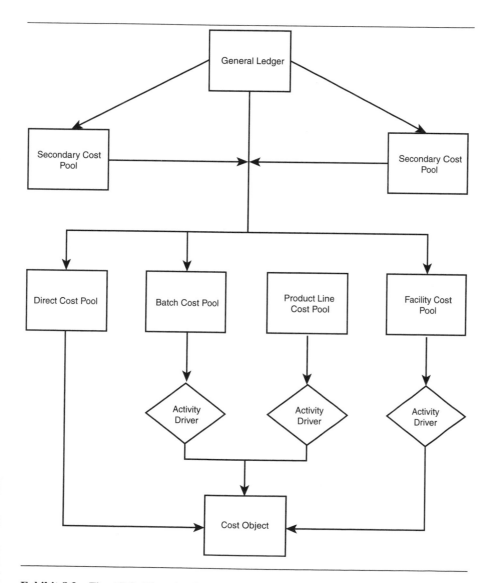

Exhibit 8.3 The ABC Allocation Process

8-3 HOW SHOULD I USE ACTIVITY-BASED COSTING?

The number of uses to which an ABC system can be put are only limited by the imagination of the user. Here are some of its more common applications:

- *How do we increase shareholder value?* When an ABC analysis is combined with a review of investment costs for various tactical or strategic options, one can determine the return on investment to be expected for each of the investment options.

- *How much does a distribution channel cost?* An ABC system can accumulate all of the costs associated with a particular distribution method, which allows managers to compare this cost to the profit margins earned on sales of products that are sold through it. One can then determine if the distribution channel should be reconfigured or eliminated in order to improve overall levels of profitability.

- *How do product costs vary by plant?* An ABC analysis will itemize the costs of each plant, and correctly allocate these costs to the activities conducted within them, which allows a company to determine which plants are more efficient than others.

- *Should we make or buy an item?* An ABC analysis includes all activity costs associated with a manufactured item, which yields a comprehensive view of all costs associated with it, and which can then be more easily compared with the cost of a similar item that is purchased.

- *What acquisition is a good one?* By using internal ABC analyses to determine the cost of various activities, a company can create a benchmark for what these costs should be in potential acquisition targets. If the targets have higher costs than the benchmark levels, then the acquiring company knows that it can strip out costs from the acquisition candidate by improving its processes, which may justify the cost of the acquisition.

- *What does each activity cost?* An ABC analysis can reveal the cost of each activity within an organization. The system is really designed to trace the costs of only the most significant activities, but its design can be altered to itemize the costs of many more activities. This information can then be used to determine which activities are so expensive that they will be the main focus of management attention, or which can be profitably combined with other activities through process centering. This is a primary cost-reduction activity.

- *What price should we charge?* An ABC analysis reveals all of the costs associated with a product, and so is useful for determining the minimum price that should be charged. However, the actual price charged may be much higher, since this may be driven by the ability of the market to absorb a higher price, rather than the underlying cost of a product.

- *What products should we sell?* An ABC analysis can be combined with product prices to yield a list of margins for each product sold. When sorted by market, product line, or customer, it is easy to see which products have low or negative returns, or which yield such low margin volume that they are not worth keeping.

- *Where are the non-value-added costs?* An ABC analysis can reveal which activities contribute to the completion of products, and which do not. Then, by focusing on non-value-added activities, a company can create significant improvements in its profitability.

- *Where can we reduce costs?* An ABC analysis reveals the cost of anything that a management team needs to know about—activities, products, or customers—which can then be sorted to see where the highest-cost items are located. When combined with a value analysis, one can determine what costs return the lowest values, and structure a cost-reduction effort accordingly.

- *Which customers do we want?* An ABC analysis can itemize the costs that are specific to each customer, such as special customer service or packaging issues, as well as increased levels of warranty claims or product returns. When added to the margins on products sold to customers, this reveals which customers are the most profitable after *all* costs are considered.

The main issue involving ABC usage is that it be addressed *before* the system is installed, for the design of the system is heavily dependent on the uses to which ABC will be put.

8-4 ARE THERE ANY PROBLEMS WITH ACTIVITY-BASED COSTING?

Though an ABC system solves a great many problems, it also has several attendant problems that have resulted in many system installation failures. One should be aware of the problems noted in this section, and resolve as many of them as possible in the earliest stages of an ABC system installation, in order to ensure a higher degree of success.

A key underlying problem is that company managers hear about the wonders of ABC and demand that it be installed at once—without considering whether the organization actually needs it. ABC is most useful in situations where the cost accounting information is extremely muddied by the presence of multiple product lines, machines that are used to process different products, complex routings, automation, and many machine setups. If a company does not have any of these criteria, it may not need an ABC system. For example, a company with a single product line, one production facility, and a small number of customers can probably generate reasonably accurate costing information from its existing general ledger system without resorting to a lengthy ABC installation. Those companies that persist in installing ABC under these circumstances may find that they have achieved only a minor improvement in accuracy at the price of having a second accounting system layered over the existing one.

Another issue is the time required to create an ABC system. This can be a lengthy undertaking, especially if the desired system is a comprehensive one that straddles multiple product lines and facilities. A project of this magnitude can easily require more than a year to complete. For work of this duration, there is a greater chance that opponents of the project will start sniping at it after a few months have passed without any tangible results. In short, the longer the project duration, the greater the chance of its being terminated prior to completion. This problem can be avoided by closely defining the scope of the ABC project into an area that can be completed, at least as a pilot project, within a much smaller time frame. By taking this approach, one can show concrete and valuable results in short order, which builds enthusiasm for a continuing series of ABC projects that gradually cover the key areas of a company's operations.

A major problem in many instances is that an ABC system draws information from and reports on the activities of many departments, which draws their ire. If a sufficient number of department managers are irritated by the reports issued by the ABC system, they can use a variety of methods to withhold information from it, so that the system no longer yields a sufficient amount of information to make it worthwhile. To avoid this problem, ensure that a high-level manager has taken personal responsibility for the ABC project, so that any interdepartmental problems can be dealt with both quickly and in favor of the ABC system. This also means that great care must be taken to hand off this project-sponsor position to succeeding individuals who have an equally high degree of enthusiasm for ABC.

A further issue is that an ABC system almost always involves the construction of a separate set of data from the general ledger. If this second database becomes so massive that it is unwieldy to use, or if the data contained in it diverges sharply from the information contained in the general ledger, there will be significant resistance to it within the accounting department. This conflict will arise because staff time must be spent on maintenance (very likely including the hiring of extra cost accounting staff) and the results of the system may be difficult to trace back to the company's financial reports, which entails additional effort by the accounting staff. Thus, a higher workload can produce resistance within the accounting department. To avoid this problem, it is necessary to properly design the ABC system so that it collects the minimum possible amount of extra information besides what is already stored in the general ledger. By doing so, data collection and maintenance requirements are reduced, while there is less trouble in tracing ABC numbers back to the general ledger. System simplification is key to avoiding this problem.

Reporting is also a problem. The users of accounting reports may have been accustomed to seeing the same accounting reports for a number of years, and might not want to put the effort into learning to read new ones. Instead, they continue to use the old reports, and ignore the new ones. The obvious solution to this problem is to phase out or restrict access to the old reports, while providing training on the use of the new reports. Follow-up training is crucial, since users may not at first understand the concept of activity-based costing.

Another issue is the trade-off between the number of cost pools used and the level of accuracy obtained. If costs are summarized into too few cost pools, the resulting level of information accuracy is reduced, while an increase in the number of cost pools (and therefore a finer level of overhead allocation) will result in more accurate costing. The trouble is that the ABC system becomes much more expensive and complex to operate if there are too many cost pools. To resolve this issue, it is useful to create an analysis of the incremental costs required to maintain each additional cost pool that is added to the ABC model, and to stop when the costs exceed a preset threshold, or when the level of complexity appears to become excessive.

A final issue is that the ABC system is frequently set up to be repeated on a project basis, which means that it requires continual reauthorization to reiterate. Because it is a project, it can be killed through reduced funding or staffpower whenever the next project renewal review occurs. ABC information is frequently derived on a project basis, because it is too expensive to continually collect and process ABC information on a continuing basis. To avoid this issue, one can alter the ABC system so that some portions of it are designed into the existing cost accounting system, so that some ABC information is constantly updated while only a small part of the information is still obtained on a project basis. Any ABC information that is easy to collect and interpret, or which yields immediate and continuing information of great importance, can be included in the ongoing ABC system. More peripheral ABC information can be collected on a project basis. This format will retain the most crucial ABC information, even if the ancillary ABC project that collects secondary data is dropped.

8-5 HOW DO JUST-IN-TIME SYSTEMS IMPACT COST ALLOCATION?

The chief difference between the types of cost allocations in a JIT environment and a traditional one is that most overhead costs are converted to direct costs. The primary reason for this change is the machine cell. Because a machine cell is designed to produce either a single product or a single component that goes into a similar product line, all of the costs generated by that machine cell can be charged directly to the only product it produces. When a company completely converts to the use of machine cells in all locations, then the costs related to all of those cells can now be charged directly to products, which leaves very little costs of any kind left to be allocated through a more traditional overhead cost pool. The result of this change is much more accurate product costs, and little debate over where allocated costs should go—since there aren't enough of them left to be worth the argument.

To be specific about which costs can now be charged directly to a product, they are as follows:

- *Depreciation.* The depreciation cost of each machine in a machine cell can be charged directly to a product. It may be possible to depreciate a machine based on its actual usage, rather than charging off a specific amount per month, since this allocation variation more accurately shifts costs to a product.

- *Electricity.* The power used by the machines in a cell can be separately metered and then charged directly to the products that pass through that cell. Any excess electricity cost charged to the facility as a whole will still have to be charged to an overhead cost pool for allocation.

- *Materials handling.* Most materials handling costs in a JIT system are eliminated, since machine operators move parts around within their machine cells. Only materials handling costs between cells should be charged to an overhead cost pool for allocation.

- *Operating supplies.* Supplies are mostly used within the machine cells, so the vast majority of items in this expense category can be separately tracked by individual cell and charged to products.

- *Repairs and maintenance.* Nearly all of the maintenance that a company incurs is spent on machinery, and this is all grouped into machine cells. By having the maintenance staff charge their time and materials to these cells, their costs can be charged straight to products. Only maintenance work on the facility will still be charged to an overhead cost pool.

- *Supervision.* If supervision is by machine cell, then the cost of the supervisor can be split among the cells supervised. However, the cost of general facility management, as well as of any support staff, must still be charged to an overhead cost pool.

As noted in several places in the preceding bullet points, a few remainder costs will still be charged to an overhead cost pool for allocation. However, this constitutes a small percentage of the costs, with nearly everything now being allocable to machine cells. Only building occupancy costs, insurance, and taxes are still charged in full to an overhead cost pool. This is a vast improvement over the amount of money that the traditional system allocates to products. A typical overhead allocation pool under the traditional system may easily include 75 percent of all costs incurred, whereas this figure can be dropped to less than 25 percent of total costs by switching to a JIT system. With such a higher proportion of direct costs associated with each product, managers will then have much more relevant information about the true cost of each product manufactured.

8-6 HOW DOES OVERHEAD ALLOCATION IMPACT AUTOMATED PRODUCTION SYSTEMS?

Traditional cost allocation systems tend to portray products made with high levels of automation as being deceptively low in overhead cost. For example, if a high-technology company decides to introduce more automation into one of its production lines, it will replace direct labor with machine hours by adding robots. This will shrink the allocation base, which is direct labor, while increasing the size of the overhead cost pool, which now includes the depreciation, utilities, and maintenance costs associated with the robots. When the overhead cost allocation is performed, a *smaller* amount of overhead will be charged to the now-automated production line, because the overhead costs are being charged based on direct labor usage, which has declined. This makes the products running through the automated line look less expensive than they really are. Furthermore, the increased overhead cost pool will be charged to those production lines with lots of direct labor, even though these other product lines have not the slightest association with the new overhead costs. The end result is a significant skewing of reported costs that makes products manufactured with automation look less expensive than they really are, and those produced with manual labor look more expensive.

8-7 HOW DOES OVERHEAD ALLOCATION IMPACT LOW-VOLUME PRODUCTS?

Traditional cost allocation systems tend to portray low-volume products as those with the highest profits. This problem arises because the overhead costs associated with batch setups and teardowns, which can be a significant proportion of total overhead costs, are allocated indiscriminately to products that have both large and small production volumes; there is no allocation to a specific short production run of the special batch costs associated with it. This results in under-costing of products with short production runs, and overcosting of products with long production runs. This results in incorrect management decisions to increase sales of short-run jobs and to reduce sales of long-run jobs, which results in reduced profits as company resources are concentrated on the lowest-profit products.

8-8 HOW DOES OVERHEAD ALLOCATION IMPACT LOW-PROFIT PRODUCTS?

Traditional cost accounting dictates that overhead costs be assigned to every product. By doing so, product margins will be reduced considerably. In some cases, margins will likely become negative. Managers will then eliminate these products, under the false assumption that the company is not earning a profit, and will be better off without them. What actually happens is that no overhead costs are eliminated along with the canceled products. Instead, the same pool of overhead costs must now be spread over a smaller pool of remaining products, which increases the allocated cost per product and makes the remaining products appear to be even *less* profitable. This can lead to a continuous series of product eliminations that leaves a company in a much less profitable situation than when it started eliminating its low-margin products.

For example, Acorn Company has three products, whose margins are shown in the following table. The company has $100,000 of overhead costs, which it allocates based on the number of units sold. Acorn sells a combined total of 15,000 units of all three of its products, so each one receives an overhead charge of $6.66 ($100,000 overhead expense/15,000 units):

	Product Alpha	Product Beta	Product Charlie	Totals
Units sold	1,500	3,500	10,000	15,000
Price each	$8.00	$12.00	$15.00	—
Variable cost each	3.00	5.00	6.00	—
Overhead allocation	6.66	6.66	6.66	—
Gross margin each	$(1.66)	$0.34	$2.34	—
Gross margin total	$(2,490)	$1,190	$23,400	$22,100

Based on this analysis, Acorn elects to stop selling product Alpha, which has a fully burdened loss of $2,490. The company does not lose any overhead expenses as a result of this product elimination, so the same $100,000 must now be allocated among products Beta and Charlie, resulting in an increased overhead charge per unit of $7.41 ($100,000 overhead expense/13,500 units). The results appear in the following table:

	Product Beta	Product Charlie	Totals
Units sold	3,500	10,000	13,500
Price each	$12.00	$15.00	—
Variable cost each	5.00	6.00	—
Overhead allocation	7.41	7.41	—
Gross margin each	$(0.41)	$1.59	—
Gross margin total	$(1,435)	$15,900	$14,465

Now the product Beta margin has become negative, with a fully burdened loss of $1,435. Acorn now stops selling product Beta. Overhead expenses do not decline as a result of this product cancellation, so now the entire cost is allocated to product

Charlie, at a rate of $10.00 per unit ($100,000 overhead expense/10,000 units). The result is shown in the following table:

	Product Charlie
Units sold	10,000
Price each	$15.00
Variable cost each	6.00
Overhead allocation	10.00
Gross margin each	$(1.00)
Gross margin total	$(10,000)

Based on the new cost allocation, Acorn cancels product Charlie as well, and now finds itself out of business! Thus we have gone from a profitable company to a bankrupt one, just because a fixed pool of overhead costs is being allocated to individual products.

A better approach is to eliminate a product *only* if its price is lower than its totally variable costs. Since these totally variable costs usually include only direct materials, there will be very few circumstances where the product price will be sufficiently low to warrant a product elimination. Instead, all products are kept if they generate any positive margin at all, since this will contribute to the overall margin being generated by the production system, allowing the company to pay for its operating expenses.

Thus, a case can be made in favor of product elimination only in situations where a specific amount of clearly defined operating expenses can be eliminated along with a product.

8-9 HOW DO I ALLOCATE JOINT AND BYPRODUCT COSTS?

To understand joint products and byproducts, one must have a firm understanding of the split-off point. This is the last point in a production process where it is impossible to determine the nature of the final products. All costs that have been incurred by the production process up until that point—both direct and overhead—must somehow be allocated to the products that result from the split-off point. Any costs incurred thereafter can be charged to specific products in the normal manner. Thus, a product that comes out of such a process will be composed of allocated costs from before the split-off point and costs that can be directly traced to it, which occur after the split-off point.

A related term is the *byproduct*, which is one or more additional products that arise from a production process, but whose potential sales value is much smaller than that of the principal joint products that arise from the same process. As we will see, the accounting for byproducts can be somewhat different.

The logic used for allocating costs to joint products and byproducts has less to do with some scientifically derived allocation method, and more with finding a quick and easy way to allocate costs that is reasonably defensible (as we will see in the next section). The reason for using simple methodologies is that the promulgators of GAAP realize that there is no real management use for allocated joint costs—they cannot be used for determining breakeven points, setting optimal prices, or figuring out the exact profitability of individual products. Instead, they are used for any of the following purposes, which are more administrative in nature:

- *Bonus calculations*. Manager bonuses may depend on the level of reported profits for specific products, which in turn are partly based on the level of joint costs allocated to them. Thus, managers have a keen interest in the calculations used to assign costs, especially if some of the joint costs can be dumped onto products that are the responsibility of a different manager.

- *Cost-plus contract calculations*. Many government contracts are based on the reimbursement of a company's costs, plus some predetermined margin. In this situation, it is in a company's best interests to ensure that the largest possible proportion of joint costs are assigned to any jobs that will be reimbursed by the customer, while the customer will be equally interested, but due to a desire to *reduce* the allocation of joint costs.

- *Income reporting*. Many organizations split their income statements into sublevels that report on profits by product line or even individual product. If so, joint costs may make up such a large proportion of total production costs that these income statements will not include the majority of production costs, unless they are allocated to specific products or product lines.

- *Insurance reimbursement*. If a company suffers damage to its production or inventory areas, some finished goods or work-in-process inventory may have been damaged or destroyed. If so, it is in the interests of the company to fully allocate as many joint costs as possible to the damaged or destroyed stock, so that it can receive the largest possible reimbursement from its insurance provider.

- *Inventory valuation*. It is possible to manipulate inventory levels (and therefore the reported level of income) by shifting joint cost allocations toward those products that are stored in inventory. This practice is obviously discouraged, since it results in changes to income that have no relationship to operating conditions. Nonetheless, one should be on the lookout for the deliberate use of allocation methods that will alter the valuation of inventory.

- *Transfer pricing*. A company can alter the prices at which its sells products among its various divisions, so that high prices are charged to those divisions located in high-tax areas, resulting in lower reported levels of income tax against which those high tax rates can be applied. A canny cost accounting staff will choose the joint cost allocation technique that results in the highest joint costs being assigned to products being sent to such locations (and the reverse for low-tax regions).

There are only two methods for allocating joint and byproduct costs that have gained widespread acceptance. The first is based on the sales value of all joint products at the split-off point. To calculate it, compile all costs accumulated in the production process up to the split-off point, determine the eventual sales value of all products created at the split-off point, and then assign these costs to the products based on their relative values. If there are byproducts associated with the joint production process, they are considered to be too insignificant to be worthy of any cost assignment, though revenues gained from their sale can be charged against the cost of goods sold for the joint products. This is the simplest joint cost allocation method, and particularly attractive, because the accountant needs no knowledge of any production processing steps that occur after the split-off point.

This different treatment of the costs and revenues associated with byproducts can lead to profitability anomalies at the product level. The trouble is that the determination of whether a product is a byproduct or not can be quite judgmental; in one company, if a joint product's revenues are less than 10 percent of the total revenues earned, then it is a byproduct, while another company might use a 1 percent cutoff figure instead. Because of this vagueness in accounting terminology, one company may assign all of its costs to just those joint products with an inordinate share of total revenues, and record the value of all other products as zero. If a large quantity of these byproducts were to be held in stock at a value of zero, the total inventory valuation would be lower than another company would calculate, simply due to their definition of what constitutes a byproduct.

A second problem with this cost allocation scenario is that byproducts may be sold off only in batches, which may occur only once every few months. This can cause sudden drops in the cost of joint products in the months when sales occur, since these revenues will be subtracted from their cost. Alternatively, joint product costs will appear to be too high in those periods when there are no byproduct sales. Thus, one can alter product costs through the timing of byproduct sales.

A third problem related to byproducts is that the revenues realized from their sale can vary considerably, based on market demand. If so, these altered revenues will cause abrupt changes in the cost of those joint products against which these revenues are netted. It certainly may require some explaining to show why changes in the price of an unrelated product caused a change in the cost of a joint product!

The best way to avoid the three issues just noted is to avoid the designation of *any* product as a byproduct. Instead, every joint product should be assigned some proportion of total costs incurred up to the split-off point, based on their total potential revenues (however small they may be), and no resulting revenues should be used to offset other product costs. By avoiding the segregation of joint products into different product categories, we can avoid a variety of costing anomalies.

The second allocation method is based on the estimated final gross margin of each joint product produced. The calculation of gross margin is based on the revenue that each product will earn at the end of the entire production process, less the cost of all processing costs incurred from the split-off point to the point of sale. This is a more complicated approach, since it requires the accountant to accumulate additional costs through the end of the production process, which in turn requires a reasonable knowledge of how the production process works, and where costs are incurred. Though it is a more difficult method to calculate, its use may be mandatory in those instances where the final sale price of one or more joint products cannot be determined at the split-off point (as is required for the first allocation method), thereby rendering the other allocation method useless.

The main problem with allocating joint costs based on the estimated final gross margin is that it can be very difficult to calculate if there is a great deal of *customized* work left between the split-off point and the point of sale. If so, it is impossible to determine in advance the exact costs that will be incurred during the remaining production process. In such a case, the only alternative is to make estimates of expected costs that will be incurred, base the gross margin calculations on this information, and accept the fact that the resulting joint cost allocations may not be provable, based on the actual costs incurred.

Chapter 9

Performance Responsibility Accounting Decisions

A subtle issue that is completely overlooked by many accountants is the proper structuring of the reports that they issue to various company employees. In addition to the creation of a single, companywide set of financial statements, a considerable amount of attention should be paid to the creation of an underlying set of reports that target specific areas of responsibility, which may be at the levels of an entire division, a department, or perhaps a single machine cell. When creating such reports, the accountant may inquire about the nature of responsibility accounting, the types of responsibility centers for which reports are created, and what types of costs should be included or excluded from them. Ancillary issues involve whether a balanced scorecard or a benchmarking system should be used; in both cases, the information selected for inclusion in reports can have a significant impact on the resulting performance of a company.

This chapter discusses the answers to all of these questions. The following table itemizes the section number in which the answers to each question posed in this chapter can be found:

Section	Decision
9-1	What is responsibility accounting?
9-2	What are the types of responsibility centers?
9-3	Should allocated costs be included in responsibility reports?
9-4	What is balanced scorecard reporting?
9-5	How does benchmarking work?

9-1 WHAT IS RESPONSIBILITY ACCOUNTING?

A key task of the accountant is to create accounting systems that ensure that costs are incurred in accordance with expectations. The best way to do so is through the concept of responsibility accounting, which is the assumption that every cost incurred must be the responsibility of one person somewhere in the company. For example, the cost of rent can be assigned to the person who negotiates and signs the lease, while the cost of an employee's salary is the responsibility of that person's direct manager. This concept also applies to the cost of products, for each component part has a standard cost (as listed in the item master and bill of materials), which it is the responsibility of the purchasing manager to obtain at the correct price. Similarly, scrap costs incurred at a machine are the responsibility of the shift manager.

By using this approach, cost reports can be tailored for each recipient. For example, the manager of a work cell will receive a financial statement that itemizes only the costs incurred by that specific cell, whereas the production manager will receive a different one that itemizes the costs of the entire production department, and the president will receive one that summarizes the results of the entire organization.

As one moves upward through the organizational structure, it is common to find fewer responsibility reports being used. For example, each person in a department may be placed in charge of a separate cost, and so each one receives a report that itemizes his or her performance in controlling that cost. However, when the more complex profit center approach is used, these costs are typically clumped together into the group of costs that can be directly associated with revenues from a specific product or product line, which therefore results in fewer profit centers than cost centers. Then, at the highest level of responsibility center, that of the investment center, one must make investments that may cut across entire product lines, so that the investment center tends to be reported at a minimal level of an entire production facility. Thus, there is a natural consolidation in the number of responsibility reports generated by the accounting department as more complex forms of responsibility reporting are used.

9-2 WHAT ARE THE TYPES OF RESPONSIBILITY CENTERS?

The most elementary form of responsibility center is the *cost center*, which itemizes all of the expenses incurred to run a specified function, but ignores the cost of capital invested in it, as well as any associated revenues. The primary form of control in a cost center is against a fixed or semivariable budget that is determined at the beginning of the year. It is not common to see a variable budget being used in a cost center, since purely variable costs tend to be most closely associated with production, for which there are associated sales; this relationship means that variable budget costs are more commonly found in profit centers than in cost centers. An example of the cost center reporting format is shown in Exhibit 9.1, where we see all the expense line items for the janitorial department listed. There is also a subtotal for those costs that are directly attributable to the department, followed by an overhead allocation for administrative costs (which is not controllable by the janitorial manager). This general format can be used for any cost center.

Though this is a good start for a company that wants to implement controls over its expenditures, it suffers from one main flaw—those responsible for cost centers are concerned only with the tight control of costs, rather than other key company goals, such as customer service, creating new products, or acquiring new customers. This can lead to counterproductive behavior. For example, the manager of the computer

Exhibit 9.1   Sample Cost Center Report

Expense Type	Actual Expenses	Budgeted Expenses	Variance
Wages	$58,000	$60,000	+$2,000
Personnel benefits	6,000	5,500	−500
Equipment depreciation	2,400	2,000	−400
Supplies	4,800	3,200	−1,600
Expense subtotal	$71,200	$70,700	−$500
Overhead allocations	6,100	6,100	0
Total expenses	$77,300	$76,800	−$500

services department, which is operated as a cost center, is determined to avoid any cost overruns. The sales manager, who is trying to increase profits, asks that a customized report be created that lists the margins for each existing customer, so that the sales team will know which customers are the best ones to sell to. However, the computer services manager refuses this request, for it will result in extra costs that will exceed her budget. This problem occurs regularly when a company is structured into many cost centers, each of which looks out for its own self-interest.

As the name implies, a *revenue center* is one where the employees located in a specific functional area are solely responsible for attaining preset revenue levels. The sales department is sometimes considered to be a revenue center. In this capacity, employees are essentially encouraged to obtain new sales without regard to the cost of obtaining them. This can be a dangerous way to run a function, unless strict guidelines are set up that control the overall spending limits allowed, the size and type of customer solicited, and the size and type of orders obtained. Otherwise, the sales staff will obtain orders from all kinds of customers, including those with poor credit records or histories of returning goods, not to mention orders that are so small that the cost of processing the order exceeds the profit gained from the sale. Other counterproductive activities associated with revenue centers are the inordinate use of travel funds to meet with customers, selling products at large discounts from the standard price, offering special promotional guarantees to customers, allowing credits on previously purchased products if the price subsequently declines, and offering to extend payment terms. For all of these reasons, revenue centers are not recommended without the addition of stringent controls to ensure that the sales staff obtains only revenues that will result in adequate levels of profitability.

The *profit center* resolves many of the problems just noted for the cost and revenue center concepts by combining the two. The manager of a profit center is primarily responsible for generating the highest possible profit (or least possible loss). This results in a strong incentive to pursue only those sales that have a sufficient margin, while also incurring expenses only if they will result in an incremental increase in revenue. An example of a profit center report is shown in Exhibit 9.2. This format is very similar to the one used for a cost center, except that it now includes a revenue line at the top and a profit amount at the bottom.

Exhibit 9.2 Sample Profit Center Report

Account Type	Actual Expenses	Budgeted Expenses	Variance
Revenue	$90,000	$92,000	−$2,000
Expenses:			
Wages	58,000	60,000	+$2,000
Personnel benefits	6,000	5,500	−500
Equipment depreciation	2,400	2,000	−400
Supplies	4,800	3,200	−1,600
Expense subtotal	$71,200	$70,700	−$500
Overhead allocations	6,100	6,100	0
Total Expenses	$77,300	$76,800	−$500
Profit	$12,700	$15,200	−$2,500
Profit percentage	14%	17%	−3%

The profit center concept is highly recommended, since it results in the strongest possible management attention to profitability. However, there are some cases where it is difficult to convert a cost center to a profit center, because there is no way for it to gain revenues by directly selling its services. Examples of such cost centers are the computer services, engineering, and production departments. These groups are all involved in the production or support of products, but it can be difficult to attribute sales directly to them. One way around this problem is to have each department charge other departments for its services. A good example is the computer services function, where many organizations create a programming cost per hour that is charged to all other departments that request changes to computer programs; it is also common to charge for the processing time used by each department's programs, as well as the cost of report processing, generation, and distribution. These are valid charges to make, for departments now have the option of outsourcing some functions, such as computer services, so that suppliers provide the same services that have previously been performed internally. If a department can find a better deal outside of the company, then it should go ahead and purchase the outside services. By using this approach, a company can force many of its cost centers to pay a much greater level of attention to their costs incurred and services rendered to other departments—if they drop below the level of outside service providers, then there will be no call for their services, and the employees in those departments will lose their jobs. This approach can be used for many functions besides computer services, such as engineering, production, and accounting.

When determining revenues for profit centers, it may be necessary to allocate revenues based on the cost of services or materials added to a product as it moves through a department. If there are cases where it becomes difficult to justify a revenue allocation, or it is impossible to prove that any value is added to a product or service, then it may be better to leave the function as a cost center.

A step beyond the profit center in its level of sophistication is the *investment center*. This is the same as a profit center, but now the responsible manager is also held accountable for any investments in the business. This added responsibility means that one additional measure is added to the normal set of measures used for a profit center: return on investment. This measures the ability of a manager not only to generate a profit, but to also create one at a sufficiently high level to offset the cost of capital on any newly invested funds.

The investment center is particularly appropriate for those cases where investment decisions must be made very rapidly in order to take advantage of changes in local business conditions. This is a particularly important issue for those companies in rapidly expanding markets, or where consumer needs change rapidly, where waiting for investment approval from a central authority may result in lost sales.

Though the investment center seems like the most sophisticated of all the various types of responsibility accounting, given its incorporation of revenues, costs, and invested funds, it is a rarely used format. The reason is that the manager of an investment center could obligate a corporation into a very large investment, and never generate a sufficient return to pay off the investment, thereby worsening the financial condition of the corporation as a whole. This problem can be restricted by adding some form of investment oversight. For example, an investment committee at the corporate headquarters or division level can be used to approve all investments over a certain amount. This approach gives the managers of investment centers total leeway to invest smaller amounts of money, while still reducing the overall corporate risk of a bad investment by requiring a more detailed analysis for large investments.

Investment centers function less efficiently when there is a highly centralized corporate management structure in place. In this instance, very few decisions are left for the local manager, and certainly not investment-related decisions, which are strictly controlled by a central capital investment review function.

The alternative corporate structure, that of decentralization, nearly *requires* the use of investment centers, since the corporate management staff goes out of its way not to become involved in operational issues at the local facility level. Thus, the overall management structure is a strong driver of the level of usage of investment centers.

9-3 SHOULD ALLOCATED COSTS BE INCLUDED IN RESPONSIBILITY REPORTS?

A common costing scenario is when responsibility reports include a variety of corporate or local overhead costs. The person who is responsible for the operating results of each department or division has virtually no control over the incurrence of these overhead costs, and so can make a reasonable argument against being judged on this number. The simplest way to avoid this issue is to restructure the responsibility financial statements by subtotaling all other financial results prior to adding in allocated costs. This approach keeps actual operating results from being obscured by allocated costs.

The decision to include or exclude an allocated cost from a responsibility report can be made by subjecting the cost to two rules. First, if a local manager has no direct ability to control a cost, then it should be excluded from that manager's responsibility reports. Second, if the cost would remain if the responsibility center were to be completely eliminated, then the cost should also be excluded from the same reports. For example, corporate overhead generally should not be allocated to any responsibility centers, because the corporate overhead costs would still exist even if the responsibility centers were eliminated.

9-4 WHAT IS BALANCED SCORECARD REPORTING?

Too often, a company focuses exclusively on its financial results. By doing so, it may be forcing attention away from other key measures that ultimately have a strong impact on financial performance and that enhance that performance in the long run. To counteract this problem, consider using the balanced scorecard. Under this approach, a company's key performance measurements are split into four areas, which are the financial, customer, internal business processes, and learning and growth areas. These areas are designed to build on each other, so that a proper level of attention to the three nonfinancial measurement areas will result in an improved set of financial measurements as well.

An example of this measurement system is shown in Exhibit 9.3. In it, we see that the learning and growth measurements, shown in the lower left-hand corner, are designed to improve the performance of employees through training as well as reduced turnover (on the grounds that fewer employee departures results in fewer new employees, hence a more experienced staff). Measurements for the last month are compared with those from previous periods, so that employees can see trends in the measurements. Success in the learning and growth area should result in an improvement in the company's internal business processes, which are itemized in the lower-right corner of the example. In this area, increased employee training has led to improved processing time for customer orders as well as the near-completion of a just-in-time manufacturing system. These process changes should result in improved customer-related measurements, which are noted in the upper-right corner. With improved product quality, on-time shipments, and customer satisfaction, we assume that financial performance will improve, which will be reflected in the final box in the upper-left corner. In this area, the financial measures are closely tied to the corporate goal, which is listed at the top of the page—that of spinning off enough cash from operations to fund new facilities and acquire competitors. Thus, the balanced scorecard reporting system results in a coherent set of interlocking measurements that are directly tied to a company's goals.

The balanced scorecard must be individualized for each company that uses it, since each one operates within a unique set of constraints. The measurements used in the example are designed for a manufacturing facility, and so would be inappropriate for use by a service company. To obtain the correct set of measurements for a balanced

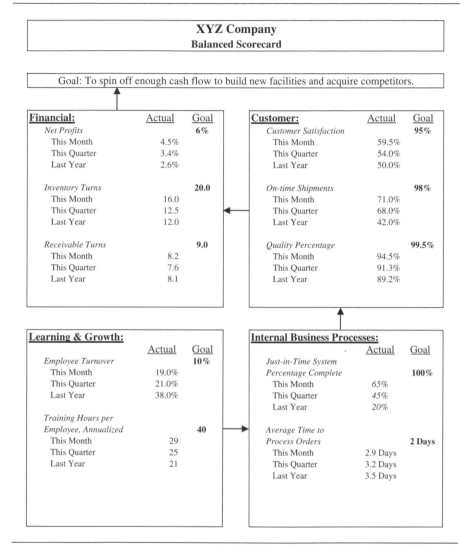

Exhibit 9.3 The Balanced Scorecard

scorecard, a company's senior management group should compile a short list of the most appropriate measures, possibly with the assistance of a trained facilitator who can keep the discussion on track. Once everyone has agreed on the most appropriate measures, there must be further agreement on how each one shall be calculated, as well as when the measures shall be sent back to the management team for periodic review. These up-front decisions will ensure that the correct measures are calculated and that they will be used by managers to improve the business.

The balanced scorecard should not supplant all previous measurement systems that a company uses to track its performance. There may be dozens or even hundreds of measures already in place that are extremely useful for the conduct of daily operations and that should be continued. The balanced scorecard is more for the use of the management group, which can use it to see how well they are directing the company's performance in reaching its major goals. To this end, it should be treated as a high-level set of measurements, under which lie a great many other measures that must be still be used to transact daily company business.

9-5 HOW DOES BENCHMARKING WORK?

Benchmarking is the process of obtaining and productively using information about how to improve one's processes, products, and strategies. It is a systematic process, rather than one that is only occasionally engaged in; this requires the ongoing use of project teams that are continually renewed with well-trained employees from all parts of an organization, and who are adequately supported at the uppermost levels of the company.

There are three types of benchmarking that one can perform, each of which is targeted at a different part of a company's operations. The first is benchmarking for internal processes. Comparisons can be made with companies from markedly different industries, since processes are readily adaptable across many industries. When one hears about how a company has conducted a benchmarking review with another company that is far outside of its normal field of competitors, it is most likely that the study addressed process changes. When processes are the subject of benchmarking, the usual justification is that there will be immediate financial results, typically through the elimination of employee positions. It can also achieve shorter processing intervals, which is readily measured. For these reasons, process benchmarking is very popular.

Another type of benchmarking is based on products or services. It uses comparisons between a company's own products or services and those of other organizations. The focus of such a study tends to be on the quality, reliability, and features of comparable products. This does not mean that benchmarking comparisons are confined to products created by companies in the same industry, since products may be broken down into their component parts, which may individually be more readily comparable with products from other industries. Product benchmarking can be performed without the approval of any other company, since one can simply buy their products and directly review them, either through reverse engineering or feature comparisons. Nonetheless, it is most useful to obtain the cooperation of the maker of each product, since the review team could glean much additional information regarding the manner in which each product was manufactured, information that is not readily apparent from a direct review of the product itself.

The final form of benchmarking is strategic; the review team wishes to discern whether there are other ways to position the company within its industry that it has not considered, but which other organizations are implementing with success. This usually requires a close look at other industries, since the industry within which a company competes may be chock-full of organizations that all have the same strategic mindset, and which therefore are not good sources of information. This type of review tends not to yield much in the way of short-term improvements, since strategic changes typically require several years of effort to implement. Thus, only the most forward-looking management teams tend to engage in this type of benchmarking, however useful it may prove to be in the long run.

How does one conduct a benchmarking study? The initial step is to decide exactly what to benchmark. Though there should already be some general idea of what is to be done, the topic initially presented may have been a broad one, within which several more specific projects could be fitted. For example, the initial proposal may have been to shorten the cycle time of the disbursements business process. However, there are a number of steps within this process, such as ordering and receiving goods, forwarding the paperwork to accounting, matching accounts payable documentation, and issuing payment. The project team may select only one of these subprocesses for a more detailed review.

Once the specific subprocess has been selected, the project team can collect information about the performance level of whatever is targeted. This information is needed in order to compare it with the results gained from a review of outside entities or other departments or divisions of the same company. For example, a review of a process might require a workflow diagram that details exactly how information flows through it, as well as the various control points and time requirements at each step in the process. Alternatively, a review of an existing product would require an analysis of its cost, as well as a complete description of its various features and level of quality.

The next step is to determine what companies to benchmark. There are a variety of ways to make a list of benchmarking targets. One is to review professional publications to see which ones are improving themselves in specific areas; another is to review general or industry-specific publications for the same information. Another source is speeches at industry symposiums. Yet another source may be networking connections between companies. If there are many company divisions, then yet another source is to call one's counterparts in those divisions.

Once a set of benchmarking targets have been selected, the project team must create a set of questions to ask the representatives of the companies with whom they will meet. This is a very important step, since the target companies are setting aside valuable time to meet with the team, and should not have their time wasted. To this end, the team should first create the largest possible list of questions, and then whittle it down to the most critical questions that can be definitely handled during the assigned meeting time with the target company. There should also be a secondary list of follow-up questions that can be used if there is still time available after the primary questions have been answered.

The completed review should give rise to a number of action items that can be used to either modify or (more rarely) replace the internal process, product, or strategy. However, before implementing any changes, this is a good time to interact with the personnel who will be impacted by them. The reason for doing so is that the person who will use the modification may be aware of internal problems that the project team is not aware of, and which will make the change inoperable.

With these preparations completed, the team should create a thorough implementation plan that describes the precise changes, when they will take place, what they will impact, and who will be responsible for them, not to mention any required training, capital purchases, or personnel changes. This plan should be carefully reviewed to ensure that nothing is missing, and that the timelines are reasonable.

A final step is to schedule a review of all changes after some time has passed during which the changes have had a chance to settle in and either succeed or fail. If they have failed, then the team must review the situation and recommend changes to the management team in regard to what further steps must now be taken. If the changes have been a success, then the benefits should be quantified and forwarded to the financial analyst who is reviewing the project, so that the management team can be informed of the return on investment of its benchmarking initiative.

Chapter 10

Product Design Decisions

The involvement of accountants with products is usually limited to the calculation of their costs for inventory costing purposes. Though this limited recordation role is useful, the accountant should become deeply involved in both the allocation of funding to new products and the analysis of costs during the product development process. The reason for this additional work is that approximately 90 percent of the cost of a product is designed into it, and cannot thereafter be altered; consequently, the accountant can have a huge impact on a company's cost of goods sold by actively providing cost accounting information to product design teams during the development process.

The key tool used to design lower costs into products is called target costing. The accountant needs to know how target costing works, how it impacts profitability, what data is needed for proper target costing analysis, how it can be incorporated into the budgeting process, and related issues. The following table itemizes the section number in which the answers to each question posed in this chapter can be found:

Section	Decision
10-1	How do I make funding decisions for research and development projects?
10-2	How does target costing work?
10-3	What is value engineering?
10-4	How does target costing impact profitability?
10-5	Are there any problems with target costing?
10-6	What is the accountant's role in a target costing environment?
10-7	What data is needed for a target costing analysis?
10-8	How do I control the target costing process?
10-9	Under what scenarios is target costing useful?
10-10	How can I incorporate target costing into the budget?
10-11	How can I measure the success of a target costing program?

10-1 HOW DO I MAKE FUNDING DECISIONS FOR RESEARCH AND DEVELOPMENT PROJECTS?

When allocating funding to research and development (R&D) projects, the traditional approach is to require all R&D proposals to pass a minimum return-on-investment hurdle rate. However, when there is limited funding available and too many investments passing the hurdle rate to all be funded, managers tend to pick the most likely projects to succeed. This selection process usually results in the least risky projects being funded, which are typically extensions of existing product lines or other variations on existing products that will not achieve breakthrough profitability. An alternative that is more likely to achieve a higher return on R&D investment is to apportion investable funds into multiple categories—a large percentage that is only to be used for highly risky projects with associated high returns, and a separate pool of funds specifically designated for lower-risk projects with correspondingly lower levels of return. The exact proportions of funding allocated to each category will depend on management's capacity for risk, as well as the size and number of available projects in each category. This approach allows a company the opportunity to achieve a breakthrough product introduction that it would probably not have funded if a single hurdle rate had been used to evaluate new product proposals.

If this higher-risk approach to allocating funds is used, it is likely that a number of new product projects will be abandoned prior to their release into the market, on the grounds that they will not yield a sufficient return on investment or will not be technologically or commercially feasible. This is not a bad situation, since some projects are bound to fail if a sufficiently high level of project risk is acceptable to management. Conversely, if no projects fail, this is a clear sign that management is not investing in sufficiently risky investments. To measure the level of project failure, calculate R&D waste, which is the amount of unrealized product development spending (e.g., the total expenditure on canceled projects during the measurement period). Even better, divide the amount of R&D waste by the total R&D expenditure during the period to determine the proportion of expenses incurred on failed projects. Unfortunately, this measure can be easily manipulated by accelerating or withholding the declaration of project termination. Nonetheless, it does give a fair indication of project risk when aggregated over the long term.

Though funding may be allocated into broad investment categories, management must still use a reliable method for determining which projects will receive funding and which will not. The standard approach is to apply a discount rate to all possible projects, and then to select those having the highest net present value (NPV). However, the NPV calculation does not include several key variables found in the expected commercial value (ECV) formula, making the ECV the preferred method. The ECV formula requires one to multiply a prospective project's net present value by the probability of its commercial success, minus the commercialization cost, and then multiply the result by the probability of technical success, minus the development cost. Thus, the intent of using ECV is to include all major success factors into the decision to accept or reject a new product proposal. The formula is as follows:

$$(((\text{Project net present value} \times \text{Probability of commercial success})$$
$$- \text{Commercialization cost}) \times (\text{Probability of technical success}))$$
$$- \text{Product development cost}$$

As an example of the use of ECV, the Moravia Corporation collects the following information about a new project for a battery-powered lawn trimmer, where there is some technical risk that a sufficiently powerful battery cannot be developed for the product:

Project net present value	$4,000,000
Probability of commercial success	90%
Commercialization cost	$750,000
Probability of technical success	65%
Product development cost	$1,750,000

Based on this information, Moravia computes the following ECV for the lawn trimmer project:

$$(((\$4,000,000 \text{ Project net present value} \times 90\% \text{ Probability of commercial success})$$
$$- \$750,000 \text{ Commercialization cost}) \times (65\% \text{ Probability of technical success}))$$
$$- \$1,750,000 \text{ Product development cost}$$
$$Expected\ commercial\ value = \$102,500$$

Even if some projects are dropped after being run through the preceding valuation analysis, this does not mean that they should be canceled for good. On the contrary, these projects may become commercially viable over time, depending on changes in price points, costs, market conditions, and technical viability. Consequently, the R&D manager should conduct a periodic review of previously shelved projects to see whether any of the factors just noted have changed sufficiently to allow the company to reintroduce a project proposal for development.

10-2 HOW DOES TARGET COSTING WORK?

The concept behind target costing is based on the realization that the bulk of all product costs are predetermined before a product ever reaches the production floor. This is because the types of materials used are determined during the design stage, as are the types of production methods used to shape and assemble the parts into a completed product. Consequently, the cost-reduction focus of any company that designs its own products should be to closely review the costs of products while they are still in the design stage, and do everything possible to keep those costs to a minimum.

The target costing methodology addresses the costs that are designed into a product with a four-step process:

Phase 1: Conduct Market Research. This involves reviewing the competitive land-scape to see what other products are in the marketplace, as well as the types of new products that competitors say they are about to release into the market. This also involves a review of which customers may buy future products, what needs they have, and what prices they are likely to pay for selected features on these products. Further, always determine the size of the market in which the new products are to be released, and the amount of market share that can likely be obtained. This gives a company the general outlines of a revenue plan, in terms of the probable number of units that can be sold and the price at which they would sell.

Phase 2: Determine Margin and Cost Feasibility. This involves clarifying what customers want for product features, based on the information gathered in the first step, and translating this into a preliminary set of product features that will go into the anticipated product design. Then determine a price point, again based on the preceding market research, at which the product is likely to sell. Then determine the standard margin to be applied to the product (which is commonly based on the corporate cost of capital, plus an additional percentage), which results in a cost figure that the product cannot exceed. Finally, conduct a preliminary review of anticipated product costs to see if the product design is in the cost ballpark. If not, cancel the design project as being unfeasible.

Phase 3: Meet Margin Targets through Design Improvements. This involves the completion of all value engineering needed to drive down the product's cost to the level at which the target price and margin can be attained, as well as confirming the viability of the material and process costs with suppliers and other parts of the company that are impacted by these design decisions. The design is then finalized, and the resulting bill of materials is sent to the purchasing staff for procurement, while the industrial engineering staff proceeds with the installation of all required changes to the production facility that are needed to implement lower-cost production processes.

Phase 4: Implement Continuous Improvement. This involves the product launch in the manufacturing facility, first through a pilot production run, and then as a launch at full production volumes. Also, the accountant begins the regular review of all supplier costs that contribute to the cost of the product, and reports on variances to management, to ensure that targeted cost levels will be maintained subsequent to the design phase.

These target costing steps are shown graphically in Exhibit 10.1.

10-3 WHAT IS VALUE ENGINEERING?

A concept called *value engineering* was noted in phase 2 of the preceding target costing steps. This is the collective term for a number of activities that are used to lower the cost of a product. Here are some of the issues that are dealt with during a value engineering review:

- *Can we eliminate functions from the production process?* This involves a detailed review of the entire manufacturing process to see whether there are any steps, such as interim quality reviews, that add no value to the product. By eliminating them it is possible to take their associated direct or overhead costs out of the product cost. However, these functions were originally put in for a

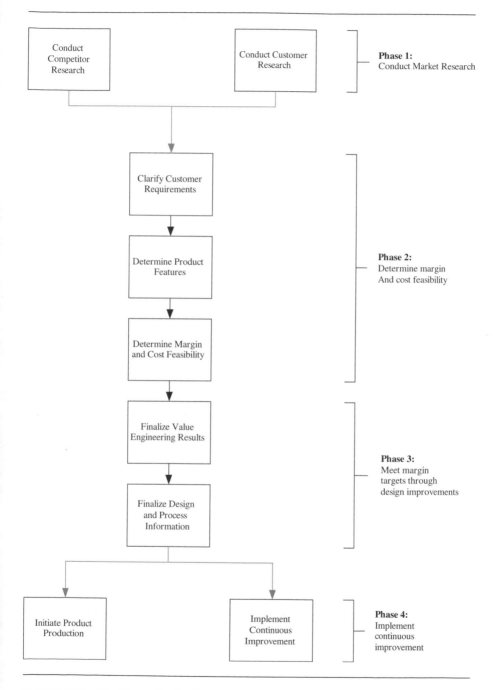

Exhibit 10.1 The Target Costing Process

reason, so the engineering team must be careful to develop workaround steps that eliminate the need for the original functions.

- *Can we eliminate some durability or reliability?* It is quite possible to design an excessive degree of sturdiness into a product. For example, a vacuum cleaner can be designed to withstand a one-ton impact, whereas there is only the most vanishing chance that such an impact will ever occur; designing it to withstand an impact of 100 pounds may account for 99.999 percent of all probable impacts, while also eliminating a great deal of structural materials from the design. However, this concept can be taken too far, resulting in a visible reduction in durability or reliability, so any designs that have had their structural integrity reduced must be thoroughly tested to ensure that they meet all design standards.

- *Can we minimize the design?* This involves the creation of a design that uses fewer parts or has fewer features. This approach is based on the assumption that a minimal design is easier to manufacture and assemble. Also, with fewer parts to purchase, there is less procurement overhead associated with the product. However, reducing a product to extremes, perhaps from dozens of components to just a few molded or prefabricated parts, can result in excessively high costs for those few remaining parts, since they may be so complex or custom-made in nature that it would be less expensive to settle for a few extra standard parts that are more easily and cheaply obtained.

- *Can we design the product better for the manufacturing process?* Also known as *design for manufacture and assembly* (DFMA), this involves the creation of a product design that can be created only in a specific manner. For example, a toner cartridge for a laser printer is designed so that it can be successfully inserted into the printer only when the correct sides of the cartridge are correctly aligned with the printer opening; all other attempts to insert the cartridge will fail. When used for the assembly of an entire product, this approach ensures that a product will not be incorrectly manufactured or assembled, which would otherwise call for a costly disassembly, or (even worse) product recalls from customers who have already received defective goods.

- *Can we substitute parts?* This approach encourages the search for less expensive components or materials that can replace more expensive parts that are currently used in a product design. This is an increasingly valid approach, since new materials are being developed every year. However, sometimes the use of a different material will impact the types of materials that can be used elsewhere in a product, which may result in cost increases in those other areas, for a net increase in costs. Thus, any parts substitution must be accompanied by a review of related changes elsewhere in the design. This step is also known as component parts analysis, which involves one extra activity—that of tracking the intentions of suppliers to continue producing parts in the future; if not, the affected parts must be eliminated from the product design.

- *Can we combine steps?* A detailed review of all processes associated with a product will sometimes reveal that some steps can be consolidated, which may mean that one is eliminated (as noted earlier), or that steps can be combined with one person, rather than having people in widely disparate parts of the production process perform them. This is also known as process centering. By combining steps in this manner, it is possible to eliminate some of the transfer and queue time from the production process, which in turn also reduces the chance that parts will be damaged during those transfers.

- *Is there a better way?* Though this step sounds awfully vague, it really strikes at the core of the cost-reduction issue—the other value engineering steps previously noted are ones that focus on incremental improvements to the existing design or production process, whereas this one is a more general attempt to start from scratch and build a new product or process that is not based in any way on preexisting ideas. Improvements resulting from this step tend to have the largest favorable impact on cost reductions, but also can be the most difficult for the organization to adopt, especially if it has used other designs or systems for the production of earlier models.

Another approach to value engineering is to call upon the services of the company's suppliers to assist in the cost-reduction effort. These organizations are particularly suited to the contribution of information concerning enhanced types of technology or materials, since they may specialize in such areas that a company has no information about. They may have also conducted extensive value engineering for the components that they manufacture, resulting in advanced designs that a company may be able to incorporate into its new products. Suppliers may have also redesigned their production processes, or can be assisted by a company's engineers to do so, resulting in cost reductions or reduced production waste that can be translated into lower component costs for a company.

A mix of all the value engineering steps noted above must be applied to each product design to ensure that the maximum permissible cost will be safely reached. Also, even if a minimal amount of value engineering is needed to reach a cost goal, one should conduct the full range of value engineering analysis anyway, since this can result in further cost reductions that will either improve the margin of the product or allow management the option to reduce the product's price, thereby causing havoc for competitors who sell higher-priced products.

10-4 HOW DOES TARGET COSTING IMPACT PROFITABILITY?

Target costing can have a startlingly large positive impact on profitability, depending on the commitment of management to its use, the constant involvement of accountants in all phases of a product's life cycle, and the type of strategy that a company follows.

Target costing improves profitability in two ways. One is that because it places such a detailed and continuing emphasis on product costs throughout the life cycle of every product, it is very unlikely that a company will experience runaway costs; also, the management team will be completely aware of costing issues, since it receives regular reports pertaining to costs from the cost accounting members of all design teams. The second way in which it improves profitability is through the precise targeting of the correct prices at which the company feels it can field a profitable product in the marketplace that will sell in a robust manner. This is opposed to the more common *cost-plus* approach, under which a company builds a product, then determines its cost, tacks on a profit, and then does not understand why its resoundingly high price does not attract any buyers. Thus, target costing results in not only better cost control, but also better price control.

Target costing is really part of a larger concept called *concurrent engineering*, which requires participants from many departments to work together in project teams, rather than having separate departments handle new product designs only after they have been handed off from the preceding department in the design chain. Clustering representatives from many departments together in a single design team can be quite a struggle, especially for older companies that have a history of conflict between departments. Consequently, only the most involved and prolonged support by all members of the senior management group will ensure that target costing, and the greater concept of concurrent engineering, will result in significant profitability improvements.

The review of product costs under the target costing methodology is not reserved for just the period up to the completion of design work on a new product. On the contrary, there are always opportunities to control costs after the design phase is completed, though the opportunities are smaller than during the design phase. Accordingly, accountants should not be pulled from a design team once the final drawings have left the engineering department. Instead, the accountants should regularly monitor actual component costs and compare them against planned costs, warning management whenever significant adverse variances arise. Also, they should take a lead role in the continuing review of supplier costs to see whether these can be reduced, perhaps by visiting supplier facilities, as well as constantly reviewing existing product designs to see whether they can be improved, and by targeting waste or spoilage on the production floor for elimination. Therefore, the accounting staff must be involved in all phases of a product's life cycle if a company is to realize the fullest extent of profitability improvements from target costing.

An issue that can get in the way of profitability is a company's type of strategy. If it is constantly issuing a stream of new products, or if it's existing product line is subject to severe pricing pressure, then it must make target costing a central part of its strategy, so that the correct price points are used for products and actual costs match those that were originally planned. However, there are other strategies, such as growth by geographical expansion of the current product line (as is practiced by retail stores), or growth by acquisition, where there is no particular need for target costing—these companies make their money in other ways than by a focused concentration on product features and costs. For them, there may still be a limited role for target costing, but it will be severely bounded by the reduced need for new products.

10-5 ARE THERE ANY PROBLEMS WITH TARGET COSTING?

Though the target costing system results in clear and substantial benefits in most cases, there are a few problems with it that one should be aware of, and guard against.

The first problem is that the development process can be lengthened to a considerable extent, since the design team may require a number of design iterations before it can devise a sufficiently low-cost product that will meet the target cost and margin criteria. This occurrence is most common when the project manager is unwilling to pull the plug on a design project that cannot meet its costing goals within a reasonable time frame. Usually, if there is no evidence of rapid progress toward a specific target cost within a relatively short time frame, then it is better to either ditch the project or at least shelve it for a short time and then try again, on the assumption that new cost-reduction methods or less-expensive materials will be available in the near future that will make the target cost an achievable one.

Another problem is that a great deal of mandatory cost cutting can result in finger pointing between various parts of the company, especially if employees in one area feel that they are being called on to provide a disproportionately large part of the savings. For example, the industrial engineering staff will not be happy if it is required to completely alter the production layout in order to generate cost savings, while the purchasing staff is not required to make any cost reductions through supplier negotiations. Avoiding this problem requires strong interpersonal and negotiation skills on the part of the project manager.

Finally, having representatives from a number of departments on the design team can sometimes make it more difficult to reach consensus on the proper design, because there are too many opinions on the team regarding design issues. This is a particular problem if there are particularly stubborn people on the design team who are holding out for specific product features. Resolving this problem requires a strong team manager, as well as a long-term commitment on the part of a company to weed out those people from design teams who are not willing to act in the best interests of the team.

For every problem area outlined here, the dominant solution is that of retaining strong control over the design teams, which calls for a good team leader. This person must have an exceptional knowledge of the design process, good interpersonal skills, and a commitment to attaining both time and cost budgets for a design project.

10-6 WHAT IS THE ACCOUNTANT'S ROLE IN A TARGET COSTING ENVIRONMENT?

Given the strong cost orientation in a target costing environment, there is obviously a considerable role for the accountant on a design team. What are the specific activities and required skills of this person?

The accountant should be able to provide for the other members of the design team a running series of cost estimates that are based on initial design sketches, activity-based costing reviews of production processes, and best-guess costing information from suppliers, based on estimated production volumes. Especially at the earliest stages of a design, the accountant will be working with vague cost information, and so must be able to provide estimates that are within a high–low range of costs, gradually tightening this estimated cost range as more information becomes available.

The accountant should also be responsible for any capital budgeting requests generated by the design team, since he or she has the most knowledge of the capital budgeting process, how to fill out required forms, and precisely what types of equipment are needed for the anticipated product design. The accountant also becomes the key contact on the design team for any questions from the finance staff regarding issues or uncertainties in the capital budgeting proposal.

The accountant should work with the design team to help it understand the nature of various costs (such as cost allocations based on an activity-based costing system), as well as the cost/benefit trade-offs of using various design or cost options in the new product.

In addition, the accountant is responsible for tracking the gap between the current cost of a product design and the target cost that is the design team's goal, which should include an itemization of where cost savings have already been achieved and in what areas of the product there has not been a sufficient degree of progress.

Finally, the accountant must continue to compare a product's actual cost against the target cost after the design is complete, and for as long as the company is selling the product. This is a very necessary step, because management must know immediately if costs are increasing beyond budgeted levels and why those increases are occurring.

Given the large number of activities for which an accountant is responsible under the target costing methodology, it is evident that the job is a full-time one for all but the smallest costing projects. Accordingly, an accountant will commonly be sent to a design team as a long-term assignment, and may even report to the design team's manager, with no or few ties back to the accounting department. This may even be a different career track for an accountant, being permanently attached to a series of design teams.

There are very particular qualifications that an accountant must have before being assigned to a target costing team. One is certainly having a good knowledge of company products, as well as their features and components. Also, the accountant must know how to create an activity-based costing system to evaluate related production costs, or at least interpret such costing data that has been developed by someone else. Further, this person must work well in a team environment, proactively assisting other members of the team in constantly evaluating the costs of new design concepts. Further, the person should have good analysis and presentation skills, since the ongoing costing results must be continually presented not only to other members of the team, but also to the members of the milestone review committee. Accordingly, the best accountant for this position is an outgoing one with some years of experience within a company or industry.

10-7 WHAT DATA IS NEEDED FOR A TARGET COSTING ANALYSIS?

The typical accountant is used to extracting data from a central accounting database that has been carefully stocked with the most accurate and reliable data, from such a variety of sources as accounts payable, billings, bills of material, and inventory records. However, the accountant who is assigned to a target costing project must deal with much more poorly defined information, as well as data that is drawn from much different sources than he or she may be accustomed to using.

In the earliest stages of a product design, the accountant must make the best possible guesses regarding the costs of proposed designs. Information about these costs can be garnered through the careful review of possible component parts, as well as comparison with the cost of existing products that bear some similarity to the designs now under review. No matter what the method, it will result in relatively rough cost estimates, especially during the earliest stages of a new product's development. To operate in this environment takes an accountant with a wide-ranging view of costing systems and the willingness to start with rough estimates and gradually polish them into more concrete information as designs gradually solidify. Accordingly, accountants with a narrow focus should not be allowed on a product design team.

Though cost estimates will be admittedly rough in the earliest stages of a new product design, it is possible to include with the *best* estimate an additional estimate of the *highest* possible cost that will be experienced. This additional information lets management know whether there is a significant degree of risk that the project may not be able to achieve its desired cost target. Though this information can result in the outright termination of a project, it is much more common for senior management to interview the project director in some detail to gain a better understanding of the variables underlying an excessively high cost estimate, as well as the chances that those costs can be reduced back to within the targeted levels. Only after obtaining this additional information should a company make the decision to cancel a product design project.

There are also new sources of data that an accountant can access. One is competitor information, which is collected by the marketing staff or an outside research agency. This database contains information about the prices at which competitors are selling their products, as well as the prices of ancillary products, and perhaps also the discounts given at various price points. It can also include market share data for individual products or by firm, as well as the opinions of customers regarding the offerings of various companies and the financial condition of competitors. This information is mostly used to determine the range of price points at which a company should sell its existing or anticipated products, as well as the features that should be included at each price point. The extra information about the financial condition and market shares of competitors may also be of use, since a company can elect to alter the pricing of its products if this will lead to a better market position against them. This database is of great value to the accountant in determining the price at which products should be released to the market.

Another database used by the accountant is one that details the cost structure of competitors. This information is compiled by a combination of the marketing and engineering staffs through a process called reverse engineering. Under this methodology, a company buys a competitor's product and then disassembles it in order to determine the processes and materials used to create them, and their costs. This information is of great value in determining the greatest allowable cost of a new product design, since a company can copy from the methods and materials used by a competitor if this will lead to a reduction in costs. The information is also of use from a pricing perspective, since it gives management some idea of the profits that a competitor is probably obtaining from sales of its products; it can then aggressively price some or all of its competing products low enough to take away some of the profits the competitor would otherwise enjoy, possibly putting it in a severe financial situation.

Another database that the accountant should peruse is that of cost data. This is not the inventory or bill of materials data that is already available in the typical accounting database, but rather the costs that are associated with specific product features or the production functions required to manufacture them. This type of information is not at all commonly found in the accounting system. Instead, the engineering staff may have compiled, over the course of numerous design projects, a set of cost tables that itemize the costs of those components or clusters of components that are used to give a product a specific feature. Also, the cost of specific production functions generally requires the in-depth analysis that can be obtained only through a prolonged activity-based accounting review. If none of this information is available, an enterprising accountant that is assigned to a product design team may take it upon herself to conduct this cost research, thereby not only improving the costing database of the current product design team, but also providing a valuable basis of information for future design teams.

Yet another database is that of engineering data. This information does not stop with the usual bills of materials, since it also includes notes on upcoming technological changes that can be used to enhance the features of existing products. There should also be information about the interaction of various components of a product, so that one can predict what cost changes are likely to arise in one subsystem of a product if a part is reconfigured in another subsystem. Further, there should be information available about the changes in costs that will arise by using a smaller or greater number of fasteners, different materials, different product sizes or weights, or a host of other factors. All of this information is not easily reduced into a standard database format, and so it tends to be partially paper based and not so well organized as the information stored in other databases. Nonetheless, this is a valuable tool for the accountant, since it yields many clues regarding how costs can be altered as a result of changes in product designs.

The final database that is available to the cost accounting member of a design team is supplier information. This should include information about the previous quality, cost, and on-time delivery performance of all key suppliers, as well as the production capacity capabilities of each one. It may even reach a sufficient level of detail to include assumed profitability levels for each supplier. The accountant can use this information to determine which standard parts are no longer acceptable for future product designs, based on a history of high costs, poor quality, or inadequate on-time delivery performance. Also, if suppliers clearly have inadequate profits, this may signal their inability to obtain further cost reductions through capital asset purchases, which may call for the need to switch to a different supplier.

Based on the wide variety of data sources noted in this section, it is evident that the accountant who is an integral member of a product design team has access to a great deal of information that is of great use in determining product prices and costs. However, few of these data sources are the same as the typical accountant is used to accessing, nor do they contain the extremely high level of data accuracy that is more common in an accounting database. Consequently, the accountant who uses this information must be well trained in its use as well as its shortcomings, and be able to use it to realistically portray expected cost and margin levels, given its imprecise nature.

10-8 HOW DO I CONTROL THE TARGET COSTING PROCESS?

A target costing program will eventually result in major cost reductions if design teams are given an unlimited amount of time to pass through a multitude of design iterations. However, there comes a point where the cost of maintaining the design team exceeds that of the savings to be garnered from additional iterations. Also, most products must be released within a reasonably short time frame, or else they will miss the appropriate market window when they will beat the delivery of competing products into the market. To avoid both of these cost and time delays, we use milestones as the principal control point over a target costing program.

There should be a number of milestone reviews incorporated into a target costing program. Each one should include a thorough analysis of the progress of the design team since the last milestone review, such as a comparison of the current cost of a design as compared with its target cost. The key issue here is that the amount of cost yet to be worked out of a product must shrink, on either a dollar or percentage basis, after each successive milestone review, or else management has the right to cancel the design project. For example, there may be a standard allowable cost variance of 12 percent for the first milestone meeting, then 10 percent at the next meeting, and so on until the target cost must be reached by a specific future milestone date. If a design team cannot quite reach its target cost, but comes very close, then the management team should be required to make a *go/no-go* decision at that time that either overrides the cost target and sends the design into production, allows time for additional design iterations, or terminates the project.

A milestone can be based on a time budget, such as one per month, or on the points in the design process when specific activities are completed. For example, a milestone review will occur as soon as each successive design iteration has been completed, or perhaps when conceptual drawings are finished, when the working model has been created, or when the production pilot has been run. In this latter case, there will be many more steps that the management group can build into the milestone review process, so that cost analyses become a nearly continual part of the target costing regimen.

10-9 UNDER WHAT SCENARIOS IS TARGET COSTING USEFUL?

Target costing is most useful in those situations where the majority of product costs are locked in during the product design phase. This applies to most manufactured products, but few services. In the services arena, such as consulting, the bulk of all activities can be reconfigured for cost reduction during the "production" phase, which is when services are being provided directly to the customer. In the services environment, the "design team" is still present, but is more commonly concerned with the streamlining of the activities conducted by those employees who are providing the service, which can continue to be enhanced at any time, not just when the initial services process is being laid out.

For example, a design team can lay out the floor plan of a fast-food restaurant, with the objective of creating an arrangement that allows employees to walk the shortest possible distances while preparing food and serving customers; this is similar to the design of a new product. However, unlike a product design, this layout can be readily altered at any time if the design team can arrive at a better layout, so that the restaurant staff can continue to experience high levels of productivity improvement even after the initial design and layout of the restaurant facility. In this situation, costs are not locked in during the design phase, so there is less need for target costing.

Another situation in which target costing results in less value is the production of raw materials, such as chemicals. In this case, there are no design features for a design team to labor over; instead, the industrial engineering staff tries to create the most efficient possible production process, which has little to do with cost reduction through the improvement of customer value through the creation of a product with a high ratio of features to costs.

10-10 HOW CAN I INCORPORATE TARGET COSTING INTO THE BUDGET?

In order to increase the level of accuracy in the budgeted cost of goods sold, there should be a linkage between the product design teams and the budgeting staff. This should involve a requirement for all accountants participating in product design teams to forward status reports to the budgeting staff for the current status of all product design projects for which target costing is used. This has the following positive impacts on the budgeting process:

- The preliminary budget can be adjusted continually to reflect the go/no-go status of each design project. Thus, if the decision is made to eliminate a prospective product, its related revenues and costs can be immediately removed from the budget model.
- The budgeted cost of goods sold for each product can be adjusted to match the estimated final cost of each new product design.

To incorporate this target costing information into the budgeting process, the budget model must already itemize revenues and costs at the individual product level. However, if the current budget model aggregates revenues and costs only at the product line level, one can at least incorporate into the model (in percentage terms) the general impact expected from a target costing program.

10-11 HOW CAN I MEASURE THE SUCCESS OF A TARGET COSTING PROGRAM?

The best measure of the success of a target costing program is the ratio of total actual product costs to target costs. The goal should be to achieve a percentage of 100 percent or less. To calculate this measurement, divide the total of actual expected product costs by the total amount of targeted costs. A footnote should accompany this measurement, stating the expected production volume at which the costs are stated. The reason for this extra wording is that component costs can change drastically if assumed volumes vary. For example, if a target cost is based on an expected unit volume of 50,000, but the actual expected costs are based on a revised unit volume of only 10,000, then it is quite likely that the cost of components will increase dramatically. The formula is as follows:

$$\frac{\text{Total of actual product costs}}{\text{Total of target costs}}$$

For example, the engineering manager for a copier design team is conducting a post-design review of the team's performance. The team did not meet its target cost goal, and the manager is wondering what could have given earlier warning of the costing problem. She has obtained the following information about design costs over the term of the project:

	Milestone 1	Milestone 2	Milestone 3	Approval
Actual cost	$2,050	$1,970	$1,880	$1,820
Target cost	$1,640	$1,640	$1,640	$1,640
Ratio of actual to target cost	125%	120%	115%	111%
Expected ratio	125%	112%	108%	100%

The measurements in the table show that the design team was on track at the first design milestone by keeping actual expected costs at a level 25 percent higher than the final target cost. However, the team slipped significantly at the second milestone, and was never able to reduce costs thereafter, resulting in a final design that was 11 percent more expensive than the target. More active management of the design process after the second milestone might have prevented this problem from arising.

The element missing from this measurement is the quality of the resulting products. A design team can quite possibly achieve a target cost and issue a completed product design, but if its associated warranty and scrap costs are too high, the lifetime cost of the product to the company will exceed the initial target cost. Consequently, this measure must be coupled with a set of minimum quality specifications; one may also want to track lifetime target costs, rather than just the initial target product costs, in order to quantify the cost of quality.

Another issue, as noted under the description of the formula, is that the individual component costs used to compile the total target cost can vary greatly, depending on the assumed volume of production; this is because components that are purchased in bulk are typically less expensive than when they are bought in small quantities, as would be the case for small production volumes.

An additional issue is that a design team usually is required to meet increasingly stringent costing targets as it moves closer to the final approval of its product design. As it passes each design milestone, its actual projected cost is expected to come a bit closer to the target cost. Consequently, it makes sense to calculate this measurement at every milestone and compare it with the target cost at that point, rather than waiting until completion of the entire project to see whether the costing goal was attained. By measuring on this trend line, management can spot design cost problems early, and correct them before designs are finalized.

Chapter 11

Pricing Decisions

The realm of price setting is an arcane one for the accountant, who is frequently asked for advice regarding the best price at which a product or service should be set. This apparently simple issue involves a multitude of questions, including how low a price can be set, how to determine long-range prices, whether to follow the pricing of the industry leader, how to set transfer prices, and what to do about predatory pricing or dumping by competitors. The answers to these questions, and more, can be found in this chapter.

The following table itemizes the section number in which the answers to each question posed in this chapter can be found:

Section	Decision
11-1	What is the lowest price that I should accept?
11-2	How do I set long-range prices?
11-3	How should I set prices over the life of a product?
11-4	How do I determine cost-plus pricing?
11-5	How should I set prices against a price leader?
11-6	How do I handle a price war?
11-7	How do I handle predatory pricing by a competitor?
11-8	How do I handle dumping by a foreign competitor?
11-9	When is transfer pricing important?
11-10	How do transfer prices alter corporate decision making?
11-11	What transfer pricing method should I use?

11-1 WHAT IS THE LOWEST PRICE THAT I SHOULD ACCEPT?

A customer may call with a special request for an order that is priced very low. The customer may be playing off the company against another one of its suppliers, or perhaps has a very large order, or maybe is just fishing for a good deal—the reason for a low pricing request does not matter. The company has to decide whether it will take the offer.

The basic rule is that the lowest price is the one that at least covers all variable costs of production, plus a small profit. Anything lower would cost a company money to produce and therefore would make no economic sense. The main issue becomes the determination of what variable costs to include in the variable cost calculation. Variable costs *may* include the following:

- Direct labor
- Direct machine costs

- Inventory carrying costs
- Materials
- Ordering costs
- Quality costs (testing, inspection, and rework)
- Receiving costs
- Scrap costs

The costs in this list are those that may vary directly with production volume. Not every item will be considered a variable cost at some companies. For example, if the purchasing staff is unlikely to be laid off as a result of not taking the customer order, then the purchasing cost is probably not a variable one; the same reasoning can be used to assume that the receiving costs and even the direct labor costs are not really variable. Also, the direct machine costs, such as for utilities and any volume-related maintenance or machine labor, may be still be incurred even if the order is not accepted, and so will not be called variable. Given all these exceptions, it is apparent that the product's list of variable costs may be quite small (possibly only the cost of materials), resulting in an equally small cost that must be covered by the customer's price.

There are several objections to the exclusion of overhead costs from the pricing formula. First, it may result in extremely low price points that will not allow a company to cover all of its expenses, which results in a loss. Over the long term, this is an accurate assessment. However, in the short term, if a company has excess production capacity available and can use it to sell additional product that generates throughput, then it should do so in order to increase profits. If its production capacity is already maximized, then proposed sales having lower throughput levels than items already being manufactured should be rejected.

Second, traditional accounting holds that a small proposed order that requires a lengthy machine setup should have the cost of that setup assigned to the product; if the additional cost results in a loss on the proposed transaction, then the sale should be rejected. However, it is quite likely that a company's existing production capacity can absorb the cost of the incremental setup without incurring any additional cost. Under this logic, if there is excess production capacity, then setups are free. This approach tends to result in a company offering a much richer mix of order sizes and products to its customers, which can yield a greater market share. However, this concept must be used with caution, for at some point the ability of the company to continually set up small production jobs will maximize its capacity, at which point there will be an incremental cost to adding more production jobs.

The third issue arises not from traditional cost accounting, but from federal government pricing rules. If a company enters into a contract to offer products or services to the federal government at a certain predetermined price, a key provision of the contract will be that the government will automatically receive the lowest price offered by the company to any of its customers. Consequently, when reviewing new pricing proposals, the sales staff should be mindful of how a new price point will impact any existing sales to and throughput arising from transactions with the federal government.

The short-term pricing concept is best illustrated with an example. A customer of the Low-Ride Bicycle Company wants to buy 1,000 bicycles from it, which it will sell in another country where it has recently opened a sales branch. The customer wants Low-Ride to offer its best possible price for this deal. The manager of Low-Ride knows that the same offer is being made to the company's chief competitor, Easy-Glide Bicycles. The company's cost to create a bicycle in a lot size of 1,000 units is as follows:

	Cost Per Unit
Direct labor	$13.50
Direct machine cost	20.17
Inventory carrying cost	None
Materials	72.15
Ordering costs	Fixed
Quality costs	3.02
Receiving costs	Fixed
Scrap costs	7.22
Total Cost	$116.06

The owner of Low-Ride has received the request for pricing at the slowest time of the production year, when he normally lays off several staff members. He sees this as a golden opportunity to retain employees, which is more important to him than earning a profit on this order. Consequently, he can charge a price of as little as $116.06 per bike, as derived in the preceding table, though this will leave him with no profit. He has recently hired the production manager away from Easy-Glide Bicycles, and knows that Easy-Glide has a similar cost structure, except for 20 percent higher scrap costs. Accordingly, he knows that Easy-Glide's minimum variable cost will be higher by $1.44. This means that he can add $1.43 to his price and still be lower than the competing price. Therefore, he quotes $117.49 per unit to the customer.

11-2 HOW DO I SET LONG-RANGE PRICES?

The pricing decisions just outlined for short-range situations are ones that will bring a company to the brink of bankruptcy if it uses them at all times, for they do not allow for a sufficient profit margin to pay for a company's overhead, not to mention the profit it needs in order to provide some return to investors on their capital. Proper long-range pricing requires the consideration of several additional costs, which are as follows:

- *Product-specific overhead costs.* This is the overhead associated with the production of a single unit of production. This tends to be a very small cost category, for if a cost can be accurately identified down to this level, it is considered to be a variable cost instead of a fixed one.
- *Batch-specific overhead costs.* A number of overhead costs are accumulated at this level, such as the cost of labor required to set up or break down a machine for a batch of production, the utility cost required to run machines for the duration of the batch, the cost of materials handlers needed to move components to the production area as well as remove finished products from it, and an allocation of the depreciation on all machinery used in the process.
- *Product line–specific overhead costs.* A product line may have associated with it the salary of a product manager, a design team, a production supervisor, and quality control personnel, customer service, distribution, advertising costs, and an ongoing investment in inventory. All of these overhead costs can be allocated to the products that are the end result of the overhead costs incurred.
- *Facility-specific overhead costs.* Production must take place somewhere, and the cost of that "somewhere" should be allocated to the production lines housed within it, usually based on the square footage taken up by the machines used in each production process. The costs of overhead in this category can include building depreciation, taxes, insurance, maintenance, and the cost of any maintenance staff.

The costs described here can greatly exceed the total variable cost of a product, as described under the preceding section. When fully applied to all products manufactured, the marketing staff will commonly find that the resulting product costs are several times higher than is the case when only variable costs are considered. This is a particular concern for companies that require a large (and expensive) base of automated machinery to manufacture their products, for they have such a large investment in overhead that they must add on a very large additional cost to their variable costs, as well as a reasonable profit, before arriving at a long-range price that will adequately cover all costs.

The size of the markup added to the variable and fixed costs of a product should at least equal the target rate of return. This rate is founded on a firm's cost of capital, which is the blended cost of all debt and equity currently held. If the markup margin used is lower than this amount, then a company will not be able to pay off debt or equity holders over the long term, thereby reducing the value of the company and driving it toward bankruptcy. It may also be necessary to increase the target rate of return by several additional percentage points, in case managers feel that the product in question may have a high risk of not selling over a prolonged period of time at adequate levels; by increasing the markup, the price is driven higher, and the company earns back its investment sooner than would otherwise be the case (assuming that customers are still willing to buy the product at the higher price).

To continue with the example from the previous question, if the Low-Ride Bicycle Company wants to determine its long-range bicycle price, it should include the additional factors noted in the following table, which covers all possible fixed costs plus a markup to cover its cost of capital:

	Cost Per Unit
Total variable cost	$116.06
Product-specific overhead costs	0.00
Batch-specific overhead costs	41.32
Product line–specific overhead costs	5.32
Facility-specific overhead costs	1.48
Markup of 12%	19.70
Total long-range price	$183.88

11-3 HOW SHOULD I SET PRICES OVER THE LIFE OF A PRODUCT?

It may not be sufficient to think of long-range pricing as just the addition of all fixed costs to a product's variable costs. Such thinking does not factor in all changes in a product's costs and expected margins that can reasonably be expected over the course of its market life. For example, if one were to compile the full cost of a product at the point when it has just been developed, the cost per unit will be very high, for sales levels will be quite small; this means that production runs will also be short, so that overhead costs per unit will be very high. Also, it is common for a company with the first new product in a market to add a high margin onto this already high unit cost, resulting in a very high initial price. Later in the product's life, it will gain greater market share, so that more products are manufactured, resulting in lower overhead costs per unit. However, competing products will also appear on the market, which will force the company to reduce its margins in order to offer competitive pricing. Thus, the full cost of a product will vary depending on the point at which it is currently residing in its life cycle.

The best way to deal with long-range pricing over the course of a product's entire life cycle is to use a company's previous history with variations in cost, margin, and sales volume for similar products to estimate likely cost changes in a new product during its life cycle. An example of this is shown in Exhibit 11.1.

Exhibit 11.1 Life Cycle Pricing

	Startup Phase	Growth Phase	Maturity Phase	Totals for All Phases
Unit Volume	10,000	200,000	170,000	380,000
Variable Cost/ea	$4.50	$4.25	$4.15	$4.21
Fixed Cost Pool	$300,000	$650,000	$575,000	$1,525,000
Fixed Cost/ea	$30.00	$3.25	$3.38	$4.01
Total Cost/ea	$34.50	$7.50	$7.53	$8.22
Expected Margin	30%	20%	15%	19%
	$44.85	**$9.00**	**$8.66**	**$9.79**
Total Revenue	$448,500	$1,800,000	$1,472,200	$3,720,700
Total Variable Cost	$45,000	$850,000	$705,500	$1,600,500
Total Fixed Cost	$300,000	$650,000	$575,000	$1,525,000
Total Margin	$103,500	$300,000	$191,700	$595,200

The exhibit shows that a company will have a considerable amount of overhead costs to recoup during the startup phase of a new product life cycle, which will require a high price per unit, given the low expected sales volume at this point. However, setting a very high initial price for a product leaves a great deal of pricing room for competitors to enter the market; accordingly, many companies are now choosing to initially lose money on new product introductions by setting their prices at the long-range price rather than at the short-range price that is needed to recoup startup costs. By doing so, they send a signal to potential market entrants that they are willing to compete at low initial price points that will leave little room for outsized profits by new market entrants. This strategy forgoes large initial profits, but may reduce the number of competitors, thereby reducing the level of competition in the long run.

The exhibit also shows that sales volumes will gradually decline as a product enters the maturity phase of its life cycle. At this point, price competition becomes fierce, as competitors strive to fill their production capacity by undercutting competitors. The company must make a decision at this point to either compete with low prices, terminate a product, or replace it with an improved one that is just starting a new product life cycle.

Based on a table similar to that shown in Exhibit 11.1, a company can determine the most appropriate pricing strategy to adopt over a product's entire life cycle, so that the company is appropriately positioned in the marketplace and can earn the greatest possible profit over the entire period during which a product is sold.

11-4 HOW DO I DETERMINE COST-PLUS PRICING?

There are some cases where a company is asked by a customer to quote a price on a project or product that is so difficult to produce that the company is at great risk of incurring large cost overruns in order to complete it. An example of this is practically any new defense project involving leading-edge technology, such as weapons that have never even been designed before, much less produced. In these cases, a company will typically quote an astronomically high price, which will give it a sufficient amount of margin cushion to yield a healthy profit on the endeavor, no matter how expensive it is to complete. The customer usually cannot support the high price, and instead offers a cost-plus pricing contract.

Cost-plus pricing is when a customer reimburses a company for all of the costs incurred to develop and produce a product that it has ordered, plus a predetermined margin. There is a strong incentive for a company to agree to such a pricing deal, for there is no way to lose—all costs are guaranteed to be covered by the customer. For this very reason, however, the customer is very concerned that only those costs are charged to it that are contractually agreed upon in advance. These allowable costs may be itemized in great detail in the contract with a customer. All variable costs will always be reimbursable; the main issue instead is how much overhead can be charged to the contract. For example, there will be a preset percentage of total plant or corporate overhead that can be charged, which cannot be exceeded. There may also be a pricing formula that allows only a certain amount of overhead to be charged to a project that is incurred for a set of projects (such as the cost of an engineering supervisor who reviews the work for several projects at once). The amounts of these allocation percentages tend to be negotiated for each contract, so they are never consistent.

There may also be stipulations in a cost-plus agreement that some portion of cost savings created by the company will be shared with the customer. This rule is required by many customers on the reasonable grounds that they are footing the entire bill for any overruns in costs, so they should be entitled to a share of any cost reductions. If this stipulation is present, then the accountant must create a tracking system that identifies and accumulates all cost savings, which can be a difficult chore.

Some contracts allow overhead to be allocated to a project (and then billed to the customer) based on a set dollar rate per unit of activity (e.g., $3.25 for every hour of direct labor incurred). Customers realize that such overhead allocation clauses can be abused, since an excessive number of units of activity charged to a project will result in an excessively large overhead cost being billed. Accordingly, the accountant must be particularly careful to charge these activities to the correct jobs, and to maintain complete records to back up this information.

11-5 HOW SHOULD I SET PRICES AGAINST A PRICE LEADER?

There may be a price leader in the marketplace who sets product prices. This tends to be a company with a dominant share of the market, and usually the lowest cost structure, and who therefore can control the price of a large share of all products sold in a particular market niche. If another company tries to sell its products at a higher price it will find that customers will not accept the increase, for they can still buy products from the price leader at a lower rate. If a company wants to sell its products for less than the prices set by the price leader, it can do so, but the leader's dominance will probably prevent the company from gaining much market share through this strategy. Consequently, most companies in such industries tend to adopt whatever price points are set by the price leader. A good example of this is the Mars Company, which has a dominant share of the candy market. It sets the prices for the products one finds stacked at the supermarket checkout lane, and all competitors are compelled to use the same pricing. In such cases as this, a company has no control over the price points at which it can sell its products.

11-6 HOW DO I HANDLE A PRICE WAR?

When there is too much production capacity in an industry and not enough available customer sales to use up that capacity, a common outcome is a price war, where one company lowers its prices in order to steal customers away from a competitor, which in turn matches or reduces these prices in order to retain its customers. During a price war, the only winner is the customer, who experiences greatly reduced prices; however, it is ruinous for companies that are slashing prices.

One way to avoid a price war is to analyze the perceived value of each feature of a company's products in relation to similar products produced by competitors. If a company can clearly identify selected product features that a competitor's offerings do not contain, then these features can be heavily promoted in order to raise the perceived overall value of the products in the eyes of customers, which allows a company to avoid a price war. However, this analysis should be conducted well in advance of a price war, so that the proper mix of high-value features will be present at all times. A discerning competitor will be able to see this differentiation, and may realize that a price war will not work.

Another option is for the accountant to conduct a competitive analysis of the company that is initiating a price war, to see if its cost structure will not allow it to cut prices to sustainable levels that are lower than what the company can support. If not, then a rational pricing move by the company is to briefly cut prices to levels below the variable cost of the competitor, thereby sending it a clear message that further price competition will put it out of business. This is a particularly effective approach if the accounting staff can discover whether the competitor is outsourcing its production. If so, the entire cost of the outsourced product is variable, as opposed to a mix of fixed and variable costs when production is kept in-house. This gives an in-house manufacturer an advantage over an outsourced manufacturer, because the in-house manufacturer has the option of not including fixed costs in its pricing calculations in the short run, whereas the outsourced manufacturer has no fixed costs to exclude. This gives the in-house manufacturer an inherent advantage in the event of a price war. For example, companies A and B produce exactly the same product. Company A manufactures it in-house, and incurs a $10 cost that is half fixed and half variable cost. Company B, however, outsources its production, and must pay $10 from its supplier for each unit it buys. This manufacturing scenario gives company A the clear advantage over company B in the event of a price war, for company A can slash its price down to its variable cost of $5, whereas B can drop prices only to its variable cost of $10. Thus, the type of manufacturing system used has a direct bearing on the competitive positioning of companies that are locked in a price war.

Another option is for the accounting staff to develop a detailed rendering of the company's cost structure and release this information to the public, perhaps through a professional magazine or newspaper interview. By doing so, competitors will access the information and realize that the company's cost structure is lower than theirs, and that waging a price war would not result in their winning it. This option, of course, is a viable one only for companies with a distinct cost advantage over their competitors.

Yet another solution to a price war is to contact key customers and offer them special long-term deals, which locks them into set pricing levels for what will presumably be the duration of the price war. This strategy has been used by most of the phone companies, where customers signed up for several years of phone service at slightly reduced prices, but which turned out to be higher prices than the going rate, as the price war drove long-distance rates ever downward. This allowed the phone companies to earn extra revenue that would otherwise have been lost.

Another strategy is to create a new product or product line, with new features and market positioning, while letting the old product gradually be eliminated by a price war. By doing so, a company allows competitors to reduce their margins to dangerous levels while it neatly sidesteps the entire problem by concentrating on a slightly different market. The approach can also be reversed by leaving the price point of the old product alone, and instead designing a new and much-lower-cost product that can more effectively compete in a price war. Yet another variation is to design a new product that is sufficiently different that customers are faced with an apples-to-oranges comparison of competing products; they cannot judge which competing product is the better value, and so the price war never gets started. Any of these approaches require a considerable amount of time to implement, and so it works best for those companies that have a significant ability to roll out new products on a regular basis.

If all of these options fail, then the only alternative left is to participate in a price war. If this becomes necessary, the best way to do so is to cut prices at the first hint of a price war, to set deeply discounted prices, and to do so with great fanfare. By taking this aggressive approach, competitors will know that a company is serious about its participation in a price war and that it intends to pursue the war until all other competitors back off. This hard-and-fast response can sometimes stop a price war before it has had time to build momentum. Some companies take this concept a step further by publicizing their intention to cut prices in the business press before anyone even attempts to initiate a price war; this tells everyone what kind of reception they can expect if they cut prices and may keep them from starting a price war.

11-7 HOW DO I HANDLE PREDATORY PRICING BY A COMPETITOR?

A company can bring charges of predatory pricing against a competitor when it feels that the competitor is creating deals with customers that either prevent them from doing business with the company or involve especially low pricing that is designed to drive the company out of business. Generally, predatory pricing is considered to be pricing activities that aim to exclude competitors from the marketplace on some other basis than internal efficiency.

These issues are addressed by three Acts of Congress. The first is the Clayton Act, which specifies that a company may not sell products or services to its customers on the express condition that they do not do business with a competitor. This exclusion of competitors can also be based on a special rebate or discount being offered to the customer. The second Act is the Robinson-Patman Act, which is actually an amendment to the Clayton Act. It states that it is unlawful to discriminate in price between different purchasers of commodities of like grade and quality, where the effect is to substantially lessen competition or tend to create a monopoly in any line of commerce; however, one can change prices based on the costs of manufacture, sale, or delivery resulting from the differing methods or quantities in which such commodities are sold. The Act does not prevent pricing changes in response to the marketability of goods, such as the deterioration of perishable goods, obsolescence, distress sales under court process, or upon the discontinuance of a business. Finally, the previously noted Sherman Act can also be applied to cases of predatory pricing, since it is a clear form of trade restriction.

The intent of these Acts is to foster competition by outlawing any predatory pricing situations that will result in the elimination of competitors from the marketplace and that lead to a reduced number of competitors that thereby have greater leeway to raise prices.

Proving a charge of predatory pricing is extremely difficult. It is necessary to show that a competitor has a specific intent to monopolize a market, that it has done so through predatory activities, and that it has a reasonably high chance of achieving its goal of creating a monopoly. The first two issues can be proven by showing that a competitor is indeed setting prices below its costs, while the probability of creating a monopoly is proven by presenting a case that the competitor is likely to recoup the costs incurred by its predatory pricing, once other companies have been driven out of the market.

The two problems that arise in proving a case of predatory pricing are the definition of a competitor's product cost, and its likelihood of recouping its lost profits. The Supreme Court has left the first issue wide open by not defining the proper measure of cost, preferring to let lower courts decide the issue on a case-by-case basis. Should it be full cost, with all overhead allocated, or variable cost, with all overhead excluded, or some point in between? In order to have a clear chance of winning a predatory pricing case, one should be able to prove that the price charged by a competitor is below its variable cost, which is the lowest possible cost that can be applied to a product. If the price charged is higher than this level, then a competitor can probably successfully defend itself on the grounds that it is making short-range marginal pricing decisions.

It is equally difficult to prove that a competitor is likely to recoup its lost profits from predatory pricing through the creation of a monopoly. One reason is that, once the competitor drives other companies out of the marketplace, it will raise prices again, which will attract new competitors to the market, thereby keeping it from raising prices to the high levels needed for it to recoup its lost profits. There must be significant barriers to entry that will allow the competitor to "own" the market for a sufficiently lengthy period of time before new competitors will arrive and drive down prices once again. Examples of such barriers are legal requirements, such as lengthy licensing procedures or patents, or capacity issues, such as long lead times to build production facilities.

Given the difficulty of proving predatory pricing, this is not a charge that is commonly won in court. However, such a lawsuit can soak up the resources of a competitor for a lengthy period, distracting it from daily business issues, and so such lawsuits will appear with some regularity.

To guard against a predatory pricing lawsuit, the accountant should build a cost tracking system that details all variable costs associated with all products sold, so that this information can be easily compiled for presentation in court. Further, there should be excellent documentation of the costing information used to make short-range pricing decisions, since these are the situations that are most likely to cause predatory pricing lawsuits to be filed. Also, this cost information should be retained for a number of years, so that it is available for all years contained within the statute of limitations for the states within which a company operates. By taking these precautionary measures, a company will be much more capable of successfully defending itself against predatory pricing lawsuits.

11-8 HOW DO I HANDLE DUMPING BY A FOREIGN COMPETITOR?

A U.S. industry can experience a severe drop in sales if a competitor located in a foreign country imports competing goods into the United States at extremely low prices. This is known as *dumping*. When this occurs, an injured U.S. company can sue the competitor directly, or can bring the issue to the attention of the Federal Trade Commission, which is empowered under the Federal Trade

Commission Act to investigate the issue and increase import duties to a sufficient level to erase the pricing advantage. This is a difficult charge to prove if one bases the dumping charges on the cost of the product, so the charge is instead based on the sale price at which the foreign company sells its products in its home market. If the price charged in the United States is lower than the price charged in the home country, then dumping is proven to have occurred. The exact text of section 72 of the Federal Trade Commission Act, which deals with this issue, is as follows:

> It shall be unlawful for any person importing or assisting in importing any articles from any foreign country into the United States, commonly and systematically to import, sell or cause to be imported or sold such articles within the United States at a price substantially less than the actual market value or wholesale price of such articles, at the time of exportation to the United States, in the principal markets of the country of their production, or of other foreign countries to which they are commonly exported after adding to such market value or wholesale price, freight, duty, and other charges and expenses necessarily incident to the importation and sale thereof in the United States: Provided, That such act or acts be done with the intent of destroying or injuring an industry in the United States, or of preventing the establishment of an industry in the United States, or of restraining or monopolizing any part of trade and commerce in such articles in the United States. Any person injured in his business or property by reason of any violation of, or combination or conspiracy to violate, this section, may sue therefore in the district court of the United States for the district in which the defendant resides or is found or has an agent, without respect to the amount in controversy, and shall recover threefold the damages sustained, and the cost of the suit, including a reasonable attorney's fee.

Dumping is of particular concern to accountants working for foreign-based corporations. They must be aware of the prices charged for their products in the entity's home countries, as well as all ancillary costs noted in the Act, such as freight and duty costs, and be prepared to defend their companies in court with this information if the need arises.

11-9 WHEN IS TRANSFER PRICING IMPORTANT?

Many organizations sell their own products internally, from one division to another. This is especially common in vertically integrated situations, where a company has elected to control the key pieces of its supply chain, perhaps to lock down the supply of key components. Each division sells its products to a downstream division that includes those products in its own production processes. When this happens, management must determine the prices at which components will be sold between divisions. This is known as transfer pricing.

Transfer pricing levels are very important in companies experiencing any of the following three transfer or operational characteristics:

1. *High volumes of interdivisional sales.* This is most common in vertically integrated companies, where each division in succession produces a component that is a necessary part of the product being created by the next division in line. Any incorrect transfer pricing in this scenario can cause considerable dysfunctional purchasing behavior.
2. *High volumes of segment-specific sales.* Even if a company as a whole does not transfer much product between its divisions, this does not mean that specific departments or product lines within each division do not have a much higher dependence on the accuracy of transfer pricing for selected products.
3. *High degree of organizational decentralization.* If an organization is arranged under the theory that divisions should operate as independently as possible, then they will have no incentive to work together unless the transfer prices used are set at levels that give them an economic incentive to do so.

Alternatively, the theoretical foundation for the calculation of transfer prices is of little importance for those organizations with a high degree of centralization, for individual divisions will be ordered by the headquarters staff to produce and transfer products to other divisions irrespective of the prices charged. This is also the case for companies that rarely transfer any products among their divisions, for such transfers, when they occur, are typically approved at the highest management levels if the transfers either are large or are so small that their impact is minimal.

11-10 HOW DO TRANSFER PRICES ALTER CORPORATE DECISION MAKING?

A company must set its transfer prices at levels that will result in the highest possible levels of profits, not for individual divisions but rather for the entire organization. For example, if a transfer price is set at nothing more than its cost, the selling division would much rather not sell the product at all, even though the buying division can sell it externally for a huge profit that more than makes up for the lack of profit experienced by the division that originally sold it the product. The typical division manager will select the product sales that result in the highest level of profit for only his or her division, since the manager has no insight into (or interest in) the financial results of the rest of the organization. Only by finding some way for the selling division to also realize a profit will it have an incentive to sell its products internally, thereby resulting in greater overall profits. An example of such a solution is when a selling division creates a byproduct that it cannot sell but that another division can use as an input for the products it manufactures. The selling division scraps the byproduct, because it has no incentive to do anything else with it. However, by assigning the selling division a small profit on sale of the byproduct, it now has an incentive to ship it to the buying division. Such a pricing strategy assists a company in deriving the greatest possible profit from all of its activities.

Another factor is that the amount of profit allocated to a division through the transfer pricing method used will impact its reported level of profitability and therefore the performance review for that division and its management team. If the management team is compensated in large part through performance-based bonuses, then its actions will be heavily influenced by the profit it can earn on intercompany transfers, especially if such transfers make up a large proportion of total divisional sales. If transfer prices are set at very high levels, this can result in the manufacture of far more product than is needed, which may lock up so much production capacity that the selling division is no longer able to create other products that could otherwise have been sold for a profit. Conversely, an excessively low transfer price will result in no production at all, as long as the selling division has some other product available that it can sell for a greater profit. This latter situation frequently results in late or small deliveries to buying divisions, since the managers of the selling divisions see fit to produce low-price items only if there is spare production capacity available that can be used in no other way. Thus, improper transfer prices will motivate division managers in accordance with how the prices impact their performance evaluations.

Finally, altering the transfer price used can have a dramatic impact on the amount of income taxes a company pays, if it has divisions located in different countries that use different tax rates. All of these issues must be considered when selecting an appropriate transfer pricing method.

Companies that are frequent users of transfer pricing must create prices that are based on a proper balance of the goals of overall company profitability, divisional performance evaluation, simplicity of use, and (in some cases) the reduction of income taxes. The attainment of all these goals by using a single transfer pricing method is not common, and should not be expected. Instead, managers must focus on the attainment of the most critical goals, while keeping the adverse affects of not meeting other goals at a minimum. This process may result in the use of several transfer pricing methods depending on the circumstances surrounding each interdivisional transfer.

11-11 WHAT TRANSFER PRICING METHOD SHOULD I USE?

The most commonly used transfer pricing technique is based on the existing *external market price*. Under this approach, the selling division matches its transfer price to the current market rate. By doing so, a company can achieve a number of goals. First, it can achieve the highest possible corporatewide profit. This happens because the selling division can earn just as much profit by selling all of its production outside of the company as it can by doing so internally; there is no reason for using a transfer price that results in incorrect behavior of either selling externally at an excessively low price or selling internally when a better deal could have been obtained by selling externally. Second, using the market price allows a division to earn a profit on its sales, no matter whether it sells internally or externally. By avoiding all transfers at cost, the senior management group can structure its divisions as profit centers, thereby allowing it to determine the performance of each division manager. Third, the market price is simple to obtain—it can be taken from regulated price sheets, posted prices, or quoted prices, and applied directly to all sales. No complicated calculations are required, and arguments over the correct price to charge between divisions are kept to a minimum. Fourth, a market-based transfer price allows both buying and selling divisions to shop anywhere they want to buy or sell their products. For example, a buying division will be indifferent as to where it obtains its supplies, for it can buy them at the same price regardless of whether that source is a fellow company division. This leads to a minimum of incorrect buying and selling behavior that would otherwise be driven by transfer prices that do not reflect market conditions. For all these reasons, companies are well advised to use market-based transfer prices whenever possible.

Unfortunately, many corporations do not use market-based transfer pricing, not because they do not want to, but because there are no market prices available. This happens when the products being transferred do not exactly match those sold on the market, or if they are intermediate-level products that have not yet been converted into final products, so there is no market price available for them. Another problem with market-based pricing is that there must truly be an alternative for a selling division to sell its entire production externally. This is a common problem for specialty products, where the number of potential buyers is small and their annual buying needs limited in size. A final issue is that market-based pricing can drive divisions to sell their production outside of the company. This problem arises in tight supply situations, where a buying division cannot obtain a sufficient amount of parts from a selling division because it is selling them externally. In this case, the selling division is maximizing its own profit at the expense of divisions that need its output. This is particularly important when the buying division adds so much value to the product that it can then sell it externally at a much higher margin than could the selling division.

Another approach is *adjusted market pricing*, where prices are set in order to simplify transfer prices and adjust for the absence of sales-related costs. For example, if market prices vary considerably by the unit volume ordered, there may be a broad range of transfer prices in use, which can be very complicated to track. A single adjusted market price can be used instead, which is based on the average shipment or order size. If a buying division turns out to have purchased in significantly different quantities than the ones that were assumed at the time prices were set, then a company can retroactively adjust transfer prices at the end of the year; or it can leave the pricing alone and let the divisions do a better job of planning their interdivisional transfer volumes in the next year. As another example, there should be no bad debts when selling between divisions, as opposed to the occasional losses incurred when dealing with outside firms; accordingly, this cost can be deducted from the transfer price. The same argument can be made for the sales staff, whose services are presumably not required for interdepartmental sales. However, these price adjustments are subject to negotiation, so more aggressive division managers are more likely to resist reductions from their market-based prices, while those managing the buying divisions will push hard for excessively large price deductions. The result may be pricing anomalies that do not yield the optimum profit for the company as a whole.

Another option is to use *negotiated transfer prices*. Under this technique, the managers of buying and selling divisions negotiate a transfer price between themselves, using a product's variable cost as the lower boundary of an acceptable negotiated price, and the market price (if one is available) as the upper boundary. The price that is agreed upon, as long as it falls between these two boundaries, should give some profit to each division, with more profit going to the division with better negotiating skills. The method has the advantage of allowing division managers to operate their businesses in a more independent manner, not relying on preset pricing. It also results in better performance evaluations for those managers with greater negotiation skills. However, it also suffers from some flaws. First, if the negotiated price excessively favors one division over another, the losing division will search outside the company for a better deal on the open market, and will direct its sales and purchases in that direction; this may result in suboptimal companywide profitability levels. Also, the negotiation process can take up a substantial portion of a manager's time, not leaving enough for other management activities. This is a particular problem if prices require constant renegotiation. Finally, the interdivisional conflicts over negotiated prices can become so severe that the problem is kicked up corporate headquarters, which must step in and set prices that the divisions are incapable of determining by themselves. For all these reasons, the negotiated transfer price is a method that is generally relegated to special or low-volume pricing situations.

What if there is no market price at all for a product? A company then has no basis for creating a transfer price from any external source of information, so it must use internal information instead. One approach is to create transfer prices based on a product's *contribution margin*. Under this pricing system, a company determines the total contribution margin earned after a product is sold externally, and then allocates this margin back to each division based on their respective proportions of the total product cost. There are several good reasons for using this approach. They are:

- *Converts a cost center into a profit center.* By using this method to assign profits to internal product sales, divisional managers are forced to pay stricter attention to their profitability, which helps the overall profitability of the organization.

- *Encourages divisions to work together.* When every supplying division shares in the margin when a product is sold, it stands to reason that they will be much more anxious to work together to achieve profitable sales, rather than bickering over the transfer prices to be charged internally. Also, any profit improvements that can be brought about only by changes that span several divisions are much more likely to receive general approval and cooperation under this pricing method, since the changes will increase profits for all divisions.

These are powerful arguments, ones which make the contribution margin approach one that is popular as a secondary transfer pricing method, after the market price approach. Despite its useful attributes, there are a number of issues with it that a company must guard against in order to avoid behavior by divisions that will lead to less-than-optimal overall levels of profitability. They are as follows:

- *Can increase assigned profits by increasing costs.* When the contribution margin is assigned based on a division's relative proportion of total product costs, it will not take long for the divisions to realize that they will receive a greater share of the profits if they can increase their overall proportion of costs.

- *Must share cost reductions.* If a division finds a way to reduce its costs, it will only receive an increased share of the resulting profits that is in proportion to its share of the total contribution margin distributed. For example, if division A's costs are 20 percent of a product's total costs, and division B's share is 80 percent, then 80 percent of a $1 cost reduction achieved by division A will be allocated to division B, even though it has done nothing to deserve the increase in margin.

- *Requires the involvement of the corporate headquarters staff.* The contribution margin allocation must be calculated by somebody, and since the divisions all have a profit motive to skew the allocation in their favor, the only party left that can make the allocation is the headquarters staff. This may require the addition of accountants to the headquarters staff, which will increase corporate overhead.

- *Results in arguments.* When costs and profits can be skewed by the system, there will inevitably be arguments between the buying and selling divisions that the corporate headquarters team may have to mediate. These issues detract from an organization's focus on profitability.

The contribution margin approach is not a perfect one, but it does give companies a reasonably understandable and workable method for determining transfer prices. It has more problems than market-based pricing, but can be used as an alternative, or as the primary approach if there is no way to obtain market pricing for transferred products.

In situations where a division cannot derive its transfer prices from the outside market (perhaps because there is no market for its products, or it is a very small one), the *cost-plus approach* may be a reasonable alternative. This method is based on its name—just accumulate a product's full cost, add a standard margin percentage to the cost, and this becomes the transfer price. It has the singular advantage of being very easy to understand and calculate, and can convert a cost center into a profit center, which may be useful for evaluating the performance of a division manager.

Unfortunately, the cost-plus approach also has a major flaw, which is that the margin percentage added to a product's full cost may have no relationship to the margin that would actually be used if the product were to be sold externally. If a number of successive divisions were to add a standard margin to their products, the price paid by the final division in line, the one that must sell the completed product

Exhibit 11.2   Comparison of Transfer Pricing Methods

Type of Transfer Pricing Method	Profitability Enhancement	Performance Review	Ease of Use	Problems
Market Pricing	Creates highest level of profits for entire company.	Creates profits centers for all divisions.	Simple applicability.	Market prices not always available; may not be large enough external market; does not reflect slight reduced internal selling costs; selling divisions may deny sales to other divisions in favor of outside sales.
Adjusted Market Pricing	Creates highest level of profits for entire company.	Creates profits centers for all divisions.	Requires negotiation to determine reductions from market price.	Possible arguments over size of reductions; may need headquarters intervention.
Negotiated Prices	Less optimal result than market-based pricing, especially if negotiated prices vary substantially from the market.	May reflect more on manager negotiating skills than on division performance.	Easy to understand, but requires substantial preparation for negotiations.	May result in better deals for divisions if they buy or sell outside the company; negotiations are time-consuming; may require headquarters intervention.

Contribution Margins	Allocates final profits among cost centers; divisions tend to work together to achieve large profit.	Allows for some basis of measurement based on profits, where cost center performance is only other alternative.	Can be difficult to calculate if many divisions involved.	A division can increase its share of the profit margin by increasing its costs; a cost reduction by one division must be shared among all divisions; requires headquarters involvement.
Cost Plus	May result in profit buildup problem, so that division selling externally has not incentive to do so.	Poor for performance evaluation, since will earn a profit no matter what cost is incurred.	Easy to calculate profit add-on.	Margins assigned do not equate to market-driven profit margins; no incentive to reduce costs.
Opportunity Cost	Good way to ensure profit maximization.	Will drive managers to achieve companywide goals.	Difficult to calculate, and to obtain acceptance within the organization.	Too arcane a calculation for ready acceptance; requires an outside market to determine the opportunity cost; the opportunity cost can be manipulated.

externally, may be so high that there is no room for its own margin, which gives it no incentive to sell the product. Because of this issue, the cost-plus method is not recommended in most situations.

A completely unique approach to the formulation of transfer prices is based on *opportunity costs*. This method is not precisely based on either market prices or internal costs, since it is founded on the concept of forgone profits. It is best described with an example. If a selling division can earn a profit of $10,000 by selling widget A on the outside market, but is instead told to sell widget B to a buying division of the company, then it has lost the $10,000 that it would have earned on sale of widget A. Its opportunity cost of producing widget B instead of A is therefore $10,000. If the selling division can add the forgone profit of $10,000 onto its variable cost to produce widget B, then it will be indifferent as to which product it sells, since it will earn the same profit on the sale of either product. Thus, transfer pricing based on opportunity cost is essentially the variable cost of the product being sold to another division, plus the opportunity cost of profits forgone in order to create the product being sold. Under ideal conditions, this method should result in optimum companywide levels of profitability.

This concept is most applicable when a division is using all of its available production capacity. Otherwise, it would be capable of producing all products at the same time, and would have no opportunity cost associated with not selling any particular item. To use the same example, if there were no market for widget A, on which there was initially a profit of $10,000, there would no longer be any possible profit, and consequently no reason to add an opportunity cost onto the sale price of widget B. The same principle applies if a company has specialized production equipment that can be used only for the production of a single product. In this case, there are no grounds for adding an opportunity cost onto the price of a product, since there are no other uses for the production equipment.

A problem with the opportunity cost approach is that there must be a substantial external market for sale of the products for which an opportunity cost is being calculated. If not, then there is not really a viable alternative available under which a division can sell its products on the outside market. Thus, though a selling division may point to the current product pricing in a thin external market as an opportunity cost, further investigation may reveal that there is no way that the market can absorb the division's full production (or can do so only at a much lower price), thereby rendering the opportunity cost invalid.

Another issue is that the opportunity cost is subject to considerable alteration. For example, the selling division wants to show the highest possible opportunity cost on sale of a specific product, so that it can add this opportunity cost to its other transfer prices. Accordingly, it will skew its costing system by allocating fixed costs elsewhere, showing variable costs based on very high unit production levels and the use of the highest possible prices, to result in a very large profit for that product. This large profit will then be used as the opportunity cost that is forgone when any other products are sold to other divisions, thereby increasing the prices that other divisions must pay the selling division.

This is a technique that is also difficult for the accounting staff to support, because the opportunity cost is not an incurred cost (since it never happened) and therefore does not appear in the general ledger. The level of understandability does not stop with accountants, either. Division managers have a hard time understanding that a transfer price is based on a product's variable cost plus a margin on a different product that was never produced. Accordingly, gaining companywide support of this concept can be a difficult task to accomplish.

A comparison of all the transfer pricing methods just discussed is noted in Exhibit 11.2, where each one's problems, ease of use, and applicability to profitability enhancement and divisional performance reviews are noted.

Chapter 12

Quality Decisions

The cost of quality can comprise an extremely large proportion of company expenditures, and yet is so diffused throughout the organization that it is difficult to compile. The accountant may be called on to determine which costs should be included in the cost of quality, as well as to develop a quality reporting system. Other likely tasks for the accountant include how to assign the correct costs to scrap and where to place quality review workstations in the production area in order to maximize profitability. This chapter provides solutions to all of these issues.

The following table itemizes the section number in which the answers to each question posed in this chapter can be found:

Section	Decision
12-1	What are the various types of quality?
12-2	How do I create a quality reporting system?
12-3	What is the cost of scrap?
12-4	How should I measure post-constraint scrap?
12-5	Where should I place quality review workstations?

12-1 WHAT ARE THE VARIOUS TYPES OF QUALITY?

There are four types of cost categories into which quality costs fall. It is useful to split quality costs into these categories, for there are so many subcategories that it can be difficult to track them all without this method of organization.

The first category of costs is *prevention costs*. These are the costs that a company incurs to ensure that product failures of various kinds do not occur either during the production process or when in the hands of a customer. These costs can also be incurred to ensure that there are fewer process-related failures. These are discretionary costs, for a company's management may choose not to expend any funds on prevention activities (though there will be an offsetting increase in failure costs). Examples of prevention costs are as follows:

- *Administration of quality-related activities*. Some staff time is required to plan for and administer quality-related prevention activities. The cost of this labor should be supplemented by the cost of related benefits and payroll taxes.

- *Education*. A very significant expense is the preparation of training materials, the cost of trainers and training facilities, and (the largest expense of all) the labor cost of all employees attending the training. This is a key prevention activity, and will be one of the largest costs in the prevention category.

- *New product trial costs.* For those organizations releasing new products, having customers test product designs is a central method for ensuring a high quality of design. Accordingly, the costs of products given to customers and survey administration can be clustered into this subcategory.

- *Preventive maintenance.* Ensuring that machinery is capable of running when needed is a key prevention activity. This includes the costs of maintenance personnel engaged in preventive maintenance, as well as any related materials and administrative costs.

- *Preventive maintenance scheduling software.* The just-noted preventive maintenance activities can be more easily accomplished if there is maintenance software available that tracks the last time such maintenance was conducted and how heavily a machine has been used since that time, and that schedules additional maintenance based on those two factors.

- *Procedure and instruction development.* A major prevention activity is the creation of machine operation instructions and other procedures that give employees complete information about how to conduct their jobs. With this information in hand, there is much less chance that any steps in the production process will be mishandled, resulting in quality problems. The cost of this subcategory includes the initial investigation of activities, procedure development, and distribution of the resulting materials.

- *Supplier qualification assessments.* Products cannot have a high quality level unless the supplier parts comprising them have high quality standards. The cost of all employee time spent in reviewing and assessing the output of suppliers must fall into this category.

- *Tool design reviews.* If a company uses a number of custom tools to create products, then those tools must be carefully reviewed in terms of their ability to produce parts at minimum specification levels, as well as their ability to do so consistently and with minimal failure rates. The costs of these reviews and any resulting tool revision costs must fall into this category.

- *Warranty reviews.* One form of prevention is to closely review all customer warranty claims in order to discern clues regarding what product problems can be prevented at the company before they can reach customers. The cost of this review and any subsequent investigation of possible problems should fall into this subcategory.

The second category of costs is *appraisal costs.* These are the costs incurred to measure products, the material components used in products, and the processes used to manufacture products. These activities are designed to reduce the number of defective products shipped to customers. These are different from prevention costs, in that they attempt to improve quality strictly through increased inspection activities.

These are also discretionary costs, for a company does not have to use any appraisal activities whatsoever—though eliminating them will increase the number of low-quality products shipped to customers. Examples of appraisal costs are as follows:

- *Incoming component testing.* If there are particularly troublesome problems with materials received from suppliers, then a company may have initiated an extensive effort to review a large proportion of those materials, which will result in costs not only for testing personnel, but also for any materials that are destroyed during the testing process.
- *Material appraisal.* It is common for the quality control staff to remove items from various stages of the production process for testing purposes. If the removed materials are destroyed during testing, then the cost of these materials should be recorded as an appraisal cost.
- *Outsourced laboratory testing.* Some of the tests conducted on materials are of such a specialized nature that a company finds it to be more cost-effective to send them to an outside laboratory for review. The fees of such laboratories should be charged to this cost subcategory.
- *Process appraisal.* The appraisal process is not confined to materials reviews. It is also necessary to periodically analyze how well the production and supporting processes are functioning; the staff time devoted to this activity should be charged to this cost subcategory.
- *Prototype appraisal.* The quality staff can spot problems with new products before they are produced by examining a variety of quality-related issues on prototype products. The cost of testing and destruction of prototypes should be grouped into this cost subcategory.
- *Testing equipment calibration.* The testing equipment used by the quality staff must be periodically recalibrated to ensure its accuracy. This task is frequently performed by certified outside calibration services, which makes it easier to identify their fees and charge them to this cost subcategory.
- *Testing equipment.* Depending on the kinds of quality tests performed, the types of testing equipment needed can be very expensive. If the cost of this equipment falls below a company's capitalization limit, then the entire cost can be charged straight to this subcategory. If higher, then the associated deprecation expense should be charged here.

The third category of costs is *internal failure costs*. These are costs incurred as a result of discovering product defects prior to shipment. At that time, products can be taken out of the production or warehouse areas, repaired or scrapped, and placed back in the production process if possible. There are a number of related costs that accompany these activities that make this a very expensive cost category. Examples of internal failure costs are as follows:

- *Correction of related paperwork.* When a product failure occurs internally, resulting in rework or scrap, there are a number of resulting paperwork activities.

One is that the production scheduling staff must schedule new production to replace the items removed from production. Also, the eliminated items must be reported to the purchasing staff, so that they can order replacement materials. Further, the accounting staff must determine the cost of the scrap or rework and record it in the financial records. The staff time required to complete all of these activities should be recorded here.

- *Lost profit on products sold as seconds.* When a company finds that it has products of a sufficiently low quality that they cannot be sold through normal sales channels, it may elect to sell them at a discount, rather than expend extra rework effort to bring them up to a higher quality standard. If so, the loss in profits that occurs when these products are sold at the lower price point should be recorded in this subcategory as a cost or a sales discount.

- *Machinery downtime.* When internal product failures are discovered, machinery downtime can be caused for two reasons. One is that the machines are now needed to rework defective product, which keeps them from being used to create new product. Also, the cause of the internal failures may be the machinery, which requires some downtime while they are investigated and repaired. In either case, the cost of the machinery downtime should be charged to this cost subcategory.

- *Redesign.* If a product continues to have high quality error rates over time, the problem may not be in the manufacturing process at all, but rather in the underlying product design. If so, the engineering staff will require extra time to develop a new design and test it to ensure that all quality problems have been resolved. The engineering time charged to this work should be summarized into this cost subcategory, as well as the costs of any inventory that will become obsolete as a result of design changes.

- *Reinspection and testing.* Once a product has been reworked, it must be inspected and tested to ensure that it now meets quality specifications, which requires extra staff time.

- *Repurchasing.* When products are scrapped, the purchasing staff may need to repurchase the components needed to create replacement products. The cost of the time needed to do this can be recorded separately here, or in the "corrections to related paperwork" subcategory that is noted earlier in this list.

- *Rework.* Depending on the extent of product rework required, there may be a separate staff devoted to this activity. If not, then production workers must be drawn from the production line (thereby taking time away from the production of other products) to perform this work. In either case, the cost of their time is charged to this account. There may also be a charge for the use of any machinery required to perform rework tasks.

- *Safety stock.* If there is a significant volume of internal product failure, the management team may think it necessary to keep on hand large quantities of extra components to make up the shortfall of components that would otherwise occur due to the scrapping of low-quality products. There is an interest cost associated with the investment in this extra inventory, as well as storage, insurance, and obsolescence costs that can be accumulated into this cost subcategory.

• *Scrap.* Some products may be of such a low quality level that they cannot be reworked, and so must be thrown away. However, some of these costs may be recouped by the income from sale of the scrap (if this is possible). For high-cost products, this is a very expensive subcategory of internal failure costs.

• *Supplier claims processing.* When internal failure costs are traced to supplier quality problems, a company must not only ship back defective supplier parts, but also process claims against the offending suppliers, so that it will not have to pay for the low-quality parts. This claims processing step can be an administrative headache, and an expensive one where there are many supplier-caused quality problems.

The final category of costs is *external failure costs*. These are the costs incurred when low-quality products are shipped to customers. This tends to be the most difficult quality cost area to measure, because it is difficult to quantify some customer-related costs (as noted in the following bullet points). There is general agreement among quality experts that these costs are the most expensive of all the various cost-of-quality categories, for the loss of customers due to low quality can have a catastrophic impact on an organization's profitability. Examples of external failure costs are as follows:

• *Customer surveys.* A company may conduct customer surveys for the sole reason that it needs feedback about the quality of products issued to them. If this is the only reason for creating and operating a survey (as opposed to one that is used by the marketing department for product positioning and pricing purposes), then the cost of the survey can be charged to this account.

• *Customer-imposed penalties.* Customers who use a company's output in their products may have considerable concerns about the quality of incoming components and will reinforce these concerns with their suppliers by charging penalties for poor-quality production. If so, these penalties should certainly be segregated into a separate account, so that management can easily determine their extent.

• *Invoice adjustments.* The cost of processing alterations to customer invoices can be very time-consuming, especially when there are a large volume of customer returns, for each transaction tends to be a unique one that requires a great deal of time. If this activity requires a significant amount of time, the associated cost can be stored separately in this account; if not, it may be rolled into the "Processing customer returns" account (as noted later in this list).

• *Loss of customers.* This is the potentially largest cost in the external failure cost category. It can be quantified by tracking those customers who are no longer buying from the company, contacting them to determine whether low quality was the reason, and then calculating the lost profit based on sales to those customers in the preceding year. Though the resulting figure will not tie to any cost recorded through a traditional accounting system, the opportunity cost of sales lost should still be itemized in this account, due to its potential size.

- *Loss of reputation.* A potentially very large expense is the reduction in a company's reputation when it continually sells low-quality products. This is a very difficult cost to calculate or even estimate, so most companies do not use this cost account, preferring instead to simply itemize the potential for this cost in the narrative sections of their quality cost reports.

- *Processing customer returns.* Whenever a customer returns a product, the receiving staff must complete special paperwork on it, store it in a special location, have it reviewed by a quality control team, and disposition it in accordance with their instructions, while the accounting staff must process a credit to the customer. The costs of all these activities should be charged to this account.

- *Product recall insurance.* If a company has a history of conducting product recalls, it may be necessary to reduce its risk of incurring further recall-related costs by procuring a product recall insurance policy. However, this can be a very expensive policy to obtain, especially if there is a recent recall history. The cost is certainly high enough to place in its own separate account.

- *Product recall.* If a company finds that quality problems with a product are sufficiently extensive, it can recall them. There are many costs when this happens, including payment for the inbound freight costs for returned products, the cost of reworking defective products, the cost of issuing replacement products, and the administrative overhead associated with these tasks. This can be an inordinately expensive cost subcategory.

- *Supplier warranty claim processing.* When customers return products, there is a good chance that the cause of their complaints is issues with product components that were sold to the company by its suppliers. If so, the company must expend considerable effort in filling out warranty claim forms to send to its suppliers in order to obtain reimbursement for shoddy components. These administrative costs should be charged to this account.

- *Warranty claim administration.* When there are many product returns from customers, a company will find it necessary to create a full-time warranty claims department. The cost of the staff for this department, as well as all associated overhead costs, should be charged to this account.

12-2 HOW DO I CREATE A QUALITY REPORTING SYSTEM?

The key issue in creating a quality measurement and reporting system is determining which costs to track. Since the cost of data collection can be considerable, the best approach is to consider the following items when determining the types of costs to be tracked:

- *Ability to measure an activity.* Some activities are extremely hard to measure. For example, the accounting staff does not have a good method for determining the time it takes each day to issue credits to customers for low-quality products that have been returned, nor does the production staff usually track the time it takes to rework low-quality products. An extremely difficult quality cost is the cost of lost sales from customers who take their business elsewhere. The accountant must evaluate the ability of the organization to collect such information, and determine whether it is sufficient to report estimated costs in lieu of "real" data.

- *Available resources.* The resources required to set up and maintain a complete quality cost tracking system will exceed the investment in a company's normal accounting systems, due to the in-depth nature of the information that must be obtained. Accordingly, always determine the cost required to collect each type of quality cost information and offset this with the benefits of the uses to which the information can be put. This will usually result in a much smaller number of quality cost items being tracked with any degree of regularity.

- *Continuing need for information.* Many organizations prefer to reduce quality costs through short-term projects that have tightly defined beginning and ending points. They do not require cost information after a project is completed, just a summary report that itemizes the success (or failure) of each project. In such cases, there is no need to continually report on issues that have long since been resolved.

- *Nonfinancial measures.* Financial measures are most commonly used by senior management, which must compare the results obtained from its investments in quality-related projects to the related investments. However, lower levels of the organization require measurements that are based primarily on units, such as percentages of scrap reduction or parts per million of rework. These measures are more relevant to their activities. Accordingly, the preponderance of information gathered by the accountant may be nonfinancial in nature.

- *Quality objectives.* The quality cost tracking system should primarily support a company's quality cost reduction efforts. This means that if management wants to focus its attention on a few specific quality issues, then the measurement system should be designed to provide the highest possible level of detail about just those areas. The next highest level of accuracy should be for measurements of areas that management has on its agenda for near-term improvements. Low-priority areas can be measured less precisely. Thus, the level of detail for quality cost measurements will vary in accordance with the current and short-term quality cost reduction goals of management.

The next issue is how to organize the selected quality costs into a data storage system. The central issue here is the structure to be used for the chart of accounts, so that these costs can be properly recorded in the general ledger. An example is shown in Exhibit 12.1, where we use a three-digit code to represent each of the four types of

Exhibit 12.1   Cost of Quality Chart of Accounts

Account No.	Description
100-00-00	**Prevention Costs**
105-00-00	Quality Administration Costs
110-00-00	Quality Training Costs
115-00-00	Supplier Qualification Review Costs
120-00-00	Equipment Preventive Maintenance Costs
125-00-00	Instruction Design Costs
130-00-00	Other Prevention Costs
200-00-00	**Appraisal Costs**
205-00-00	Receiving Inspection Costs
210-00-00	Test Equipment Calibration Costs
215-00-00	Outsourced Testing Costs
220-00-00	Inspection Labor Costs
225-00-00	Test Equipment Depreciation Costs
230-00-00	Other Appraisal Costs
300-00-00	**Internal Failure Costs**
305-00-00	Rework Costs
310-00-00	Scrap Costs
315-00-00	Repurchasing Costs
320-00-00	Downtime Costs
325-00-00	Cost of Processing Claims Against Suppliers
330-00-00	Other Internal Failure Costs
400-00-00	**External Failure Costs**
405-00-00	Product Liability Insurance Costs
410-00-00	Product Liability Costs
415-00-00	Warranty Costs
420-00-00	Field Service Costs
425-00-00	Customer Complaint Processing Costs
430-00-00	Other External Failure Costs

quality costs. In the example, there are additional spaces in the chart of accounts numbering system, in case the accountant decides to further subdivide the costs. For example, when using the code for equipment preventive maintenance costs (which is 120), one may decide to further subdivide costs for each machine in the facility; so if we assign a subcode of 27 to a specific machine, then the maintenance cost for that machine becomes 120-27. We can further subdivide the costs if it seems necessary to further refine the cost tracking system. For example, if we want to break down the materials, labor, and other maintenance costs for each machine, we can add a few more digits to the account code; to trace the labor cost of preventive maintenance for machine 27, we can use the code 120-27-01. By using increasingly detailed chart of accounts codes in which to store the cost of quality data, an accountant can subdivide

Exhibit 12.2   Summary Cost of Quality Report

Cost Type	Detail	Summary
Prevention Costs		
Quality Administration Costs	$7,500	
Quality Training Costs	2,500	
Supplier Qualification Review Costs	4,000	
Equipment Preventive Maintenance Costs	21,000	
Instruction Design Costs	2,400	
		$37,400
Appraisal Costs		
Receiving Inspection Costs	$5,900	
Test Equipment Calibration Costs	2,300	
Outsourced Testing Costs	5,000	
Inspection Labor Costs	15,000	
Test Equipment Depreciation Costs	8,100	
		$36,300
Internal Failure Costs		
Rework Costs	$51,000	
Scrap Costs	43,000	
Repurchasing Costs	1,900	
Downtime Costs	3,500	
Cost of Processing Claims Against Suppliers	900	
		$100,300
External Failure Costs		
Product Liability Insurance Costs	$8,000	
Product Liability Costs	88,000	
Warranty Costs	29,500	
Field Service Costs	60,200	
Customer Complaint Processing Costs	43,000	
		$228,700
Total Quality Costs		**$402,700**

the information in more ways, allowing her to create and issue a greater variety of reports.

The information accumulated through the new chart of accounts can be presented in a variety of ways to suit the needs of the recipient. One format is shown in Exhibit 12.2, which itemizes the various costs that roll up into each of the four main cost categories. Its primary uses are to communicate costs to senior management and to show what cost line items are the largest, and are therefore worthy of more in-depth discussion. For example, the exhibit shows that scrap and rework costs are by far the largest internal failure costs, while field service and customer complaint processing expenses are the largest external failure costs. However, this

Exhibit 12.3 Report on Components of Cost of Quality

Cost Type	Materials	Labor	Other	Summary
Prevention Costs				
Quality Administration Costs	$0	$5,000	$0	$5,000
Quality Training Costs	0	1,000	250	1,250
Supplier Qualification Review Costs	0	1,750	450	2,200
Equipment Preventive Maintenance Costs	1,200	10,200	0	11,400
Instruction Design Costs	0	1,400	0	1,400
	$1,200	$19,350	$700	$21,250
Appraisal Costs				
Receiving Inspection Costs	$0	$3,000	$0	3,000
Test Equipment Calibration Costs	0	0	1,500	1,500
Outsourced Testing Costs	0	0	2,500	2,500
Inspection Labor Costs	0	7,500	0	7,500
Test Equipment Depreciation Costs	0	0	4,350	4,350
	$0	$10,500	$8,350	$18,850
Internal Failure Costs				
Rework Costs	$10,000	$16,000	$0	$26,000
Scrap Costs	22,000	0	0	22,000
Repurchasing Costs	0	1,000	0	1,000
Downtime Costs	0	2,000	0	2,000
Cost of Processing Claims Against Suppliers	0	500	0	500
	$32,000	$19,500	$0	$51,500
External Failure Costs				
Product Liability Insurance Costs	$0	$0	$4,200	$4,200
Product Liability Costs	0	0	47,000	47,000
Warranty Costs	0	14,000	0	14,000
Field Service Costs	8,000	22,000	3,000	33,000
Customer Complaint Processing Costs	0	20,000	1,500	21,500
	$8,000	$56,000	$55,700	$119,700
Total Quality Costs	$41,200	$105,350	$64,750	$211,300
Percentage of Total Costs	19%	50%	31%	100%

report format does not break down the cost line items into a sufficient level of detail to be of much use to the lower levels of management where cost reports are scrutinized most intensively. They need information that is broken down by department or location.

A more detailed report is shown in Exhibit 12.3. It is more specific about the types of costs incurred—materials, labor, or other (these costs categories can be swapped

Exhibit 12.4   Cost of Quality versus Budget

Cost Type	This Month Actual	This Month Budget	This Month Variance	Year to Date Actual	Year to Date Budget	Year to Date Variance
Prevention Costs						
Quality Administration Costs	$7,500	$7,000	–$500	$16,000	$14,000	–$2,000
Quality Training Costs	2,500	3,000	+500	5,200	6,000	+800
Supplier Qualification Review Costs	4,000	3,200	–800	8,500	6,400	–2,100
Equipment Preventive Maintenance Costs	21,000	20,000	–1,000	44,500	40,000	–4,500
Instruction Design Costs	2,400	2,000	–400	5,000	4,000	–1,000
	$37,400	**$35,200**	**–$2,200**	**$79,200**	**$70,400**	**–$8,800**
Appraisal Costs						
Receiving Inspection Costs	$5,900	$6,000	+100	$12,000	$12,000	$0
Test Equipment Calibration Costs	2,300	4,000	+1,700	7,000	8,000	+1,000
Outsourced Testing Costs	5,000	2,500	–2,500	6,100	5,000	–1,100
Inspection Labor Costs	15,000	10,000	–5,000	30,700	20,000	–10,700
Test Equipment Depreciation Costs	8,100	8,100	0	15,500	16,200	+700
	$36,300	**$30,600**	**–$5,700**	**$71,300**	**$61,200**	**–$10,100**

Internal Failure Costs

Rework Costs	$51,000	$50,000	−$1,000	$99,900	$100,000	+100
Scrap Costs	43,000	40,000	−3,000	78,700	80,000	+1,300
Repurchasing Costs	1,900	3,000	+1,100	6,900	6,000	−900
Downtime Costs	3,500	2,100	−1,400	6,500	4,200	−2,300
Cost of Processing Claims Against Suppliers	900	1,000	+100	2,050	2,000	−50
	$100,300	**$96,100**	**−$4,200**	**$194,050**	**$192,200**	**−$1,850**
External Failure Costs						
Product Liability Insurance Costs	$8,000	$7,250	−$750	$17,100	$14,500	−$2,600
Product Liability Costs	88,000	65,000	−23,000	167,000	130,000	−37,000
Warranty Costs	29,500	30,000	+500	60,000	60,000	0
Field Service Costs	60,200	60,000	−200	119,600	120,000	+400
Customer Complaint Processing Costs	43,000	41,000	−2,000	87,200	82,000	−5,200
	$228,700	**$203,250**	**−$25,450**	**$450,900**	**$406,500**	**−$44,400**
Total Quality Costs	**$402,700**	**$365,150**	**−$37,550**	**$795,450**	**$730,300**	**−$65,150**

with others, depending on a company's specific needs). One can also add many more columns, if it seems necessary to itemize the report for more types of costs. This extra level of detail allows managers at the facility level to more easily track down and reduce quality costs.

Another reporting possibility is to construct reports that itemize the budgeted and actual quality costs for each period, as well as the variance between the two figures. In Exhibit 12.4, the report also includes additional columns for year-to-date information. This type of report structure is essential for those organizations with enough historical budgeting information to conduct comparisons, and with a long-term plan to use this information as the basis for long-range quality cost reductions. It is also very useful for conducting performance evaluations of those managers who are responsible for controlling quality costs.

The preceding reports have focused on splitting specific accounting categories of costs into finer levels of detail. These formats are useful for locating and reducing specific types of costs. However, they do not draw management's attention to the specific processes within an organization that are causing problems. An example of a format that resolves this problem is shown in Exhibit 12.5, where we have sorted the four main types of quality costs by the steps in an injection molding production process. By using this approach, managers can quickly tell which production steps are incurring the majority of quality-related costs, and can focus their attention accordingly on the major offenders. In the exhibit, the injection molding process is incurring the majority of costs, while the assembly operation is a distant runner-up.

By comparing the costs of problems and the costs to correct them, management can determine which corrections will result in the largest net increase in profits. An example of the reporting format that contains the cost-benefit trade-off of each correction activity is shown in Exhibit 12.6. The example lists the root causes of quality problems down the left side, along with correction activities for each one. Then the costs of each root cause are reduced by the cost of each correction activity to determine the net change in costs.

Exhibit 12.5   Cost of Quality Report by Operation

	Prevention Cost	Appraisal Cost	Internal Failure Cost	External Failure Cost	Total Cost
Mold Setup	$0	$0	$3,500	$0	$3,500
Machine Preparation	500	750	3,000		4,250
Injection Mold Processing	1,020	80	4,200	8,720	14,020
Part Trimming	500	500	2,200	500	3,700
Labeling				500	500
Hot Stamping	250		500		750
Assembly	500	600		3,000	4,100
Boxing	0	0	0	0	0
Total	$2,770	$1,930	$13,400	$12,720	$30,820

Exhibit 12.6 Cost-Benefit Tradeoff Report

Root Causes	Correction Activities	Quality Cost	Associated Quality Cost	Net Change in Costs
Inaccurate assembly instructions	Audit and reissue assembly instructions.	$24,000	$13,500	+$10,500
Inadequate assembler training	Create training materials and conduct classes.	$60,000	$27,000	+$33,000
Inadequate performance specifications	Revise purchasing specifications for all purchased parts.	$60,000	$42,000	+$28,000
Inadequate supplier certification	Create certification program, screen suppliers, and drop those with poor performance.	$120,000	$120,000	$0
Missing operator instructions	Correct and reissue operator instructions.	$84,000	$50,000	+$34,000
Faulty machine setups	Create training program for all machine operators, with periodic updates.	$264,000	$110,000	+$154,000
	Totals	$612,000	$362,500	+$249,500

12-3 WHAT IS THE COST OF SCRAP?

Under traditional cost accounting, the cost of any scrapped item will be its fully absorbed cost. For example, the following table shows that a product passing through a series of work centers will accumulate the cost of each work center, and will have a progressively higher scrap cost if it is scrapped later in the production process:

Work Center	Work Center Cost Added	Work Center Cumulative Cost	Product + Variable Cost	Total Scrap = Cost
No. 1	$2.05	$2.05	$8.25	$10.30
No. 2	0.35	2.40	8.25	10.65
No. 3	1.15	3.55	8.25	11.80
No. 4	4.80	8.35	8.25	16.60
No. 5	1.80	10.15	8.25	18.40

Instead, the location of the constrained resource should dictate the cost of the scrap. If scrap occurs prior to the constrained resource, then the cost of the scrap is strictly the variable cost of the work-in-process, which is usually only its material cost. No additional cost is assigned based on the number of work centers involved in processing the scrapped item, because these upstream workstations have excess capacity, and so can easily process replacement inventory for free. The basic concept for this type of scrap is that a work center's production capability is free as long as it has excess capacity.

However, the cost assignment scenario changes radically if scrap occurs either at the constrained resource or anywhere downstream from it. If scrap occurs in these areas, it must be replaced with another part that will use up additional time at the constrained resource. Thus, the cost of scrap occurring either at or following the constrained resource is the lost throughput that would have been realized if the item had not been scrapped. The calculation of post-constraint scrap is to compile the constraint hours spent to produce all scrap occurring at or after the constraint, and then multiply this by the average throughput per hour generated by the constraint.

The preceding scrap example is presented again below, but now we assume that the constrained resource is work center no. 3. In the example, we assume that the average throughput per hour generated by the constrained resource is \$2,000, and that one unit of a scrapped item requires three minutes of operating time by the constrained resource, which translates to an opportunity cost of \$100 (\$2,000 $\times$ 3/60):

Work Center	Throughput Opportunity Cost	Product + Variable Cost	Total Scrap = Cost
No. 1	\$0.00	\$8.25	\$8.25
No. 2	0.00	8.25	8.25
No. 3	100.00	0	100.00
No. 4	100.00	0	100.00
No. 5	100.00	0	100.00

Quality improvement investments at or downstream from the constrained resource are an excellent idea, since they prevent the loss of constraint time. For example, the Candy Stripe Company, maker of two-tone toothpaste, is evaluating a proposal to reduce the scrap rejection rate of its product. The company is currently throwing out 1,000 tubes of toothpaste per hour, all downstream of the constrained resource. Its constrained resource is the packaging machine, which uses a multi-nozzle dispenser to fill different colors of toothpaste into the toothpaste tube. The machine produces 5,000 tubes of toothpaste per hour, which is \$2,500 of throughput per hour. The proposal is intended to eliminate downstream bursting of the tubes through overfilling, which requires an investment of \$250,000 in a replacement multinozzle dispenser that more precisely fills each tube. The dispenser will require replacement once a year.

All scrap is downstream from the constraint, so the average hourly throughput rate of \$2,500 is the appropriate cost to apply to the scrap. The scrap rate is 20 percent of hourly production, so the scrap cost is 20 percent of the average hourly throughput rate, or \$500 per hour. If the company invests in the new multinozzle dispenser, it will require 500 hours of throughput to repay the investment (\$250,000 investment/\$500 per hour of throughput savings). Since the company runs on an eight-hour day, this means that the investment will be recouped in just over two months, leaving nearly 10 more months in which to generate additional throughput from the investment. Thus, the investment proposal should be accepted.

In summary, never assign an accumulated overhead cost based on how far inventory has come in the production process before being scrapped; instead, assign scrap costs based on the simple criterion of whether scrap occurs before or after the constrained resource.

12-4 HOW SHOULD I MEASURE POST-CONSTRAINT SCRAP?

An excellent way to increase the total amount of system throughput is to avoid scrap that occurs after the constraint. These items have already been processed by the con-strained resource, and so have used up bottleneck capacity that cannot be recovered. Consequently, one of the best throughput-related measurements is for scrap occurring after the constrained resource. The measurement is to compile the constraint hours spent to produce all scrap occurring after the constraint, and then multiply this by the average throughput per hour generated by the constraint. The calculation follows:

(Constraint hours spent to produce scrap) × (Throughput per hour)

Conversely, scrap occurring before the constrained resource does not impact constraint utilization, and so is much less important from the perspective of throughput generation.

For example, the primary component of the Dumper Wheelbarrow Company's legendary HaulMax Wheelbarrow is its oversized, heavy-gauge steel tray. The company's constrained resource is a sheet metal–bending machine required to produce each tray. Subsequently, holes are drilled in the tray so that it can be bolted to the wheelbarrow frame. If the holes are drilled off-center, then the wheelbarrow must be scrapped.

A number of trays are being scrapped because of this drilling problem. Dumper's controller wants to determine the cost of post-constraint scrap. To do so, she accumulates the number of scrapped trays in the past month (120 trays) and uses routing documents to determine the average amount of constraint time used for the production of each tray (0.15 hours). She then calculates the constraint's average throughput per hour as $1,850. With this information, she compiles the cost of post-constraint scrap as follows:

(120 Scrapped trays × 0.15 Hours) × ($1,850 Throughput per hour) = $33,300

Wooden frames for the HaulMax do not use the constrained resource at all, but are still subject to drilling problems that require many frames to be discarded. Dumper's controller calculates the cost of these scrapped items as the number of units scrapped

(190 in the past month) multiplied by the variable cost of each frame ($17), which is a total cost of $3,230. Clearly, Dumper should concentrate its efforts on fixing the downstream tray drilling problem rather than the unrelated frame drilling problem in order to more quickly maximize its throughput.

12-5 WHERE SHOULD I PLACE QUALITY REVIEW WORKSTATIONS?

The placement of a quality review workstation in the production area can have a major impact on profitability. If placed just in front of the constrained resource, it keeps low-quality items from using up valuable processing time at the constraint. If these work-in-process items were to pass through the constrained resource and then be thrown out as scrap, then the capacity of the constraint used to produce them would have essentially been wasted. Thus, the correct analysis for the installation of a quality workstation is to weigh the cost of the additional quality review staff and equipment against the throughput saved by not running all detected scrap through the constrained resource.

What if the quality review station were to be shifted a few yards to the downstream side of the constrained resource? This would mean that no constraint time would be saved, while the company would still be investing in the additional quality review staff person and related equipment. In this case, there is no change in throughput, but an increase in expenses and invested capital. Consequently, merely moving the quality workstation to one side or the other of the constrained resource can have a significant impact on corporate profitability, either up or down.

Index

Account reduction, 30
Activity-based costing, 199–209
Activity drivers, 203
Adjusted market pricing, 257–258
Adobe Acrobat, 80
Appraisal costs, 265–266
Audit, inventory, 164

Balanced scorecard, 222–224
Benchmarking, 224–226
Benefits administration outsourcing, 156–157
Best practices, budgeting, 29–35
Bill of materials accuracy, 187–188
Billing controls, 102–103
Biometric timeclock, 145
Bonus scale, 36
Bottleneck analysis, *see* Constraint
Breakeven point, 110–115
Budget
    Best practices, 29–35
    Cash, 9
    Capital, 8, 24–25
    Controls, 35–37
    Cost of goods sold, 7, 17–18
    Direct labor, 5–6, 13–15
    Facilities, 8, 23
    Financing, 27–28
    Flex, 28–29
    Interlocking, 1–10
    Inventory, 4, 12
    Marketing, 7, 19–20
    Model, 10–
    Overhead, 6, 16
    Preloading, 32
    Production, 3–4, 12–13
    Purchasing, 5, 13–14
    Research and development, 1–3, 23–24
    Revenue, 3, 11, 38–40
    Sales department, 7, 17–19
    Staffing, 8, 21–22
    Summary-level, 33
    Throughput impact on, 37–43
Byproduct cost allocation, 213–216

Capital asset disposition form, 108
Capital expenditure
    Budget, 8, 24–25, 44–68
    Discounting, 60–62
    Post-completion analysis, 65–67

    Project ranking, 33
    Proposal form, 62–64
    Request form, 51–52
    Strategy linkage, 50
Capital request form, 107
Cash
    Collection acceleration, 81–82
    Forecast, 9–10
    Receipt controls, 103–104
Cash-on-delivery payment terms, 89
Chart of accounts, 271
Collection
    Agencies, 89–90
    Call optimization, 82–83, 85–86
    Legal action, 90–91
Constraint
    Cost, 45–47
    Identification, 47–49
    Investment in, 49
    Sales funnel, 42–43
    Scrap measurement, 279–280
    Staffing analysis, 137–139
Controls
    Billing, 102–103
    Budgeting, 35–38
    Cash receipts, 103–104
    Credit management, 94–95
    Fixed asset, 106–109
    Inventory, 101–102, 183–186
    Need for, 92–93
    Order entry, 93–94
    Payables, 100–101
    Payroll, 104–106
    Procurement card, 96–100
    Purchasing, 95–96
Cost drivers, 33
Cost of capital
    Calculation, 54–58
    Incremental, 58–60
Cost of goods sold budget, 7, 17–18
Cost pools, 201
Cost variance analysis, 121–127
Cost-plus pricing, 259
Credit
    Application, 72–73
    Approval stamp, 94
    Controls, 94–95
    Granting system, 74–76
    Policy, 70–72

Credit (*continued*)
   Reports, 73–74
   Terms, 76–77
Customer contact information, 83–85
Cycle counting, 163–164

Deductions database, 87
Direct deposit, 149–150
Direct labor budget, 5–6, 13–15
Discounted cash flow analysis, 51–54
Dollar value LIFO method, 176–178
Dumping, 253–254
Dunning letters, 88–89

Early payment discounts, 82
Efficiency variance, 125
Electronic child support payments, 152–153
Employee payroll portal, 147–148
Employment verification outsourcing, 155–156
Expected commercial value, 228–229
External failure costs, 268–269
External market pricing, 256–257

Facilities budget, 8, 23
Financing budget, 27–28
First-in, first-out costing, 171–174
Fixed asset
   Controls, 106–109
   Serial number database, 106
Fixed overhead spending variance, 125
Flex budgeting, 28–29
Flowcharts
   Budgeting, 31, 34
   Target costing, 231
Forms
   Capital asset disposition, 108
   Capital investment, 63
   Capital request, 52, 107
   Credit application, 72–73
   Distribution of, 148–149
   Invoice, 78–79
   Missing procurement card, 99
   Procurement card missing receipt, 98
   Procurement card statement of account, 97

General and administrative budget, 7–8

Internal failure costs, 266–268
Inventory
   Accuracy, 160–165, 189–190
   Budget, 4, 12
   Controls, 101–102, 183–186
   Disposal, 167–169
   Dollar value LIFO method, 176–178
   First-in, first-out costing, 171–174

Last-in, first-out costing, 174–176
Link chain method, 178–180
Lower of cost or market, 169–171
Measurements, 187–192
Obsolescence, 102, 165–166, 191
Ownership by suppliers, 194–195
Returnable, 191–192
Specific identification method, 183
Weighted average method, 181–183
Investment center, 221
Invoice
   Delivery, 80–81
   Format enhancement, 78–79

Joint cost allocation, 213–216
Just-in-time system costing impact, 209–211

Labor efficiency variance, 126
Labor price variance, 122–125
Last-in, first-out costing, 174–176
Link chain method, 178–180
Lockbox, 81, 103
Lockbox truncation, 81–82
Lower of cost or market rule, 102, 169–171

Marketing budget, 7, 19–20
Materials price variance, 121–122
Materials review board, 165–166
Materials yield variance, 125–126
Metrics
   Inventory, 187–192
   Target costing, 241–242

National Association for the Exchange of
   Industrial Resources, 168–169
National Association of Credit Management,
   73–74
Negotiated transfer pricing, 258
Net present value, 60–62

Obsolete inventory, 165–166, 191
Opportunity cost pricing, 262–263
Order entry controls, 93–94
Outsourcing
   Analysis, 137
   Benefits administration, 156–157
   Employment verification, 155–156
   Payroll, 153–155
Overhead
   Allocation issues, 211–213
   Budget, 6, 16
   Calculation, 197–199

Payables controls, 100–101
Payback period, 64–65

Payment
    Deductions, 86–88
    Terms, 76–77
Payroll
    Controls, 104–106
    Cycles, 157–158
    Deduction simplification, 146–147
    Employee portal, 147–148
    Form distribution, 148–149
    Frequently asked questions, 158–159
    Outsourcing, 153–155
    Paycards, 150–152
    Remittance automation, 153
Petty cash, 104
Policies, credit, 70–72, 94
Post-completion analysis, 65–67
Predatory pricing, 252–253
Prevention costs, 264
Price protection costs, 195–196
Price leader, 249–250
Price war, 250–252
Pricing
    Cost-plus, 249
    Impact on breakeven, 114–115
    Long-range, 245–247
    Lowest acceptable, 243–245
    Predatory, 252–253
    Transfer, 254–263
Procedure
    Budgeting, 30–31
    Lower of cost or market, 171
Procurement card controls, 96–100
Product mix analysis, 115–116
Production
    Batch sizing, 4
    Budget, 3–4, 12–13
    Outsourcing, 137
Profit center, 219–220
Profitability analysis
    New product, 139–142
    Services, 128–130
    Volume change, 135–136
    Working days, 130–131
Purchase orders, 95
Purchasing budget, 5, 13–14

Quality
    Costs, 264–269
    Reporting system, 269–277
    Review workstation placement, 280

Radio frequency identification
    tag tracking, 109
Reporting periods, reduction of, 30
Research and development
    Budget, 1–3, 24–24
    Funding analysis, 131–133, 227–229
Responsibility accounting, 217–218
Responsibility centers, 218–221
Revenue budget, 3, 11, 38–40
Revenue center, 219

Sales department budget, 7, 17–19
Sales funnel bottleneck, 42–43
Scrap
    Cost, 277–279
    Post-constraint, 279–280
Service levels, 192–194
Services profitability analysis, 128–130
Site selection considerations, 67–68
Small claims court filing, 90
Specific identification method, 183
Sprint capacity, 49–50
Staffing budget, 8, 21–22
Step costing, 4, 32, 112–113
Strategy, capital budgeting linkage to, 50
Supplier
    Inventory ownership, 194–195
    Naming convention, 100

Target costing, 229–230, 233–242
Telephone timekeeping, 145–146
Throughput
    Analysis model, 133–135
    Budgeting, 37–43
Timeclock data collection, 144–146
Tooling setups, 5
Transfer pricing, 254–263

Value engineering, 230–233
Variable overhead efficiency variance,
    126–127
Variable overhead spending variance, 125
Variance analysis, 121–127
Vendor master file, 100
Volume change profitability analysis, 135–136

Warehouse consolidation, 193
Weighted average method, 181–183
What if analysis, 116–121